Using Information Technology Effectively in Teaching and Learning

Studies in pre-service and in-service teacher education

Edited by
Bridget Somekh and Niki Davis

London and New York

First published 1997
by Routledge
11 New Fetter Lane, London EC4P 4EE

Simultaneously published in the USA and Canada
by Routledge
29 West 35th Street, New York, NY 10001

Reprinted 1998, 1999

Routledge is an imprint of the Taylor & Francis Group

Typeset in Garamond by Keystroke, Jacaranda Lodge, Wolverhampton
Printed and bound in Great Britain by
TJ International Ltd, Padstow, Cornwall

British Library Cataloguing in Publication Data
A catalogue record for this book is available from the British Library

Library of Congress Cataloging in Publication Data
A catalog record for this book is available from the Library of Congress

ISBN 0-415-12131-0 (hbk)
ISBN 0-415-12132-9 (pbk)

Contents

List of figures and tables viii
List of contributors ix
Preface x
Charles Desforges
Introduction 1
Bridget Somekh and Niki Davis

Part One IT as a learning tool: the potential and the teacher's role

Introduction to Part One 11

1 Can quality in learning be enhanced through the use of IT? 14
Niki Davis, Charles Desforges, John Jessel, Bridget Somekh, Chris Taylor and Gay Vaughan

2 Children writing words and building thoughts: does the word processor really help? 28
John Jessel

3 Number education for very young children: can IT change the nature of early years mathematics education? 40
Gay Vaughan

4 Do electronic databases enable children to engage in information processing? 50
Helen M. Smith

5 Does data logging change the nature of children's thinking in experimental work in science? 63
Roy Barton

6 Can design software make a useful contribution to the art curriculum? The experience of one school 73
John McGowan

7 Children exploring the Queen's House in hypertext: has the hype any educational potential? 85
John Jessel and Vicky Hurst

Part Two Learning to use IT as a teaching tool: strategies for teacher training

Introduction to Part Two 97

8 Computers and the teacher's role 100
Peter Scrimshaw

9 Classroom investigations: exploring and evaluating how IT can support learning 114
Bridget Somekh

10 Using IT in classrooms: experienced teachers and students as co-learners 127
Malcolm Bell and Colin Biott

11 Getting teachers started with IT and transferable skills 138
Bridget Somekh and Niki Davis

12 Partnership in initial teacher education 150
Graham Byrne Hill

13 Do electronic communications offer a new learning opportunity in education? 167
Niki Davis

Part Three The management of IT development in educational institutions

Introduction to Part Three 183

14 IT and the politics of institutional change 187
Bridget Somekh, Geoff Whitty and Rod Coveney

15 Managing change in educational institutions: reflections on the effects of quality audit and a staff development project 210
Rod Coveney

16 Organising IT resources in educational institutions 228
Chris Taylor

17 Managing curriculum development: using school teacher appraisal to find the means 238
Jon Pratt

18 Strategies for staff and institutional development for IT in education: an integrated approach 255
Niki Davis

Index 269

Figures and tables

FIGURES

4.1 Graph of children in Year 3 57
4.2 Graph of distance travelled to school 57
5.1 Predicting graph shapes 70
8.1 Curricular elements of the pre-computer classroom 101
17.1 Appraisal Man 238
17.2 Appraisal phases 247
17.3 Features of effective learning in Information Technology 249
17.4 Tally systems 251

TABLES

8.1 Types of software and their educational characteristics 104
9.1 Subject disciplines of the secondary teachers who carried out action research in PALM 118
9.2 The project officers' retrospective assessment of teachers' level of competence with computers at time of joining the PALM project 118
16.1 Requirements to comply with basic health and safety regulations for extended computer use 232
17.1 Communicating information 252
18.1 The greatest problems of IT co-ordinators 266

Contributors

Roy Barton, University of East Anglia, Norwich
Malcolm Bell, University of Northumbria at Newcastle
Colin Biott, University of Northumbria at Newcastle
Graham Byrne Hill, Goldsmiths' College, University of London
Rod Coveney, Worcester College of Higher Education
Niki Davis, University of Exeter
Charles Desforges, University of Exeter
Vicky Hurst, Goldsmiths' College, University of London
John Jessel, Goldsmiths' College, University of London
John McGowan, Arthur Mellows Village College, Cambridgeshire
Jon Pratt, Cambridge Curriculum Agency
Peter Scrimshaw, The Open University
Helen M. Smith, King Alfred's College, Winchester, Hampshire
Bridget Somekh, Scottish Council for Research in Education
Chris Taylor, University of Exeter
Gay Vaughan, Worcester College of Higher Education
Geoff Whitty, Institute of Education, University of London

Preface

How can developments in IT be put to the service of learning? This was the central question that faced the collaborators in Project INTENT. It is a multi-faceted question, each facet raising more questions of both a theoretical and practical kind. What is quality learning? What are the relationships between curriculum and learning? How can pupils be engaged in quality learning through the management of classroom work? How can classroom work be promoted through IT? How can teachers at all levels of experience be enskilled in IT for learning? How should the promotion of IT for learning be managed in teacher education institutions in order to support teachers in their work?

These questions are inter-connected and any one of them creates a need to know – a need to know more and a need to know different. And each required a sceptical stance: little could be taken for granted. Project INTENT was thus a research project very close to practice and a practical development project riding incessantly on the research of the participants.

The participants, all working in teacher education, evinced a wide range of IT and management experience. Some were from the cutting edge of research and development in technology and its curriculum implications. Some, including me, were novices in IT use.

Some had managerial responsibility at the classroom or course level whilst others had whole-institution management responsibility. It was a carefully chosen rich mix, a mixture that never allowed the group to stray far from the imperatives of high-quality learning and the practicalities of resource limitations – including people skills, technical skills and time and money.

The products and some of the processes of our thinking are presented in this book. The editors have carefully selected and organised the material to focus on matters which endure rather than matters of some moment in the mid-1990s. The questions always will endure. Our way of working, shaped as it was by our skills and circumstances has less permanence but, I feel, no less relevance now than it did at the time of the project. In banal terms we were collaborative action researchers promoting institutional change in the name of student learning through IT. Time was never on our side: it is not now. We worked intensely as we must work now.

Our broader canvas was the so-called Learning Society, a society committed at all levels to continuous learning in order to make the most civilised adjustments to social change driven by economic competition and catalysed by developments in IT.

If our society is to adjust and avoid turmoil, alienation and the threat of disintegration, then the impact and potential of IT must be at everyone's fingertips. The lessons we learned in INTENT are offered here as part of that bigger social project. They were exciting lessons to learn and they left us all wanting more. The editors have, I feel, captured this broad canvas, the technical details, the feelings of competence and mastery in lessons learned and the feelings of excitement about lessons yet to be learned.

Charles Desforges

Introduction

Bridget Somekh and Niki Davis

This is a book about the development of effective learning and teaching. It comes about through our research and development of information technology in education and so a major focus of the book is IT in education. New technologies have a surprisingly emotional effect on people for something that is essentially inanimate. While we do not feel passionate about the technology itself, we have found it to be extraordinarily provocative in encouraging teachers, senior management and teacher educators to re-appraise how they manage and develop learning and its organisation.

Our approach has been in depth over time as co-workers using action research together. We have been engaged in the development of effective teaching and learning in a wide range of partnerships. The partnerships are with our colleagues in university departments of education, with teachers in schools and with our senior managers and students. These collaborative teams have given us, the agents, an enormously enriching experience of professional development and, we believe, an understanding of the processes through which to strive for effective use of IT in teaching and learning. It is this understanding that we aim to share with you.

THE PURPOSES AND STRUCTURE OF THIS BOOK

First, and most importantly, this book explores ways in which IT can make a difference to the experience and quality of learning. We begin with the understanding that learning is not neutral and unemotional. Learning involves intellectual excitement and emotional commitment but it is also an 'act' involving practical skills. All the learners whose work is represented in this book – children in schools, practising teachers, student teachers, mentor teachers, tutors in university departments of education – have brought both their intellects and their emotions to the learning process. We have all, in the broadest sense of the term, been *researchers* – exploring ideas, gathering and interpreting evidence and constructing knowledge. But we have all, also, been *active learners* because changes in the way that we carry out daily tasks, interact with others and use a variety of learning tools – including IT – have been an integral part of our learning.

Second, this book presents an approach to learning to use IT which takes account of some of the psychological and cultural factors which strongly influence how it is used. Computers are not often associated with passion in our culture. The word computer is more likely to conjure up images of robots, machines, remote control and technology. Yet most people respond initially to using computers with very strong emotions – excitement, enthusiasm and 'hype', or anxiety, anger and a sense of threat. These emotions tend to be polarised into positives and negatives depending upon whether we see the computer as an opportunity or a threat, which in turn depends a great deal upon our past experience. We all have a well-developed sense of our own identity – a self-image – which for reasons deeply rooted in our culture often means that we see ourselves as either technophiles or technophobes. In both cases this strongly emotional response can prevent us from learning how to use IT effectively as a tool: anxiety and anger tending to result in non-use or minimal use, and uncritical enthusiasm in unthinking – and therefore often low-level – use. This tendency to cast ourselves as 'pro' or 'anti' computers is, of course, strongly influenced by practicalities such as: whether or not we have guaranteed access to a computer on our desk; the availability or not of a person who can provide us with support; and whether or not the hardware and software are easy to use. All this depends increasingly on the management and structure of the organisation in which we work.

Third, therefore, this book presents an approach to managing change which takes account of some of the sociological factors which influence how IT is used in an educational institution such as a school or a university department of education. For example, computers are costly and can usually only be purchased at the expense of something else, thus creating 'winners' and 'losers'; and computers take up space and their introduction often means a re-organisation of rooms, again resulting in 'winners' and 'losers'. Thus the introduction of computers into an educational institution disturbs the existing balance of power between individuals and groups, and creates opportunities for those with political acumen to increase their personal and/or departmental power and status. An understanding of this process, and the ability to use it as a lever of change while limiting its negative consequences, are crucial to those who have a role in co-ordinating or managing IT development.

We have divided the book into three sections which broadly approximate to these three foci. Part One explores the potential of IT as a tool which can influence the experience and quality of learning. Part Two looks at strategies for teachers' professional development to enable them to use IT effectively as a learning tool in the classroom. Part Three looks at strategies for co-ordinating and managing IT development across a whole school or university department of education.

However, the three parts of the book intentionally have many overlaps, because students, teachers and managers are all learners and can be more effective if they take on aspects of each other's roles. To take just one example,

IT development across a whole school or university department cannot be successfully managed by a small group of people who hold formal decision-making powers in the institution. Instead, IT development depends upon many individuals sharing the responsibility for managing change and learning how to be effective as managers within the limitations imposed upon them by institutional structures. The chapters in Part Three are written with this particularly in mind. They uncover some of the complexities of management and are intended to provide those without – as well as those with – a formal management responsibility with an understanding of how to develop their own effectiveness in the process of managing change.

THE SOCIAL AND EDUCATIONAL CONTEXT

Information technology has become part of our society: the so-called information society of the late twentieth century. The aim of many policy-makers in the UK and around the world is to encourage evolution into a learning society for the next century: one in which all people are responsible for their own learning throughout their lives. Access to information and learning will often depend on new technologies as well as on an approach to teaching which encourages and supports collaborative professional development.

Governments in Europe and around the world have already recognised the need to review traditional educational practices and incorporate new technologies. Their view is of a vocational imperative and one in which IT will increase the efficiency and quality of learning itself. In the UK IT has been designated as a basic skill both in the National Curriculum and in National Vocational Qualifications. In England and Wales it has its own National Curriculum assessment point and is to be used where appropriate in most disciplines. In Scotland it is an integral part of the 5–14 curriculum, to be used where appropriate in the five curriculum areas. IT is also a statutory right for students with special educational needs where it can give them access to the curriculum of which they were previously deprived. For these reasons it is clearly essential that teachers and senior managers consider how to use IT effectively in teaching and learning. However, for many educators, including ourselves, it is the opportunity to enhance education that most excites and motivates us in this work.

Professional development for teachers requires a holistic view. Neither learners nor their teachers work in isolation and it is not possible to make changes at one place without affecting the others. In terms of the curriculum, the introduction of IT challenges the traditional approaches to each discipline and its assessment. An example is the introduction of the pocket calculator in mathematics. This has eliminated the teaching of tedious methods of calculation, such as long division, and enabled some topics to be taught at school which were previously considered university level, such as iteration. The practice and management of teaching are also challenged. For example, a classroom teacher cannot adopt a new approach such as using a word processor to draft and redraft language work unless the organisation provides the resources and a supportive environment. Where one teacher attempts this alone the result can only be a pilot, because the learners' experience is across many classrooms. In initial teacher education, redesign of teaching and learning spans all the education organisations involved in the process, and they need to develop the most efficient, supportive environment together. For example, changes in courses should involve partner schools as well as initial teacher education establishments. All three components of education – curriculum, practice and institutional management – are challenged by the introduction of IT and effective use requires the challenges to be met together.

HOW THIS BOOK CAME TO BE WRITTEN

The book has its origin in the Initial Teacher Education and New Technology Project, 1990–92 (INTENT) which was set up by the National Council for Educational Technology (NCET) in response to a perceived need to develop more effective use of IT in initial teacher education (DES, 1989). INTENT was funded by NCET in association with Chester College, Goldsmiths' College University of London, Liverpool Polytechnic, the University of Exeter and Worcester College of Higher Education and co-ordinated from the Centre for Applied Research in Education at the University of East Anglia. It had four aims:

- developing the quality of teaching and learning with IT;
- providing support for tutors integrating IT across the curriculum for initial teacher education;
- developing management strategies to support these developments;
- monitoring the processes of institutional change.

In each institution, INTENT was led by a partnership of staff development tutor(s) and senior manager, who shared responsibility for staff development and institutional change. Both partners adopted an action research approach to their own roles in the change process. As many colleagues as possible in each institution were involved in the work of the project, and many carried out research into their use of IT with their students. The style of INTENT's organisation was strongly collaborative. There were regular residential meetings where the institutional partners and co-ordinator came together for discussion of both practical issues and insights from research into the process.

The present book goes well beyond the boundaries of INTENT, drawing also upon a range of further research undertaken by the seventeen authors. However, we have been able to build upon the considerable shared understanding that results from a large-scale, collaborative research and development project. Many of the authors have worked together over a long period and know each other well. Bridget Somekh was co-ordinator of INTENT, Niki Davis led development work at the University of Exeter, and most of the other authors worked with INTENT, either as team members, participants in network activities, or members of the editorial board of INTENT's publications (INTENT, 1992, 1993; Somekh, 1993).

The book also draws upon the work of the Pupil Autonomy in Learning with Microcomputers Project (PALM), funded by NCET and Cambridgeshire, Norfolk and Essex LEAs, which Bridget Somekh co-ordinated during 1988–90. PALM's aims were:

- to work in partnership with teachers to research the role of IT in developing pupil autonomy in learning;
- to investigate the effectiveness of action research as a means of teacher professional development in the IT innovation.

PALM worked with teachers in twenty-four schools. Like INTENT, it was strongly collaborative in its style and working methods. PALM publications include thirty-six reports of action research studies written by teachers and a number of articles setting out what was learnt about action research as a strategy for supporting change. For a fuller account of PALM's approach to IT development and references to publications see Chapter 9 by Bridget Somekh.

THE APPROACH TO CHANGE PUT FORWARD IN THIS BOOK

In this book we present a particular approach to change which springs from the working methods and outcomes of these two projects. We see change as resulting, first and foremost, from individuals' active learning. Through our research, we have come to understand that effective use of IT as a tool for learning, effective staff development in IT, and effective IT development across a whole school or university department, do not usually result from traditional training courses. Real change (as opposed to the mere appearance of change) always involves individuals exploring and experimenting so that their learning is integral with action and development. Therefore, change can be promoted by involving individuals in some form of research into their (our) own practice. This may be through a detailed study, or it may be through something much smaller in scale. In the latter case research is defined very simply as collecting evidence and then interpreting the meaning of this evidence through a process of self-reflection and dialogue. There may be an additional written outcome, but dialogue is always important because we know from many studies that talk is a key component of successful learning – for adults just as much as for children.

This approach fits well with what we know to be the learning experience of most of those who are already competent and confident IT users. When we talk to these colleagues – or reflect on our own early learning – it is clear that initial interest was sparked through some situation or opportunity involving 'need-to-know' and thereafter the acquisition of competence was largely self-taught and incremental. The key ingredient brought to the learning was confidence to 'have a go'. In other words, these individuals were not held back by the anxieties and negative assumptions that so often block the development of IT competence. Those teachers who believe in the need to be seen to be experts by students and colleagues face an almost impossible challenge, since they are very unlikely to have either the easy access to computer equipment outside the classroom or the large amount of time which would make this possible. Therefore, whether in schools or university departments, teachers who are competent IT users usually share another important characteristic. This is a willingness to investigate IT use with their students rather than presenting themselves as experts. They are prepared to admit to lack of expertise, and to explore the possibilities of computers with curiosity and enthusiasm in partnership with their students. This characteristic is not only important when teachers are in the early stages of computer use, but continues to be important in enabling them to keep up with the rapid pace of technological change.

Teachers involved in this kind of exploration and experimentation with IT need particular kinds of support from colleagues and senior managers. First, they and their students need reasonable access to hardware and software that is in good working order (and preferably reasonably new) – because this is *a necessary but insufficient condition* of carrying out interesting work with IT. Second, they need technical backup so that they are not too much troubled by the equipment itself and can focus on development of learning and teaching. It's difficult to maintain enthusiasm in the face of non-functioning hardware – such as printers that don't print or networks that are desperately slow. Third, they need an institutional culture which is non-judgemental and non-punitive so that experimentation feeds curiosity and leads to learning. Fourth, they need an administrative structure which encourages sharing rather than grudging penny-pinching over competition for resources.

This book is intended to be interesting and informative. It is not a book of 'tips for teachers and lecturers'. Every chapter contains ideas that we believe can be taken and turned into practical use. All the chapters are grounded in research so that the ideas they present are tried and tested. We hope that you, our readers, will feel inspired to use IT in new ways, while critically reviewing your professional practice. We also wish to provide all the professionals engaged in education with a vision and an understanding of the positive part IT can play in the curriculum, in professional and course development and in their management. The aim is to encourage an understanding of roles and responsibilities across all levels so that everyone may work together within partnerships developing effective teaching and learning with IT. This collaborative development of education incorporating IT could become a model for the future learning society. The approach is likely to involve you, our readers, in your own enquiry-based learning, and we trust that although its focus may start on IT you, like us, will ultimately focus on enhancing the quality of learning.

REFERENCES

DES (Department of Education and Science) (1989) *Information Technology in Initial Teacher Training*: the report of the expert group chaired by Janet Trotter. London: HMSO.

INTENT (Initial Teacher Education and New Technology Project) (1992) *Developing Information Technology in Teacher Education*, numbers 1–7. Coventry: National Council for Educational Technology.

—— (1993) *Strategy Cards: A Series of Five Discussion Documents.* Coventry: National Council for Educational Technology.

Somekh, Bridget (1993) *Project INTENT, 1990–92: Final Report.* Coventry: National Council for Educational Technology.

Part One

IT as a learning tool

The potential and the teacher's role

Introduction to Part One

The aim of this book, first and foremost, is to communicate the potential of information technology for learning. The chapters in Part One have been chosen to illustrate a range of ways in which IT changes the learning process across all phases of education. Although any one application, such as a word processor or database, can be used across a range of subjects, each requires a particular kind of thought process. It also implicitly suggests a particular approach by the user and therefore offers a particular kind of opportunity for teaching and learning. Part one provides examples of a range of teaching approaches stimulated by IT in contexts across primary and secondary education.

Chapter 1 introduces the theoretical ideas which underpin this approach to the use of IT. To prepare for writing, the six authors worked together intensively over a three-day period to hammer out ideas in the light of recent research into learning. The chapter focuses upon the use of IT as a tool which complements and extends our existing set of tools (including, for example, language and number); upon ways in which the IT tool may be used within the curriculum; and upon the challenges and opportunities of integrating IT into classrooms.

The other chapters in Part One draw directly upon the authors' research, so that the processes of learning with IT can be examined in depth and in particular contexts. Each author explores a sequence of thought processes that one particular IT tool can enhance. For example, rising five-year-olds explore number using a robot; primary children create stories together using a word processor; and secondary pupils are encouraged to think as scientists with a data logger and its graphing software. The authors also identify common problems that arise for teachers because, like any tool, IT can be used skilfully or it can be abused. The teacher's role is seen as the key to skilful use.

Teachers' skills with IT can be classified into a range of competences. We find this useful as a framework for professional development, assuming – as we do – that competences are not perceived as a set of separate behaviours but rather as integrated elements of a teacher's professional role and activities. (Reynolds and Salters, 1995, provide a useful overview of three differing models of competence.)

The National Council of Educational Technology's guide (NCET, 1995) lists seven elements:

- positive attitudes to IT;
- understanding the educational potential of IT;
- ability to use IT effectively in the curriculum;
- ability to manage IT use in the classroom;
- ability to evaluate IT use;
- ability to ensure differentiation and progression;
- technical capability to use an appropriate range of IT resources and to update these skills.

Each chapter illustrates the relevance of one or more of these competences, by challenging our easy assumptions about IT and looking at ways in which it can *in reality* have a positive impact on learning. For example, in Chapter 2, John Jessel observes primary-age children using a word processor to write in pairs. He asks the question: Does the word processor, and the interaction it stimulates between children using it collaboratively, really help to build thoughts? He concludes that the potential value of the word processor in this respect is great, but that a great deal depends upon teachers helping children to view the task of writing in new ways.

In Chapter 3, when exploring number with rising fives, Gay Vaughan asks us to re-consider the traditional restrictions built into the nursery curriculum, now that IT is available as a tool for nursery-age children. Young children can appreciate large numbers and they enjoy this challenge when supported by IT. In Chapter 4, Helen Smith investigates children's use of databases in a primary classroom. She challenges the assumption that this kind of data processing necessarily supports children's learning, showing, for example, that the interpretation of graphs requires careful teaching – and that it is easy to lose sight of this because of the ease with which IT produces graphs.

In Chapter 5, Roy Barton looks at the new opportunities for practical work in science now that portable computers are available to log data while experiments are actually taking place. He stresses the important role of the teacher in encouraging secondary pupils to use this tool to predict outcomes and test them experimentally. Chapter 6 also draws upon work in the secondary school. John McGowan describes how IT created new opportunities in art and design education at his school. He describes how his department experimented with strategies to teach the use of rather complex software in a normal classroom setting. IT permitted pupils to gain new understandings of design concepts such as colour. It also enabled the teachers to make significant and timely one-to-one interventions with pupils more easily. A further interest of John McGowan's chapter is that it sets the development work with art and IT at his school within the complexity of changing national curriculum policies.

In the final chapter in Part One, John Jessel and Vicky Hurst report a study of primary children using hypertext. This new form of communication is neither linear nor dependent on text. It prompts John and Vicky to consider new modes of learning while observing children exploring this new form of information storage and communication. They speculate on the educational value of models and artefacts created by scientists, engineers and the children themselves. Perhaps this is a more abstract form of IT as a tool: one which is created by the learner for learners. Novel approaches such as these may increase the value of the partnership between teachers and learners. Teachers can evaluate and support IT deployment, permitting learners to learn for themselves and their peers. Increasingly teachers are able to stand back from the provision of information and concentrate on the role of facilitating learning. IT appears to be an effective catalyst in this process.

REFERENCES

NCET (National Council for Educational Technology) (1995) *Training Today's Teachers in IT: Elements of Capability.* Coventry: NCET.

Reynolds, M. and Salters, M. (1995) 'Models of competence and teacher training'. *Cambridge Journal of Education*, 25, 3, 349–59.

Chapter 1

Can quality in learning be enhanced through the use of IT?

Niki Davis, Charles Desforges, John Jessel, Bridget Somekh, Chris Taylor and Gay Vaughan

The primary focus for this chapter is not information technology itself, but quality teaching and learning in which information technology is used as a tool.

Many of the aspirations for quality teaching and learning with information technology are synonymous with those for the curriculum as a whole. However, we will argue that they are promoted and facilitated by new information and communication technologies and therefore can more easily become a reality in everyday classroom practice. What then are our aspirations for quality teaching and learning with information technology? 'Our', not only in terms of the writers of this chapter, but also in terms of both the overt and covert views expressed by government-funded organisations. One 'covert' aim for information technology which might have been regarded as an aspiration by some is the more effective achievement of existing educational goals. Another aspiration is that information technology should act to 'liberate' learners. What precisely is meant by this rather broad and sweeping statement? The central issue is empowerment, that is the pupil's degree of autonomy over the pace and content of his or her learning. The questions which might be raised are: how precisely is this viewed as facilitating quality teaching and learning? In what ways would giving greater control to learners equate with a corresponding increase in quality learning? Indeed, what do we mean by learning and how do we find evidence for it? These are some of the issues which will be explored in depth later in this chapter.

'Quality' is currently a contested term. If education is viewed as a system for preparing young people to make a valuable contribution to our society in adult life, quality may be seen in terms of the cost-effective use of teacher time and resources and the functional effectiveness of school-leavers in the job market. However, if the aims if education are seen in terms of fostering individual achievement and maximising human potential, quality may be seen in terms of the intrinsic value of educational experiences and the individual achievements and personal fulfilment of school-leavers. These contrasting views are an indication of the extent to which educational debate has currently become politicised – representing extremes between the functionalism of the free market and the individualism of liberal humanism. In looking at quality in teaching and learning we do not wish to align ourselves with either of these extremes. To an extent, what is good for the society is good for the individual and vice versa. However, any discussion of quality in teaching and learning has to recognise its problematic nature. Within a system of mass schooling there has to be a tension between what is ideal for each individual and what is possible for all. It is perhaps in alleviating this tension that information technology tools may be able to make a difference. Let us begin by looking at the implications for teachers if IT gives greater control to pupils over their own learning.

The traditional role for teachers has been as presenters of ready-made information and as organisers of learning experiences. One way in which information technology can be used in the classroom is to take over these presentational and organisational roles. This has implications for both teachers and learners: the computer, by providing an additional or alternative source of knowledge and information, may reduce the dependency of students upon the teacher. The aspiration is that this will liberate the teacher's time and enhance the student's repertoire of learning skills, enabling greater student autonomy. This would allow students to maximise their active role in learning and help to prevent teaching from being construed by teachers as a technical procedure of transmitting knowledge to passive learners. It would also allow a change in the teacher's role: student autonomy in learning means that teachers no longer need to adopt a didactic approach, but gain the freedom to function increasingly as 'enablers of quality learning experiences' (Somekh and Davies, 1991, p. 156). They need to take on a more active and creative role. Through student autonomy, teachers gain the time and mental space to 'see and influence more of the learning process' (POST, 1991, p. 3). This in turn allows greater opportunities for teachers and students to engage in the kind of quality communication which generates mindful, deliberate deployment of higher-order thinking processes such as synthesising, interpreting and hypothesising. As a result of this change in the nature of interaction, the roles of teachers and learners can become less distinct. Indeed, the roles may even be reversed at times, as students find themselves having to explain their thinking to teachers, in order to enable teachers to understand. Operating in such a classroom environment necessitates active cognitive involvement on the part of learners and teachers: it is precisely this aspiration relating to the use of information technology in developing metacognitive or thinking skills to which we must now turn.

INTELLECTUAL TOOLS

The term 'intellectual tool' is generally attributed to Vygotsky (Wertsch, 1985). Vygotsky noted that nature endows humans with certain elementary mental functions (including, for example, memory, attention and the capacity to make associations based on contiguity). We use these basic functions to make sense of our environment. Vygotsky also observed that human culture has invented higher forms of intellectual mediation of experience. In this view it is natural to be able to discriminate an object from its background and to note another and another of the same kind. Here, say, is a sheep and another sheep. To cut notches on a tree to help us recall that we have a specific number of sheep is, however, not natural. It is to use a cultural artefact, an *aide-mémoire*. Vygotsky termed these artefacts in support of intellect 'intellectual tools'.

Culturally invented tools may become increasingly decontextualised. Notches may be cut on a stick so that the *aide-mémoire* becomes moveable from its setting. The notches may represent cows or sheep or pigs and this use creates the possibility of inventing the notion of the twoness of two. From here a whole number system may be invented with all the possibilities which that generates for representing and examining quantitative relationships. Each of these modes of representing observations – notches as icons, numbers as symbols, statistics as relationships – is a culturally invented intellectual tool. The examples given become increasingly decontextualised from the direct experience of observation. Vygotsky described all such tools as 'higher mental functions' to distinguish them from innate or lower mental functions. Among higher mental functions he distinguished between rudimentary higher functions (such as icons) and advanced higher mental functions, in recognition of increasing decontextualisation.

Other forms of culturally invented intellectual tools include literacy (broadly conceived as symbolic representation and including, for example, the use of print for speech, maps for land and notations for music). The analogy with physical tools is very productive. Tools empower the tool user. They facilitate memory and hence release attention for thinking and reflection. They permit creativity. Literature and mathematics are endlessly generative of new forms. The analogy with mechanical tools enforces the point that intellectual tools not only expand human consciousness and production, they also make demands on the tool user. The tool use has to be learned and practised; its limits may be explored. And there are limits: hammers do not make good screwdrivers. Scientific theories foster observation but they also blind the observer to alternative perspectives.

Adding a particular tool to a tool-kit and learning and exploring its scope and limits are demanding processes which may be generative. Developments seem endless, for example, with basic tools such as rulers or pens. Developments from intellectual tools – in the form, for example, of literature and technology – are even more impressive.

One of the most important challenges to an educational system is to empower the young with the intellectual tools of the culture. Children are perfectly capable of incidental learning based on their natural mental functions. The acquisition of more advanced forms of tool use, however, must be deliberate and must proceed in the full understanding of the power of the tool, of its generative capacity and of the demands made on the user during the period of learning. What does this look like in respect of information technology?

INFORMATION TECHNOLOGY AS A TOOL

Information technology is such an adaptable intellectual tool that it may be better visualised as many tools. Like any other sort of tool, these may be embedded within each other and used in conjunction with other tools and materials in a number of subject disciplines. For example, number is a tool that may be used within mathematics which in turn is used when analysing scientific data, providing access to scientific thinking to those who have difficulty with mathematics. We take, as a guiding principle, Vygotsky's concept of elementary and higher-level functions in relation to the degree of abstraction or decontextualisation of learning. Tools can, of course, support learning at different levels. Kozma (1991) identifies particular features of information technology systems which are of importance in relation to learning: (a) the speed of their processing; (b) the way in which they proceduralise information ('operating on symbols according to specific rules'); (c) their transformation capabilities (for example, from text to voice, or from equation to graph); and (d) the way in which they 'can help novices build and refine mental models so that they are more like those of experts'. In this discussion of IT tools we shall take four areas of IT capability which are widely used within the UK:

- communicating ideas and information;
- handling information;
- modelling;
- measurement and control.

While considering each in turn, we may be able to illustrate how IT tools can be effective in supporting learners engaged in increasingly decontextualised learning.

Communicating ideas and information

There are many information technology tools which can assist communication and frequently they permit the learner to develop ideas and engage in a creative process. The most widely used of these tools must be a word processor. Those who have difficulty using a pen and paper may experience an intense delight and pride in producing writing in print. At a more sophisticated level, a word processor permits the writer to rework the text without having to 'remember' it as a whole, cut and paste many pieces of paper or rewrite manually. For some, a change in the way text is presented increases its value and provides some 'mental distance' from its production, both of which encourage critical rewriting. Therefore the word processor as a tool speeds the process, reduces the demand on memory and enhances creativity. It also has an effect on the way in which we may work on writing. Collaborative groups of authors can share a screen more easily than a book and the ease of changing or recovering writing increases risk taking. Teachers can organise collaborative writing with a word processor to encourage children to engage in critical review of each other's work (Graves, 1983). Where the teacher takes the role of co-editor, he or she can encourage metacognition and deepen learners' knowledge about language.

A sense of audience is recognised to be of critical importance in the production of any text. Desktop publishing tools increase the professional appearance of the final artefact and make it literally more readable. Electronic communications offer an extended potential audience, perhaps of other learners in another country, and may enhance motivation by the speed of communication and the opportunities to experiment with writing in a foreign language. Other information technology applications also enhance communication. Music software can permit those without instrumental skills to compose and edit their own tunes. Some of the new IT tools promise an apparent explosion of opportunity for communications, in particular in control over the selection and presentation of multimedia material drawn from video, compact disk and satellite sources.

Handling information

Much learning takes place within the context of a large volume of information. For example, historical inquiry necessitates reviewing evidence in order to interpret historical events. However, the volume of information can obstruct learning, and in practice teachers normally present children with only a small selection of information, thereby considerably reducing the authenticity of the task. Information technology provides a range of information-handling tools which can help to alleviate this problem. At the elementary tool level a relational database may be viewed as representing records in the manner of a card index archive. One such presents the Totnes Workhouse register for 1891. It permits the learner to browse and select records. The display of a pie chart of age or occupation quickly reveals differences with the present time. However, a price must be paid for the power of this tool: learners find it difficult to visualise the structure of the information, to organise their interrogation and to interpret the information provided by a database (Underwood and Underwood, 1990). The tool makes demands on the user to think in a similar way to the structure that the software imposes on the information. Other data structures which are more easily understood may be more supportive of learning: for example, 'decision tree' software which assists the learner to sort or classify objects in relation to questions with yes/no answers.

Programs which process data into graphs and pie charts reduce the time and skill required to draw them and thereby increase the time available for data analysis. Speed in displaying data is particularly important when dealing with concepts which learners may find difficult. For example, children learning physics can explore velocity graphs by walking in front of a motion detector and seeing the computer plot their own velocity. Information-handling software can search, sort and represent information in graphs and charts, dealing with a range of media including pictures and sound. The data sources can either be local on CD-ROM or video disk, or on a remote computer accessible by means of either a telephone line or a digital line. Recent developments in the volume and quality of information available have already revolutionised pursuits such as journalism, and have implications for the ways in which teachers can use resource-based learning, now and in the future. For example, a learner who needs to find the meaning of a new word may gain more by comparing ten examples of its use obtained from a CD-ROM containing all the issues of a newspaper for two years, than by finding its 'dry' definition in a dictionary.

Modelling

The most highly publicised modelling environment is the programming language, LOGO (Papert, 1980). At the elementary level learners explore directional movement through a trundling robot which accepts commands to move it forwards and backwards, left and right. This supports learners with left–right and spatial difficulties. The robot permits them to view the consequences of their instructions without confounding them with delays in time or distance. The lines drawn by the robot or screen turtle's movement may also be treated in an abstract way, as a representation of geometry. More detailed uses of LOGO require teaching of programming strategies, such as writing procedures and engaging systematically in debugging. Learning to program in LOGO has the advantage that it largely uses natural language with a reduced number of predetermined commands. Programming does take a toll in time with the demand that learners formalise their strategies of problem-solving, but the rewards are rich in enabling the construction of elaborate models made up of text, sound and graphics – or a combination of all three.

Computer modelling also provides support in learning to handle abstract concepts, for example in science. At an elementary level, the spreadsheet tool simply presents rows and columns in the form of a table. However, formulae can be set up which automatically calculate and recalculate results as data are added or changed, hence taking away the need for mathematical calculation and leaving the learner free to concentrate on the scientific concepts under discussion. The facts that the screen can be shared and the model stored for further use on another occasion permit more discussion than a blackboard or overhead transparency. At a more abstract level the rows and columns of boxes may be structured to represent variable factors, and formulae can represent the rules of defining relationships. In this way learners are empowered 'to play' with complex models such as predator–prey relationships so vital to the environment. The IT tool reduces attention to memory and calculation while increasing speed and accuracy, and so permits learners to be creative in adding factors or changing relationships. Replication allows patterns to be observed and from such patterns learners can generalise and then theorise and so become more formal in their statements of abstract theory drawn from the patterns.

Spreadsheets are a good example of tools which enable learners to operate a high level of abstraction in setting up the model and understanding the way in which a table with changing numbers represents a system in the natural world. These tools have generated other more specific modelling tools, often called simulations: for example, in a simulation, learners might control factors which affect life in a pond displayed on the computer screen. The graphics programmed into the simulation limit the range of applications, unless they are wholly abstract. An example of the latter for science teaching is Stella, which represents numbers in the form of the water level in a container and formulae as stopcocks on pipes which connect the containers. Another limitation, or strength, of this type of modelling tool is that it is only as accurate as the formulae used to represent the rules or relationships. Simulations have the drawback that they are only capable of representing a rule-governed system – for example, being unable to take account of unpredictability and hazard in the life of the pond. In this way they inevitably misrepresent some aspects of what they simulate; and the model itself needs to be subjected to critique by the learner so that its shortcomings stimulate understanding rather than it becoming a tool for misunderstanding.

Such IT modelling tools enable methods of teaching in which learners can pose 'What if . . . ?' questions, such as 'What if gravity was zero?' In mathematics the use of a graphic calculator or other IT tool which calculates with speed has also changed the way in which some topics are taught: for example, iteration (repeated recalculation until a target figure is achieved) is now a practical means of solving quadratic equations. In this way, IT tools have replaced other tools such as slide rules and log tables, and brought about new ways of using algebraic methods.

Measurement and control

Computers and related devices are also used as measuring tools. The calculating speed of information technology can be used to represent either very swift events, such as dropping an object to calculate the coefficient of gravity, or very slow events, such as the process of photosynthesis. An example already mentioned is the use of motion detectors to plot velocity graphs. Information technology can also permit learners to take many more accurate measurements and so engage in creative exploration of a phenomenon, taking into account more factors than would otherwise have been possible. The drawback, once again, is in the way IT tools may mediate and structure the learning experience, but this is a drawback which up to a point is common to all tools.

Control at an elementary level was illustrated within modelling when we described directional use of a trundling robot. At more abstract levels, control permits learners to appreciate complex interrelationships when they construct systems with electronic switches under the control of a computer program. Many IT tools may be controlled at one time. Themselves made up of electronic systems, IT tools provide the opportunity, for the first time, for learners to explore other electronic systems.

The most abstract and powerful IT tools are frequently created from a number of more elementary IT tools. An integrated package of word processor, database, spreadsheet, graphics and communications software is an example. They are now available on portable 'notebook' computers which easily fit into a school bag or briefcase. We are only just beginning to appreciate the ways in which learning may be enhanced with such tools. Other new tools currently becoming available include expert systems modelled on neural networks with parallel processing of more than one interacting computer system. These may have been set up by 'learning' from an expert, so that children and other users can be encouraged to learn by imitation and playful investigation of an expert's reasoning. Alternatively, some are based on such sophisticated models that they begin to appear to operate with a degree of unpredictability and creativity. The teacher's role may move further towards that of an expert co-learner to support the learner's development of metacognition. There will also be a crucial new role for the teacher. As with all increasingly sophisticated tools there is a risk that the process of learning will become increasingly decontextualised, and the teacher must provide the context linking the learning to the real world.

THE INFORMATION TECHNOLOGY TOOL IN THE CLASSROOM

Classrooms are not ideal learning environments; they are working compromises in mass education systems. In classrooms it is difficult for teachers and children to remain centrally focused on learning tasks. Teachers are always short of resources: space, books, equipment, and above all time to meet the demands of a large number of children. Jackson's seminal work (1968) reports teachers engaging in 'as many as 1000 interpersonal interchanges each day'. In this context four salient features of school life for pupils are: delay – in waiting for the teacher's attention; denial – in being ignored or refused by the teacher; interruption – in being asked to stop work at an inopportune time in relation to the task; and social distraction – in other children's demands for attention. Frustration levels can be high, noise levels can rise, and the authority of the teacher can be called into question. As a result teachers have a central need to gain (and remain in) control of the class, to organise the children in task-oriented activity and to pace their own work (for example, in keeping the children working at the same pace rather than at the pace which best suits their own needs and abilities). This tends to make teachers managers of learners rather than managers of learning.

Adapting to classroom culture, many teachers concentrate their efforts in planning contexts in which they believe learning is likely to take place, and which at the same time fulfil the conditions necessary for well-organised group activity. Learning can be inferred from the accounts learners give of their thinking, or from an analysis of their products. Additionally, the likelihood of learning taking place can be inferred from an analysis of classroom tasks. Doyle

(1979) distinguishes different types of task, depending upon the cognitive demands they make on pupils. The tasks which demand higher-level cognitive operations place pupils in situations of high ambiguity (in which they have to take decisions and solve problems) and high risk (in which they may fail to accomplish the task successfully). These tasks are not only harder for pupils to undertake, but also make classroom organisation much more difficult for teachers because pupils can no longer be assured of doing well in assessment. In Doyle's analysis of the ecology of the classroom, teachers and students normally establish routines and patterns of behaviour which make their respective jobs easier. Through complex and sometimes covert patterns of negotiation they engage in a process of 'exchanging performance for grades', in which teachers set tasks which are less demanding cognitively or socially and students work more efficiently and reliably on those tasks. In contrast, as Stenhouse (1975) points out, when teachers set more cognitively demanding tasks, some students will have quality learning experiences while others may fail altogether to learn what was intended.

This is the classroom context within which learning tools are used. Whether they are specialist tools such as textbooks, or more generic tools such as the symbolic systems of literacy and numeracy, they have to be assimilated into the task structures and organisational patterns of classroom life. Thus, a mathematics scheme may serve a useful function in keeping children busily engaged in pleasant but relatively undemanding activity such as colouring or practising many examples of the same problem (Desforges and Cockburn, 1987). And a computer may serve a useful function as a reward system for those who comply with the teacher's demands, or as a motivator of those who fail to engage with other classroom tasks. Just as with any other tool, if computers are used primarily to service the teacher's needs for organisation and control, they will make little impact on children's learning. To enable quality learning, IT tools need to support children in undertaking cognitively demanding tasks.

Effective use of information technology, like any other tool, has to be acquired. You have to learn how to use a knife to cut a notch in a stick. Equally, without some facility in using software it is impossible to make effective use of a computer. The more complex the tool, the more arduous the process of learning its use: hence the huge amount of resources devoted to teaching children how to read, write and work with numbers. Computers are complex tools and, potentially, each new piece of hardware or software demands the acquisition of new skills in tool use. This poses a real dilemma for teachers, particularly in secondary schools, where spending time on learning *how* to use information technology may not appear to be justified in terms of knowledge gains in subsequently learning *with* information technology. There is a partial solution to this problem with more 'friendly' user-interfaces and moves towards common interface standards (all software designed to operate with similar commands) which make it much easier to use computers with a traditional keyboard. In addition, there are increasing numbers of alternative input devices such as touch screens, Concept keyboards, light pens and speech-sensitive devices. These may largely overcome the barrier of typing skills and enable communication with a computer to be integrated with 'natural' communication skills such as pointing and speaking. In some recent experiments with virtual reality the whole body becomes part of the interface in the sense that the computer responds to body movement. Nevertheless, an element of technical skill will always be necessary to use a computer, comprising a combination of practical knowledge of how the software works and psychomotor skills to operate it via an input device.

It is difficult to teach someone else a skill which demands the interrelationship of cognitive purpose with physical co-ordination. How do you teach someone to use a hammer? How do you teach someone to swim? In both cases learning is only possible by doing, and the motivation to acquire the skill will be greatest if the learner has a purpose in learning this new skill. To a limited extent it may be possible to teach IT skills, in a classroom, decontextualised from purposeful use, but this will be limited and constrained by the differences in group members' prior experience, and the well-defined, predictable but purposeless nature of the learning tasks. IT skills are likely to be more easily learned in the context of some other pursuit, focused on more open-ended tasks in which individuals can engage at their own speed; in this context learning to use information technology tools has an obvious purpose which provides the motivation to learn. Individuals may be able to participate in the task at different levels but still have a basis for the interactive dialogue which many identify as important in supporting the learning process.

The importance of learning a technical skill by doing translates easily into the importance of cognitive engagement for all learning. In his book, *Personal Knowledge*, Polanyi begins with the example of learning to use a hammer, and compares this with learning to exercise connoisseurship in medical diagnosis (Polanyi, 1958, p. 58). Elsewhere in the same book he writes of 'indispensable intellectual powers, and their passionate participation in the act of knowing' (p. 17). The key factor in this continuum of 'active' learning is the degree of decontextualisation of the knowledge with which the learner is interacting. Sometimes – as in learning to swim or ride a bicycle – the business of learning and doing are almost the same activity, but the greater the decontextualisation the less relationship there is between overt 'doing' and the operation of the tool. For example, you cannot see the most important facets of a writer's tool use – the intellectual processing before and during the business of writing. This has implications for teaching. If we take IT as an illustration, it is relatively easy to teach skills in using software but difficult to teach (and learn?) mindful, decontextualised use of the intellectual power of information technology tools. To have a positive impact on the quality of learning, the aims for information technology in education must go beyond the acquisition of skills – say to access a database – and engage at a higher cognitive level by asking, 'What questions can I now ask, with the help of this database, that I couldn't ask before – and what supplementary questions may there be?'

In considering the quality of learning with IT tools the most important question seems to be to what extent they change the nature of children's cognitive engagement with classroom learning tasks. In particular, can computer-mediated tasks provide more authentic learning activities? Much recent work has suggested that a crucial determinant of cognitive learning is the authenticity of the task. Tasks are or are not authentic depending upon whether or not they are supported by, or integral to, the learning context. In this way, when learning mathematics in a mathematics research centre the learner is supported by observing the activities of mathematicians and listening to their talk, as well as by having access to the tools of mathematics (see Brown *et al.*, 1989). In a school classroom, as we have already noted, the context is the school iteself, which does not provide the same context of working practice for the learner of mathematics. Activities truly authentic to classroom culture teach children how to manage classroom work. This may be an unfortunate diversion of cognitive energy. Activities which engage children in quality learning – in terms of intellectual engagement with valued objectives – need to be authentic with respect to inquiry in a particular discipline or field of study, or in terms of artistic performance. An example might be when children and their teacher work with a professional writer on writing and desktop publishing a collection of short stories or poetry, provided, of course, that a genuine collaborative partnership is established between the teacher, the writer and the children.

To improve the quality of learning there is a need to achieve the best possible match between these two kinds of authenticity: authenticity to the classroom and authenticity to a particular discipline or field of study. For example, Bereiter and Scardamalia (1985) describe a procedure for managing learners' experience while engaging in writing, through a schedule for self-questioning. The whole area is greatly complicated by the fact that central to the context of learning is the learner's own prior experience. This means that a task will be more or less authentic depending upon whether it can be easily integrated with the learner's existing mental models. Authenticity is relative, not absolute. To an extent it depends upon the learner's perceptions of the task and career aspirations, so that it is possible for a task to achieve a kind of authenticity by its academic nature if a pupil aspires to university, or by its vocational utility if a pupil perceives it to be a good preparation for a job.

Despite their limitations, classrooms can be designed to be more (or less) supportive of quality learning. There is a growing body of evidence – supporting our aspirations – that information technology tools can change the social dynamics of classrooms. Their use disturbs the established classroom routines either by enforcing pair or group work, or by necessitating the movement of the whole class to a specialist computer room for part of their time. This disturbance of routine is a necessary, but insufficient, condition for change. In many cases new routines are quickly established which neutralise the disturbance and re-establish the negotiated compromises of Doyle's 'exchange of performance for grades'. However, IT tools can be used as a means of circumventing some of the classroom constraints on setting cognitive learning tasks. Computer tasks, of the kind described earlier, can be more authentic than traditional tasks. For example, through the wide range of information sources that it makes available, information technology can provide many more opportunities for the kind of spontaneity in learning which is characteristic of learning away from classrooms. In addition, the structure of support can be more flexible to the learner's needs in carrying the task through. The degree of interactivity in the software – whether it be through extensions and modifications of the task in response to the learner, or through the demand on the learners to decide upon appropriate questions for interrogating an information bank, or through the tangible products of creativity (in writing, design work or music) – can sustain a higher than normal degree of on-task engagement and 'mindfulness'. This fills a gap otherwise left by the teacher's inability, through pressure of time, to provide sufficient appropriate interventions to sustain the task. Group work around a computer may be more genuinely collaborative than other group work, thereby enabling more focused group talk. This in turn may enable learners to go further in developing their powers of hypothesising and problem-solving without needing to resort to the teacher for help. In these ways IT tools appear to be able to support learners in what Vygotsky (1978) calls the 'zone of proximal development' in which *with interactive support* they are able to use skills and concepts they have only partially mastered (Pea, 1987; Salomon, 1988).

It would appear that the conditions for classroom learning can be improved by information technology tools. But, equally, teachers can use information technology to create a new set of mundane tasks which negate the opportunities for quality learning. Word processors can be used solely to produce display copy of previously hand-written work. Chunks of writing can be copied from large information banks to concoct the answers to teachers' questions without any gain in understanding. Simulations can be used to replace experimental work on chemicals or plants, so that instead of close reflection upon one experiment using natural entities, pupils investigate a large number of abstracted examples on the computer screen. In a mass education system the use of IT tools to enable quality learning experiences depends upon the teacher. The need is for teachers to interact creatively with this resource and 'shape its use' (Sheingold, 1987) through the setting of 'framing tasks' (Somekh and Davies, 1991). In this way, computer-mediated tasks are embedded within a wider framework of learning tasks, which are themselves part of the process of task-negotiation between teacher and children.

This chapter has been concerned with looking at the impact of information technology on learning within the existing schooling system. It raises questions about the extent to which information technology tools offer opportunities to 'liberate' learners in classrooms – by giving them a degree of individual control at each stage of the learning process, and by giving teachers freedom from mundane organisational tasks in which to pay more attention to learners' individual needs. There is, however, the possibility that IT tools may lead to a radical restructuring of the education system itself. The impact of these tools is permeating through the infrastructures of our society, making fundamental changes to financial and communication systems, ushering in the concept of the 'global village' and radically changing conditions in the workplace (by no means always for the better). The information and learning tasks presented to young people through new media are already affecting the notion of authentic learning by changing the learning context. IT tools are currently revolutionising school administration – it is possible that in the not too distant future they may also revolutionise school structures. The 'electronic classroom' does not depend upon teachers and learners working in a single location for regular set periods of time: it holds the potential for breaking down the walls of the classroom as we know it and enabling a new form of mass education tailored to individual needs and controlled by individual learners.

ACKNOWLEDGEMENTS

We should like to thank the other members of the INTENT team, Maureen Blackmore, Katrina Blythe, Graham Byrne Hill, David Clemson, Rod Coveney, Andrew Hamill, Malcolm Glover and Geoff Whitty, who helped us to formulate the ideas contained in this chapter.

REFERENCES

Bereiter, C. and Scardamalia, M. (1985) 'Cognitive coping strategies and the problems of "Inert Knowledge"', in S.F. Chipman *et al.*, *Thinking and Learning Skills*, vol. 2: *Research and Open Questions*. Hillsdale, N.J. and London: Lawrence Erlbaum Associates.

Brown, J.S., Collins, A. and Duguid, P. (1989) 'Situated cognition and the culture of learning', *Educational Researcher*, 18, 1, 32–42.

Desforges, C. and Cockburn, A. (1987) *Understanding the Mathematics Teacher: A Study of Practice in First School.* London, New York and Philadelphia: Falmer Press.

Doyle, W. (1979) 'Classroom tasks and students' abilities', in P.L. Peterson and H.J. Walberg, *Research on Teaching: Concepts, Findings and Implications*. Berkeley: McCutchan, National Society for the Study of Education.

Graves, Donald H. (1983) *Writing: Teachers and Children at Work*. London: Heinemann Education.

Jackson, P.W. (1968) *Life in Classrooms*. New York: Holt, Rinehart & Winston.

Kozma, R.B. (1991) 'Learning with media', *Review of Educational Research*, 61, 2, 179–211.

Papert, Seymour (1980) 'Microworlds: incubators for knowledge', in *Mindstorms*, Brighton, Sussex: Harvester Press, pp. 120–34.

Pea, R.D. (1987) 'Integrating human and computer intelligence', in R.D. Pea and K.Sheingold, *Mirrors of Minds*. Norwood, N.J.: Ablex Publishing Corp.

Polanyi, M. (1958) *Personal Knowledge: Towards a Post-critical Philosophy*. London: Routledge & Kegan Paul.

POST (Parliamentary Office of Science and Technology) (1991) *Technologies for Teaching: The Use of Technologies for Teaching and Learning in Primary and Secondary Schools*, vol. 1. London: Parliamentary Office of Science and Technology, House of Commons.

Salomon, G. (1988) 'AI in reverse: computer tools that turn cognitive', *Journal of Educational Computing Research*, 4, 2, 123–34.
Sheingold, K. (1987) 'The microcomputer as a symbolic medium', in R.D. Pea and K. Sheingold (eds), *Mirrors of Minds*. Norwood, N.J.: Ablex Publishing Corp.
Somekh, B. and Davies, R. (1991) 'Towards a pedagogy for information technology', *Curriculum Journal*, 2, 2, 153–70.
Stenhouse, Lawrence (1975) *An Introduction to Curriculum Research and Development*. London: Heinemann Educational Books.
Underwood, J.D.M. and Underwood, G. (1990) *Computers and Learning*. Oxford: Blackwell.
Vygotsky, L.S. (1978) *Mind in Society: The Development of Higher Psychological Processes*. Cambridge, Mass.: Harvard University Press.
Wertsch, J.V. (1985) *Vygotsky and the Social Formation of Mind*. Cambridge, Mass.: Harvard University Press.

Chapter 2

Children writing words and building thoughts

Does the word processor really help?

John Jessel

Being able to capture and represent our thoughts in the form of written text and have them available for further scrutiny is an important ingredient in thinking and learning. Text can convey ideas, and the recording of text allows ideas to be re-read and reflected upon. Used in this way writing may be viewed as a means of unburdening the memory so that the mind is free to attend to further lines of thought. The act of writing can thus allow us to reflect, revise and build upon our thoughts. However, in addition to making an initial draft of ideas, this act of writing can, just as importantly, include working with that draft and making changes, or redrafting, as our thoughts progress. If we wish children to take advantage of this then it is important to encourage them to view writing as a mutable entity: something to be experimented with in the process of their learning.

The materials we use may influence the way in which we get writing to work for us. While paper and pencil may be a more flexible medium in comparison to, say, a stone and chisel, there are nevertheless limitations as to what a surface such as paper can take. Children rapidly acquire a sense of how many alterations are possible before the surface they are working on becomes too congested or disintegrates under the eraser. Even if they obtain fresh supplies of materials they may lose continuity in the pattern of ideas that had been evolving. There may also be a sense of commitment with regard to any representing mark that is about to be made on a new sheet of paper. It is possible that factors such as these conspire to inhibit the development of thinking through writing. The possibilities afforded by electronic media may, however, stand in contrast to more traditional materials. Children may acquire both a sense of non-permanence and permanence in the marks that they make. In terms of non-permanence, there is a freedom in that word processors, drawing and painting programs alike all allow editing to take place easily; electronic surfaces do not wear out. Equally, however, children are aware of the option to record or display the results of their endeavours whenever they wish. Seen in this light, writing could take on a form where ideas can be explored, extended and reviewed. The redrafting entailed in this could have important consequences for cognitive development (Fisher, 1990).

The potential of the word processor as supportive in the process of redrafting in terms of ideas and content has been widely acknowledged (e.g., Calkins, 1983; Graves, 1983), and writers such as Daiute (1985), Sharples (1985), and Maxted (1987) have argued the benefits of word processing for children's writing. This viewpoint is also endorsed in the Kingman Report, namely:

> Through the use of word processors pupils are drawn into explicit discussion of the nature and likely impact of what they write. They will begin to talk about appropriate structure, correct punctuation and spelling and the vocabulary appropriate for their audience.
>
> (DES, 1988, p. 37)

While arguments such as these have been frequently expressed, evidence supporting them appears somewhat lacking, especially for younger children (Cochran-Smith, 1991; Peacock and Breese, 1990). This lack of evidence is, perhaps, a disappointment in view of the widespread availability and use of the word processor. Since children may frequently find themselves using a word processor in classroom situations where detailed direction and supervision is minimal it is of interest to find out what kind of activity might occur at the keyboard. To what extent might the word processor automatically assist any cognitive functions of writing where ideas can be put together, reviewed and developed? Can writing and thinking become more integrated in this way?

It was in view of the above questions that I observed some nine- and ten-year-old children at a South London primary school who were using a word processor in a writing activity in which it was thought redrafting could occur. I was interested in assessing the extent to which children, as the Kingman Report suggests, become drawn into explicit discussion of the nature and likely impact of what they write. Is this spontaneous? Further questions were concerned with how any discussion might be reflected in the process of what was drafted and redrafted at the keyboard. These questions, of course, relate both to the effect of the word processor and to collaboration in writing. Effective redrafting in terms of ideas and content may, for example, arise from an interaction of the writing medium and working in collaboration. With this in mind I was also interested to see how writing approached collaboratively at the word processor may compare with that produced when children work on their own.

All the children I observed were used to working both individually and with others in a variety of classroom activities. The computer that they worked on was permanently available in the classroom and regularly used. Since discussion might be an important catalyst in the redrafting process, I observed children working in pairs as well as individually. Here the assumption was that pairing children at the word processor might allow ideas to be developed collaboratively, with each child being exposed to the viewpoint of the other, as Mehan (1989) has noted with children between seven and eleven years of age. Other observations have also been supportive of this (e.g. Dickinson, 1986; Tobin and Tobin, 1985). The children were asked to write a story so that, in addition to allowing creative thought, it would be possible for collaborators to address content relevant to common interests and experiences, or which could be related to other classroom work. In addition to writing to a mutually agreed title, I also asked some of the children to write a story that would end with a sentence which they had previously agreed upon; the latter being regarded as a device which might also encourage some forward thinking or discussion.

OBSERVING SOME YOUNG WRITERS AT THE WORD PROCESSOR

Maria and Darren had chosen to work on the computer together. They had both used the word processor on earlier occasions and were already aware that any text they typed could be altered, saved and printed. The word processor was set up and they were reminded how to use the basic editing facilities. These were used in establishing what the story was to be about; a possible ending to a story was typed in and underwent a series of modifications until the words 'and that is why three girls and a boy were looking guilty on top of a ladder' were finally agreed. The children took turns to work at the keyboard. Maria suggested: 'One morning Tracy and her two sisters woke up . . .', she paused while Darren caught up with the typing, '. . . and went down stairs and looked out of the window.' Some of these words were voiced hesitantly. Darren continued to type, looking mostly at his hands rather than at the screen. It was then Maria's turn at the keyboard. She continued with her train of thought: 'They saw their neighbour in her dressing gown crying *Get my cat out of the tree.*' When Maria stopped typing both children read aloud what had been written. Two typing errors were spotted and put right. Darren thought for a moment and said: 'They saw a boy trying to get the cat down but he fell out of the tree', and Maria typed it in. This pattern of events continued; a sentence would be suggested and typed in, sometimes this would be read back and a suggestion for a further sentence made. Occasionally there were alternative suggestions; these were offered, accepted or rejected on the basis of a 'decision' process which generally took the form of a further amendment accompanied with minimal comments such as 'No', or 'That's better.'

On the whole work at the keyboard was divided evenly between the two writers without the possibility of an imbalance appearing to be an issue. Maria, however, tended to dominate with suggestions to be typed in. Eventually a screen full of text was produced, with the story ending in the way that had been agreed. Both children read through their story aloud together and, apart from some very minor details concerning spelling and punctuation, they seemed happy with what they had done. Referring to the story in its present form, I asked what had woken Tracy and her two sisters. Some suggestions were offered and, after some prompting, the beginning of the story was changed to: 'One morning Tracy and her two sisters were woken up by shouting outside. They went downstairs and looked out of the window.' Both children thought that this was an improvement. The possibility for further changes was investigated and, again after some prompting, Darren eventually noticed the repetition of 'them' in 'One of them went and got a ladder and all of them climbed up the tree.' This sentence was duly modified and one more change of a similar nature was made before the story, standing at 118 words, was regarded as finished, the whole session having lasted about one hour. It was now playtime.

It may appear from the above episode that Darren and Maria did not engage in substantial redrafting. The composing process manifested itself as a series of alternating suggestions which were typed in rather than discussed. Although both children knew how to operate the word processor and had been involved in the use of editing facilities immediately prior to beginning their story, unprompted alterations were of a superficial nature. Any redrafting in terms of content that did occur was carried out after the story was complete as a first draft rather than during the initial writing. Furthermore, redrafting was confined to modifying sentences with, at best, minimal insertions. Both children were articulate and regarded by their teacher as good writers. They did not appear to lack an appropriate vocabulary and had a good command of sentence structure. While composing, there was no pressure to write at speed or to produce a lengthy piece of work. There were many opportunities to pause and consider what had been written and to discuss. Although their keyboard skills were by no means fluent this did not appear to slow things down unduly. The attitude of both children towards the computer was positive, they found it fun to use; Maria commented 'the keyboard doesn't ache your hand'. Maria and Darren had chosen to work together and it appeared that they were helpful towards each other and seemed to enjoy what they were writing.

The above observations were not untypical: Jason and Samuel spoke little when they began to compose; the odd word that was exchanged referred to syntax rather than ideas for their story. Jason was quite adept at using the keyboard and the editing functions on the word processor. The story in its initial form was short (about sixty words) and limited in content. With some prompting some insertions were made. At one point, however, some discussion did arise; referring to the sentence which was to come at the end of their story Sam said: 'But why is he worried?' This comment was answered with a further suggestion to be typed in.

Jonathan and Laura also worked together in a similar way. Often they would alternate at the keyboard in mid-sentence when one or other of them suggested an extension to the words already on the screen or produced an alternative to a suggestion that had just been verbalised. Apart from this approach, the only discussion that occurred was concerned with the name of one of the characters; the intention in this case was to find a name that could be associated with one of the other children in the class. When they had finished their first draft and were asked if they wanted to do anything to make the story more interesting, Jonathan's response was to replace 'Once upon a time' with 'Long long ago'. Again, these children enjoyed working on the computer and also liked working towards a given ending because, as Jonathan observed, 'you know where to go'.

In this way Ross and Claire also liked the idea of working towards an ending; this was summarised in Ross's comment: 'more of something to think of when you write'. Daniel, after writing collaboratively, also said that having an end is better 'because you work your way down to what it says at the end and you have to think it out before you actually write it'. In spite of having said this, Daniel's behaviour when composing was similar to that of the other children as far as any discussion was concerned. This latter observation is of interest because it could suggest that any thinking ahead that was going on was not being discussed with his partner; it would have been merely the product of any thinking that was offered as a suggestion.

Accounting for the evident lack of discussion and revision may not be straightforward. Even though the writing took place in a relaxed classroom atmosphere there may have been a variety of organisational, social or inter-personal factors that may have inhibited discussion. Factors such as these will be discussed later. First, however, it may be instructive to consider some of the intellectual demands which, even in relatively ideal circumstances, may have been placed upon our writers when engaged in the task of composing a story.

WHERE DO STORIES COME FROM?

Thinking up a story is a potentially complex process. What is a story, and how do children come by their notions of what a story is? If it is a report of something witnessed, then how is that 'something' identified? If it is fictional, then upon what is the fiction based? Decisions have to be made about who or what to have in a story, what will happen and in what kind of sequence. What do you want to leave in and, perhaps just as importantly, what do you want to leave out? In Bereiter and Scardamalia's (1987) terms, ideas have to be 'accessed', content 'selected' and the selection 'encoded' into writing. A difficulty here may be that in the process of accessing an array of story elements it may not be easy to find a focus for discussion. Any plot or meanings may not easily be captured within a few words and, instead, pervade the resulting text so that any precise localisation is eluded. This in turn may make it difficult for collaborating parties to assess and discuss their ideas. This may be particularly relevant before anything has been written. How do you talk about something which isn't there? Do you need to justify your intentions to your collaborator, and if so, how? In this situation working collaboratively may not only involve having thoughts and expressing them but also having thoughts and expressing a rationale for them. Working concurrently in this way may make intellectual demands which many nine- or ten-year-olds find difficult to meet.

In view of the possible difficulties, any thinking or discussion might have been mediated through suggestions in the form of tangible products which could be modified or built on repeatedly. This may also have been why the children opted for relatively simple story structures consisting of familiar elements organised in terms of a plausible chronology. Within this broad strategy the extent of any planning that may have occurred could have been at sentence level. The hesitations and minor adjustments that were often made as sentences were suggested may have been indicative of such planning in progress while words were being voiced. This in itself could be seen as a form of reformulation or redrafting. It is possible that the children regarded this as sufficient for the task of writing as they perceived it.

Once writing had begun there would have been scope for reflection, further discussion and revision. However, significant activity of this nature was not apparent. Again, this outcome is subject to different interpretations. Being a reflective writer also has implications for being a critical reader. In addition to reading for meaning, a new demand at this stage would have been for the children to detach themselves from their writing in order to discern what they mean from what they have expressed in words. Critical review also means spotting infelicities in one's writing, and on occasion this occurred with some of the children. However, there is also the distinction between having the receptive ability to know that something does not read well and the productive ability to know how to analyse it and create an alternative (Wood, 1988). Analysis, then, implies explicit knowledge of a rule system which children may not have at their disposal. There is a difference, therefore, between knowing something, which may be regarded as a form of intuition, and accounting for what you know. This may constitute a further intellectual demand if effective discussion and analysis is to take place.

The intellectual demands that have to be met when children work together to initiate and revise ideas for a story may underlie some of the more manifest reasons why effective collaboration did not occur. In this respect it was of interest to find that although all the children appeared to have enjoyed writing together, with hindsight most of them would have preferred to work on their own. Sarah, one of the most able children in the class, thought she could work faster without Sam. She preferred the idea of writing her own story. This may have been reflected in the fact that she said very little when working collaboratively. Sam, for his part, however, also expressed a similar preference: 'You have more ideas if you work on your own, the other person puts you off.'

Although, for many of the children, mutual inhibition might have limited the scope of the redrafting process it was also observed that, when the same children worked on their own, redrafting again did not occur. For example, the main revision made to Sarah's story occurred when the sentence 'It was so bright it nearly blinded me' was changed to 'It was so bright it nearly made me blind.' Sarah was relatively fluent at the keyboard as well as being a very good reader, but in spite of these abilities revision was still minimal. However, this story of some 400 words was nearly three times longer than the story which she wrote collaboratively two days earlier; both writing sessions lasted slightly in excess of one hour. Maria and Daniel also produced significantly longer pieces of work when writing individually rather than collaboratively, and again this was matched by a lack of redrafting. A similar pattern of observations was obtained regardless of whether the children wrote to a given ending or, more conventionally, to a given title. It appears that in all these instances working collaboratively affected the quantity of writing rather than the extent of any redrafting at the keyboard.

The differences in length between individual and collaborative writing may have occurred for a number of reasons; perhaps, most simply, because time is spent on such acts as vocalising suggestions and swapping at the keyboard. In many respects, writing collaboratively is, in itself, something that has to be learned, and children may need to have much more experience of this approach. It is also possible that if the dominant mode of writing in the school setting is individual, then writing collaboratively might have been seen by the children as a different venture which could be taken less seriously; this presupposes that children produce a level of output that they feel is expected of them, certain associations having been built up in relation to different forms of activity.

A further reason why revisions were not frequent is that the children observed may have considered that they were not sufficiently adept at using the word processor, or that their typing skills were lacking. Although the quantity of work produced in a given time by individuals at the word processor was of a similar order to that which was handwritten, this observation alone can be misleading; for example, unless one is well in control of a word processor there may be the feeling that changing something can also mean losing something. With this in mind Sarah's remark that she preferred writing by hand might have been significant; she was relatively adept at operating the word processor. Remarks such as 'you don't need to use a rubber' were frequently expressed, however; it is one thing to be aware of the existence of editing facilities and quite another to use them when the occasion requires it.

During the writing sessions that I have considered it is also possible that there may not have been enough time for redrafting to develop; ideas can take time to incubate. This contrasts with the pattern of writing with which many of the children were familiar: a rough draft written on one occasion, commented on by the teacher, and a fair copy produced some days later. However, here it should also be noted that inspection of rough and final copies of the children's handwritten stories revealed little in the way of substantial changes in terms of ideas or structure.

WHERE NOW?

Earlier I put forward some arguments concerning the potential role of the word processor as a tool to help children in the process of developing their thoughts and ideas through writing. If the nature and extent of discussion and redrafting is assumed to be a measure of this process, then that potential was not realised with the children who were observed. Similarly, substantial redrafting was not evident when children worked individually. It is possible that extended experience in word processing may lead to the development of different thinking and writing strategies. Equally, it is possible that there might have been another outcome if the writing activities were introduced differently or set in another context. Regardless of these possibilities, however, it is clear that use of the word processor alone does not automatically have an immediate impact on the quantity and quality of writing at primary level. So what can we do?

With regard to the extent to which the word processor can play a useful role to aid children to build upon their thoughts through writing, there are central questions concerning developmental factors. Drafting and redrafting in terms of ideas and content can make considerable intellectual demands. In particular, from the story writing activities observed I have argued that further demands may arise as a result of collaboration. Perhaps future work will usefully elaborate on this. If children do have the intellectual apparatus to allow reflection and revision in their thinking, then it is possible that a number of techniques could be developed to encourage this process. Techniques which specifically encourage redrafting in terms of ideas should, however, occur within a curriculum context. The processes involved in some curriculum areas can lend themselves easily to this. For example, with Key Stage 2 and Key Stage 3 pupils I have attempted to link writing with such activities as developing observation in science and developing ideas for investigation. In these instances one strategy has been for pupils to approach their drafting initially in terms of lines of text consisting of no more than a single word or a short phrase. Each word or phrase, for example, represented a particular observation which was then progressively refined; the writing in this form provided a record which the pupils found they could easily assimilate and modify (Jessel, 1994). For this work I used small laptop word processors. The portability and size of the laptops was relevant in so far as it allowed ease of use amidst a classroom activity and avoided any effects that might have arisen due to the physical dominance of a computer acting as a barrier to separate the writing from what was being written about. This could be an important factor if the act of writing is to be effectively integrated within a range of classroom activities.

A further issue arising from this work with the laptops concerns their availability. There were sufficient machines for pupils to use regularly on a long-term basis. Over an initial period spanning several weeks both primary and secondary groups had control over how they used their word processors. However, although these pupils were becoming familiar with the editing facilities available, as in the case of the story-writing pupils discussed earlier, they were still not automatically disposed to redraft in terms of ideas. In sum, then, regardless of whether word processors are used occasionally or regularly, it appears that careful planning is important if the editing facilities are to be used effectively to encourage thinking through writing.

If word-processing facilities were to become more widely available then one could foresee many young writers becoming receptive to encouragement and guidance; here Vygotsky's (1978) theory might be applicable as a 'zone of proximal development' is reached in terms of editing and redrafting. Guidance could take place within a context such as that cited by Scrimshaw (1993) where the teacher becomes an active communicative participant in learning, the word processor allowing new possibilities. Furthermore, this kind of partnership could be important in developing a more conscious awareness of thinking about writing as well as thinking about thinking. Manipulation of text that is effective in the development of ideas could, for example, be modelled on a regular basis. Currently, however, it cannot be assumed that the ability to exemplify this is widespread among teachers.

The role of the teacher as an active agent in encouraging the process of redrafting has implications for professional development and initial teacher education. If the word processor is to be instrumental in effective redrafting then it could be advantageous for language curriculum specialists to accept a level of responsibility here rather than assuming that the operational skills imparted by a computer specialist may suffice. However, if we regard activities in all curriculum areas to be concerned with the nature of children's thinking and focus on the possible role that writing may play in this, then, in turn, the role of the word processor has a wider domain which must be addressed by all.

At this juncture it may help to consider any initiatives regarding the use of the word processor in relation to a wider context within which writing occurs. In particular it may be necessary to consider children's perceptions of the function of writing. Children may assume that they write for many purposes other than to develop their own thinking. For many, writing may be about dealing with a verbal code and be seen in terms of such surface details as neatness in letter formation and accuracy in spelling and punctuation. This perception may be reinforced in different ways: for example, social context may be a factor. Deviations from convention in terms of such aspects as spelling and punctuation can be easily spotted. In comparison, meaning is more difficult to assess; this is always potentially original, more subtle and, as has already been noted, can pervade a given text. Assessing writing in such terms as the quality of the ideas and underlying thinking it represents is more difficult than assessing writing in terms of surface detail. When children write they will for the most part be operating within such a social setting; both peers and adults may be quick to comment on surface detail. As a result, preoccupation with such detail can arise at the expense of meaning.

The fact that in many classrooms children are encouraged to work their ideas out in rough may be seen as support for the role of writing in developing ideas. Equally, however, those same children are also likely to have a fair copy demanded of them which, furthermore, may be put on display for all to see. Such a demand again raises important questions regarding children's perceptions of the role of writing; it is not just an aid to their thinking, it is also a communication beyond the self. This may, again, have implications for attention to such aspects as spelling and punctuation. Other people may wish to read and understand what has been written. Within this context it may be argued that conventions regarding surface detail have not evolved without good reason. Rightly or wrongly, a child may give weight to the notion of writing as a tangible product which, for others to read, must meet certain conventions in terms of certain details and will thus approach it in those terms. In turn this can influence how a child approaches working in rough. In particular, working in rough may not necessarily be seen as an opportunity for experimenting with ideas or expressing tentativity and revising in these terms; flexibility in these respects may be somewhat limited. In some ways, then, rough work may be approached as if it were a final draft; the only difference being that there will be a chance to put right some of the details relating to a given verbal code. If a rough draft is to be used by children in the first instance, such a device may need to be carefully examined. In particular it may be necessary to explore children's notions of a rough draft and compare these with teachers' expectations. These notions, of course, may influence, and be influenced by, the writing implements chosen, such as the word processor. If pupils at both primary and secondary level are part of a culture where certain expectations about writing hold, then any changes in patterns of working with words at the word processor and the broadening of expectations could take time.

If the timescale for effective use of the word processor in the process of composing is a long one, then the balance of this in relation to alternative activities involving the computer will have to be carefully considered, especially if computing resources continue to be relatively limited. If word processors are used extensively in schools, one must ask if the time is well spent. However, difficulties in relation to encouraging effective redrafting may not in themselves be a reason for discontinuing the use of the word processor. The abilities to present writing neatly and to make relatively superficial changes to text can do much to engender self-confidence in writing, which in turn may have a motivational value. Indeed, through using the word processor children may see their writing as a presentable product and feel a sense of professionalism in their work. In this context we might view children as taking on the mantle of the professional writer, which could lead in some way to their utilising the word processor to develop ideas through writing in the same way as has been done by many professionals (e.g. Moran, 1983; Zinsser, 1983). However, it should also be noted that most children in the classroom may be working to a quite different agenda from that of the professional. Early in their schooling many children know that a given activity may last only one or two class sessions; furthermore, they know that there may be a variety of other activities that they may either wish or will be expected to do. In this way other constraints may come into force. From previous encounters with writing it is known that there are expectations concerning what a piece of work is, how long it should be, and how much time should be taken for its completion. For example, if it is a story that is being written, does a child consider it to be part of his or her life's work, or something to be done by playtime?

The function of writing as a means of allowing children to focus on and to develop their ideas may be compromised in many ways. Indeed, through investigating the functional aspects of children's writing we may begin, as

Bereiter (1980) has suggested, to find out more about the school system than about children. The use of the word processor, then, must be seen in relation to ways of working with words which are already established. Although use of the word processor may extend children's powers in terms of their thinking and writing, the extent to which this will occur within the normal constraints of the classroom remains an issue. From the present observations it appears that some of the assumptions voiced in this respect are not always borne out immediately. If we consider it desirable to develop the use of the word processor in this way then we must consider these developments as integral to much of what already goes on in the classroom. In order to make progress here we may have to return to some fundamental questions concerning thinking and writing. Another question, of course, is whether or not the word processor will allow us any further insights into the process of thinking and writing itself.

REFERENCES

Bereiter, C. (1980) 'Development in writing', in L. Gregg and E. Steinberg (eds), *Cognitive Processes in Writing*. Hillsdale, N.J.: Lawrence Erlbaum Associates.

Bereiter, C. and Scardamalia, M. (1987) *The Psychology of Composition*. Hillsdale, N.J.: Lawrence Erlbaum Associates.

Calkins, L. (1983) *Lessons from a Child*. Portsmouth, NH: Heinemann Educational Books.

Cochran-Smith, M. (1991) 'Wordprocessing and writing in elementary classrooms: a critical review of related literature', *Review of Educational Research* 61, 1, 107–55.

Daiute, C. (1985) *Writing and Computers*. Reading, Mass.: Addison-Wesley.

DES (Department of Education and Science) (1988) *Report of the Committee of Inquiry into the Teaching of English Language*. London: HMSO.

Dickinson, D. (1986) 'Integrating computers into a first and second grade writing program', *Research in the Teaching of English*, 20, 357–78.

Fisher, R. (1990) *Teaching Children to Think*. Oxford: Blackwell.

Graves, D. (1983) *Writing: Teachers and Children at Work*. Exeter, Devon: Heinemann Educational Books.

Jessel, J. (1994) 'Writing in science: second report'. Submitted to the National Council for Educational Technology, Coventry, as part of the Portable Computers Pilot Project, unpublished.

Maxted, D. (1987) 'Wordprocessing and special needs', *Educational Computing*, 8, 4, 25–6.

Mehan, H. (1989) 'Microcomputers in classrooms: educational technology or social practice?', *Anthropology and Education Quarterly*, 20, 4–22.

Moran, C. (1983) 'Wordprocessing and the teaching of writing', *English Journal*, 72, 113–15.

Peacock, M. and Breese, C. (1990) 'Pupils with portable writing machines', *Educational Review*, 42, 1, 41–56.

Scrimshaw, P. (1993) 'Teachers, learners and computers', in P. Scrimshaw (ed.), *Language, Classrooms and Computers*. London: Routledge.

Sharples, M. (1985) *Cognition, Computers and Creative Writing*. Chichester, Sussex: Ellis Horwood.

Tobin, K. and Tobin, B. (1985) 'The one-computer classroom: applications in language arts', *Australian Journal of Reading*, 8, 158–67.

Wood, D. (1988) *How Children Think and Learn.* Oxford: Blackwell.
Vygotsky, L.S. (1978) *Mind in Society: The Development of Higher Psychological Processes.* Cambridge, Mass.: Harvard University Press.
Zinsser, W. (1983) *Writing with a Word Processor.* Boston, Mass.: Houghton-Mifflin.

Chapter 3

Number education for very young children

Can IT change the nature of early years mathematics education?

Gay Vaughan

This chapter examines some of the traditional theories regarding young children's cognitive processes which have led to assumptions about the teaching of number, in particular the assumption that mathematical knowledge must be taught linearly in small incremental steps. It reports on research in which rising five-year-olds were encouraged to use a a floor robot, a computer with turtle graphics, Concept keyboard and a counting program to explore the concept of number. Drawing on the theories of Vygotsky (1935), the chapter describes how an adult (the researcher) was able to use information technology as a tool to 'scaffold' the children's learning of the concept of number, by enabling them to explore double-digit numbers and, where appropriate, hundreds and thousands. The chapter ends by suggesting that IT might have the power to transform the teaching and learning of all mathematics.

THE BELIEFS THAT UNDERPIN THE PRESENT FORM AND CONTENT OF EARLY YEARS MATHEMATICS EDUCATION

Traditionally mathematics education has been conceptualised in terms of a linear hierarchy. 'Concepts' have been analysed into their 'component parts' and these component parts have then been 'ordered' by adults with regard to their 'increasing level of difficulty', the assumption being that such analysis would enable teachers to present learners with a carefully structured, 'logical' framework within which to build their conceptualisation. In consequence of this approach to the learning of mathematics, upon entering school young children are almost invariably restricted to working with natural numbers below ten. It is 'reasoned' that any other numbers would be 'too difficult for them to understand'. Then, when they have 'demonstrated' that they can perform certain tasks 'competently', which is taken to be indicative of their level of understanding, they are allowed to progress to working with 'larger numbers', these 'larger numbers' being only slightly larger, the reasoning being that controlling the pace of access will prevent confusion.

According to this conceptualisation of mathematics learning, effective learning is dependent upon 'correct' decisions being made with regard to the next content to be presented to the learner; these 'correct' decisions being made with reference to a pre-established order of difficulty which has been arrived at by mathematicians who have taken decisions regarding the order of conceptual items. Their decisions have had the power to become accepted as the dominant view. Difficulty has thus come to be perceived as being objective, it resides outside the learner and can be determined without reference to the learner. The role of the teacher, in this case, is to draw off the next dose of content and administer it to the pupil. Commercial texts reflect, and in doing so reproduce, this approach; thus over time the ordering comes to be regarded as the correct ordering.

This acceptance of a learning hierarchy for mathematics has had a profound effect on the syllabus presented to pupils. It has resulted in the child's access to concepts being tightly controlled and, as a result, restricted. Such restriction could be said to have resulted in a self-fulfilling prophecy in that it has placed a ceiling on children's experiences and thus has prevented them from exhibiting capability at 'higher' levels. The purpose of the research reported on in this chapter was to explore the 'truth' of beliefs relating to hierarchical ordering by presenting children with opportunities to experiment with numerical ideas far 'above' those perceived as being appropriate for their age.

THE RESEARCH

Selection of children for the study

Four children, two boys and two girls aged between four years nine months and five years, were selected for a study which took place in the autumn term over nine weeks in weekly sessions of one and a half hours. The children were drawn from a reception class in a school that serves a working- to middle-class catchment area. My only criteria for selection were that all four children should be regular attenders and articulate. A decision was made not to consider their 'mathematical ability' as perceived by their class teacher as there is no evidence that children of different abilities actually think in different ways. The difference seems, rather, to be their capacity to make sense of new ideas and concepts.

Choice of style of data gathering

The children were interviewed in the first and final data collection episodes, to ascertain the current state of their numerical knowledge. As the children were very young and did not know me, I decided to pair them for the first interview. I believed that they would be less intimidated if they were in the company of another of their peers and therefore more willing to respond. I also felt that they were likely not always to give the same answer to the same question and that such differences would provide opportunities for debate and dicussion. In the final episode the children were interviewed alone, as by then they were relaxed in my presence and I felt that this would enable an in-depth assessment of all responses made. In both instances a semi-structured style was used; this was felt to be better suited to the age of the children and the needs of my research. First, a degree of flexibility was essential as at any time during the interview requests for further clarification might need to be made by me or by the children. Second, revisions of and substitutions to my questions might need to be made as the children might understand the questions in quite different ways to how I imagined they would. Rather than asking specific questions in a particular order, my aim was to develop a conversation with the children and to ask questions as and when seemed to be an appropriate time, appropriateness being dependent on the children's responses and initiatives.

To encourage the children to speak, various strategies were used. Derogatory statements supposedly made by adults about young children's lack of knowledge of numbers were made and their comments were sought; one child in a pair was asked to comment on the other child's response, and contradictory responses made by the same child were brought to his or her attention. Additionally, stimuli and tasks were introduced. For example, in the first session, a calculator was produced and the children were asked to make it show a big number; in the final session, the children were presented with cards with numerals on them and asked to place them in order. After the initial interview, a decision was made regarding what would be an appropriate task to present to the children on the next occasion. Successive decisions were dependent on analysis of the children's responses in the preceding session. All tasks were microprocessor based; a computer or a robotic device was used to create environments in which the children's thinking would be challenged. COUNTER was used for one session, LOGO for four and ROAMER for two. The intention was to discover whether microprocessor environments could act as cognitive scaffolding for numerical concepts.

Pseudonyms have been used throughout to protect the identity of the children.

THE CHILDREN'S KNOWLEDGE BASE AT THE START OF THE STUDY

With regard to their ability to recite the number names in order, Edwin could say the names correctly from 1 up to 30, Terry up to 29 and Hazel up to 10. Sarah made no mistakes until reaching 25, at which point she skipped to 50 and then skipped to 60 after 54, before finally stopping at 65. When they stopped their recital, they were asked what came next. This was done to check that they had made a deliberate decision to stop rather than stopping at some arbitrary point. Sarah and Hazel both stated they didn't know what came next, Terry tentatively offered 22 as coming after 29, whereas Edwin began counting again from 21, missed out 30, skipped to 40 and, after 49, offered an assortment of previously occurring names and an occasional name from later in the number name sequence.

The fact that the children could recite numbers accurately up to these points did not mean that they did not have conceptions regarding numbers further along the number line. This emerged as a result of Terry spontaneously commenting on the fact that his sister who was six could count up to 100. This in turn led to Hazel reflecting that her sister who was eight could probably count up to 20, whereas Terry thought 122 would be more likely. Using this family scenario which clearly made human sense to the children (Donaldson, 1979), Hazel conjectured that her even older sister could count up to 21. Terry was unsure what number to give as could be seen by his response: 'I think she could count up to about a hundred.' I interpreted his response as indicating that the edge of his knowledge base was being reached. However, later in the interview, when asked to consider what numbers their parents would be able to count up to, Terry offered that his dad would be able to count up to 125. This line of questioning which appeared to be very effective with these two children was ineffective when applied to the other pairing: Sarah could not be encouraged to reflect on her sister's counting ability, and although Edwin hypothesised that maybe his brother would be able to count up to 100, he was unable to offer an explanation as to why there was a difference between his counting ability and that of his brother.

The fact that three of the children could apparently respond 'appropriately' with regard to questions relating to age and counting ability did not, however, mean that they could make sense of requests for successively larger numbers. 'Larger' when used in an everyday sense invariably demands a concrete, visual comparison to be made in terms of relative size, whereas in a numerical context a comparison is required to be made within an abstract frame of reference; indeed, any visual comparisons should be disregarded. Terry, in contrast to the other three children, appeared able to distinguish between the everyday use of 'larger' and its mathematically specific meaning. For example, when Hazel entered '7' on the calculator after he had entered '9', he protested and was able to justify this.

Knowledge of symbolisations

All four children could display the numbers 1, 2, 3, 4 on a calculator screen and knew their number names. Sarah displayed uncertainty with regard to 5 and sometimes called it 2, and both Sarah and Edwin frequently confused 6 and 9. All the children could recognise the symbolisation for 7 and 8; Hazel could correctly select and display all numbers up to 10; Terry up to 12; and Edwin up to 14. Sarah knew which digits to use for double-digit numbers up to 14, but reversed the digits in every case.

TASKS PRESENTED TO THE CHILDREN

The Spaceship task using LOGO

Three of the children seemed not to have a discernible strategy for deciding which of two single-digit numbers was the bigger in a numerical sense and the other child's knowledge of symbolisations was quite restricted when compared with his understanding of number names and their magnitude. So they were presented with an activity which gave them an opportunity to experiment with symbolisations whilst at the same time allowing them to experience the magnitude of numbers in a visual way. The activity devised took on board Terry's apparent linking of 'larger' with numbers getting physically higher.

LOGO primitives were used to write a short procedure which resulted in vertical lines of different lengths being drawn on the monitor screen, the length of the line being dependent on the magnitude of the number inputted. The larger the number, the greater the length of line drawn and the higher the position of the end point. To help the children make a connection between the lengths of lines and the relative magnitude of numbers, the procedure was altered such that the size of each unit was increased by a multiple of ten. This was to make a more noticeable visual difference between the lengths of lines for consecutive numbers. In order to make the task meaningful and motivating for the children, the task was presented in the scenario of a space journey. The children were informed that the screen turtle, a small triangle, was a space rocket and their task was to help the astronauts inside the rocket to travel to a star, which was to be stuck on to the screen. With this intention the procedure was defined as 'Spaceship':

```
TO SPACESHIP
PRINT [FORWARD]
MAKE 'N RL
FD (FIRST :N) X 10
SPACESHIP
END
```

When loaded, the prompt FORWARD appeared on the screen and the children were asked to type in a number to make the Spaceship move. Initially all the children experimented exclusively with single-digit numbers, and only Terry's choice indicated an understanding that 8 and 9 were better numbers to choose than those appearing earlier in the sequence. However, after a few turns Hazel referred to 1, 2 and 3 as slow numbers and other single-digit numbers as fast numbers. By my formulating questions which required reflection on the relative speed of different numbers she was able to advance her thinking further:

Me: What's the fastest number?
Hazel: Nine.

Me: Is six faster than nine?
Hazel: No.
Me: Is ten faster than nine?
Hazel: I want to press eleven.

Using children's own constructions, in this case related to the relative speed of numbers, it is possible to encourage them to think about their own thinking, and often as a result they are able to advance their conceptions.

This task appeared to be extremely effective in advancing all the children's single-digit numeric conceptions. It seemed that the LOGO scenario enabled the children to evoke their own mental images which made it possible for them to make sense of the words 'a larger number' within a numerical frame of reference. The computer allowed the children to have complete freedom to decide on numerical inputs: they were not limited to those numbers deemed to be appropriate for children of their age. As learners they had control over their own learning. Unless they are allowed this power, we will never be able to discover children's potential. LOGO is an example of an item of software which can provide us as teachers and children as learners with such an environment in which to explore this potential.

COUNTER

COUNTER is another such example. It displays a large numeral on the monitor screen and can be set to count forwards or backwards in steps of selected magnitude and at a speed determined by the user. My intention in using the program was to explore successive symbolisations to see if the children were able to perceive the structure of the patternings in the sequence – successive being related to my conception of structuring the task in a logical controlled manner. How difficult it is to realise aspirations related to setting aside restrictions! However, the children soon removed the ceilings for me. Edwin suggested an alternative task: 'Let's try to get it to a thousand.' How should one react to such a response? Take a deep breath and stay silent is my advice! Edwin filled the silence by commenting: 'Then we'll have lots of zeros.' A discussion ensued relating to how many zeros; it became clear that none of the children felt they knew exactly how many zeros would be needed to symbolise 1,000 and the discussion turned to how to symbolise 100.

Eventually agreement was reached as to the correct symbolisation for 100 and the task became to stop the counter when it was displaying 100. When 70 was displayed Edwin commented: 'That's nearly to a hundred.'

Hazel appeared to interpret Edwin's 'nearly' as a cue that they needed to stop soon, so she shouted 'stop' when the display showed 72. Edwin and Terry were indignant; however, Hazel responded by saying: 'They've got to say what number it is!' Here was another example of a child defining the task. It seemed clear that the computer environment was not only allowing but encouraging the children to take control. The two boys did not question Hazel's right to set them a task and they responded immediately. Terry noticed that there was a Concept keyboard attached to the computer and used this to locate a matching symbolisation. A Concept keyboard is a touch-sensitive input device divided into cells. Each had been assigned a number from 0 to 128. Edwin commented that he had thought 72 was 17, but having noticed the correct symbolisation for 17, he recognised his mistake. Edwin's difficulty was related to the fact that 17 is a teen name and a similar sounding word 70 is a decade name; in fact, he mumbled to himself: 'Seventeen two?' After explaining the sequence of decade names up to 70, Hazel, who I was worried might be completely lost by this activity, commented: 'And I know where eighty is', and immediately pointed to the correct symbolisation.

As a result of the computer activity and the responses generated, Hazel had been able not only to understand and extend the -ty patternings but had been empowered to discover the decade symbolisations. She had been able to use her peers' responses as cognitive scaffolding (Bruner, 1986). Through the social interaction which may be generated by the common focus of a computer-generated display, ideas which initially appear to be beyond a child's understanding may become accessible. The advice must be to let the children show what they can do and be careful not to let your assumptions prevent them from exhibiting their capabilities.

Using a Concept keyboard to structure the Spaceship task

Sometimes we wish to add a structure to the experiences we present to children as a way of focusing their attention and encouraging them to experiment in particular ways. One such example of this was the use of prepared Concept keyboard overlays in conjunction with the Spaceship scenario. To encourage Hazel and Sarah to experiment with double-digit numbers, an overlay was constructed which had three rows, 1 to 10, 11 to 20, 21 to 30; additionally 40 and 50 were shown in their correct positions. To enter a number, the children simply pressed the required number on the Concept keyboard. As a further encouragement to use larger numbers, the children were told that the original Spaceship had broken down and they had to use this less powerful Spaceship, which moved half as fast, until the other one was mended.

The overlay influenced the children's choices from the outset, for when Sarah suggested 2, Hazel shook her head violently and pointed out 25 which she said was a faster number. Additionally, they were encouraged to make predictions about the result of symbolisations. Hazel predicted that 50 would go past the star. The fact that the overlay was offered rather than being insisted on was important. Sarah first used the overlay to experiment with the effect of inputting 2, then 22, but then used the keyboard to input 3, then 33 and then 4 and 44. If a structure is offered with the intention of empowering learners, learners must be allowed to use the structure in their own way or even ignore the given structure and invent their own.

Knocking down the tower using ROAMER

This task appeared to be very different to the 'reach the star' activity but was identical in terms of requiring them to relate the difference in distance travelled to the symbolisation. The task was to command a microprocessor-controlled robot, the trajectory of which was set so that it would travel in a straight line to knock down a tower constructed out of wooden building bricks. In order to instruct the robot to move forward a number had to be entered; entering one would result in the robot moving forward 1 centimetre. All four children gradually developed their own strategies for trying to form two-digit numbers which would make the robot travel the greatest possible distance. Hazel and Terry independently came up with the idea of keeping the final digit of their numbers constant at 9; Sarah experimented with keeping both digits the same and compared successive attempts; Edwin explored consecutive digits (34, 67).

Traditional approaches to the teaching of number have tended to focus exclusively on physical quantity, with children being involved in counting out a number of items and later making comparisons by one-to-one correspondence to ascertain which number is greater. The IT tasks presented allowed the children to explore a different conception of the magnitude of numbers based on a number line. From the children's responses it seemed that they were able to make sense of what might be regarded as a rather abstract conceptualisation. The application of microprocessor technology to the teaching and learning of mathematics seems to present an empowering cognitive tool.

DISCUSSION

In this study, the children were presented with microprocessor-based activities which allowed them to explore numerals and constructions which would be deemed far too difficult by existing commercial schemes. The children were allowed to experiment freely without assumptions being made as to whether the focus of their exploration was too difficult for them to gain any understanding. Preconceptions were set aside in order to gain insights into the children's potential. A conscious attempt was made to ask the children questions of a far higher level of difficulty than are usually asked and to set them 'truly' challenging tasks. The children themselves were allowed both to change the direction of planned tasks and to suggest and pursue completely different lines of inquiry. Edwin's request that the computer be made to count up to 1,000 was one such example.

A task of this type would not appear in any commercial scheme as it would be deemed to be inappropriate for rising five-year-old children, yet the discussion arising out of the task proved to be a potent source of cognitive challenge and provided a rich environment for psychological interaction. Interestingly, even when consciously attempting to present the children with challenging tasks, occasionally they claimed that the tasks were too easy. For example, in the final session, Terry was presented with a task which I felt would be challenging to him and which would have been considered far too difficult according to the ordering given in commercial texts. He was required to order a sequence of numbers in the thousands, 6,000, 2,000, 8,000, 4,000. He protested about the ease of the task, completed it immediately and asked to be given a really hard one. Taking this request on board, I asked him to place in order of magnitude a mixture of three- and four-digit numbers, 5,000, 900, 2,000, 700, 1,000, 9,000, 7,000. He thought for about ten seconds, then identified the smallest and largest numbers in the set and proceeded by arranging in order the thousands, then the hundreds. Upon being asked whether 700 was smaller or larger than 1,000, he responded by confidently picking up the hundreds and placing them in their correct order in the sequence.

It is clear that great caution needs to be exercised when making decisions as to what tasks are too difficult for young children. Account needs to be taken not only of their actual understanding but their potential understanding. For instance, when working with Hazel, an activity which first appeared to be far beyond the limits of her understanding, experimenting with symbols up to 100, moments later proved to be within them. Through witnessing the interactional sequence between me, Edwin and Terry, she was able to use the responses of her peers to scaffold her understanding and as a result become an active participant. All the time we are interacting with children we need to challenge our own conceptions of the limits of their potential capabilities.

CONCLUSION

In deciding what is appropriate mathematical content for young children we must look beyond authoritative textbooks and national guidelines, for such literature constitutes only what has been traditionally accepted as appropriate content. We must investigate further the potential of information technology and discover how to make it an empowering tool for teachers and learners alike.

I offer the examples given in this chapter as tentative explorations of the form and content of early years mathematics education if we step outside our conceptual prisons and take on board the empowerment for learners which information technology offers. As a parting thought, I ask you to consider the implications of this study for all mathematics teachers and learners. If access to concepts were not restricted and learners were allowed the freedom to explore mathematics freely, then the form and content of mathematics education would in all likelihood undergo a radical change. Some idea of the potential for change is already apparent through research undertaken into how calculators can alter teaching and learning throughout all phases of education, primary, secondary and tertiary (Shuard *et al.*, 1991). Given its myriad forms, it seems very likely that information technology has the power to transform mathematics education as we know it. The question is: are we brave enough to do as these children did and travel beyond our present horizons to explore what lies beyond?

ACKNOWLEDGEMENTS

I should like to thank the head teacher, the reception teacher and the four children at Comberton First School, Kidderminster, and my supervisor, Professor Leone Burton, without whose help this study would not have been possible.

REFERENCES

Bruner, J. S. (1986) *Actual Minds, Possible Worlds.* Cambridge, Mass.: Harvard University Press.

Donaldson, M. (1979) *Children's Minds.* Glasgow: Collins.

Shuard, H., Walsh, A., Goodwin, J. and Worcester, V. (1991) *Calculators, Children and Mathematics.* Hemel Hempstead, Herts.: Simon & Schuster.

Vygotsky, L. S. (1935) 'Educational implications: interactions between learning and development'. Reprinted in M. Cole v John-Steiner, S. Scriber and E. Souberman (eds), *Mind in Society: The Development of Higher Psychological Processes.* Cambridge, Mass.: Harvard University Press, pp. 79–91.

Chapter 4

Do electronic databases enable children to engage in information processing?

Helen M. Smith

What can children achieve through interaction with electronic databases? This chapter explores the processes associated with file creation and interrogation. Data handling is considered as a process of critical inquiry, in which pupils actively raise questions, gather information, test ideas and explanations, and communicate findings. The National Curriculum requires that pupils are taught to use computer applications to manipulate data.

DATABASE STRUCTURES USED IN SCHOOLS

Underwood and Underwood (1990) have described typical educational database applications. While hierarchical (tree) databases exist, the most familiar is the two-dimensional tabular form. The structure may be represented as a table organised under headings, or *fields*. Each *entity*, or object about which data have been collected, is mapped to a row: each row constitutes a *record*. The model may also be represented as a card index. Many educational applications require entry on 'forms', but display data in tabular format. School databases are not simply scaled-down versions of real world applications. They cannot be applied to the same diversity of contexts, since complex relationships between data groups cannot be accommodated.

Within the tabular database, all records conform to the same format. Retrieval and statistical analysis are bound to the field structure. Precision and accuracy are demanded: categories within the data must be described consistently, otherwise subsets cannot be retrieved through searching, nor compared through graphical display.

Searching is essentially a matching process, conducted on specified fields. Text searches may demand exact matching or the inclusion of a text string. Mathematical relations, such as *less than* or *equal to*, are applied to numeric fields. Negative searches, where non-matches are counted, are available. Simultaneous searching on more than one field involves Boolean operators. AND narrows down, whereas OR widens the sample to include records which match a second specification.

Frequency bar charts, histograms and pie charts are widely implemented.

Direct data plots, derived from individual records, are unusual: a potentially large number of bars cannot be displayed. Graphs thus enable examination of groupings, distribution and trends, rather than illustrations of individual records.

Does the user of an electronic database manipulate data, information or knowledge? Kist (1989) has distinguished *data*, or serially arranged collections of facts, from *information*, which results from our imposition of order. *Knowledge* arises from the application of human judgement and expertise. However, many people use 'information' as an umbrella term for all three.

The extent to which computers contribute to knowledge has been questioned. According to Chandler (1990), data-handling systems limit and distort knowledge, since they can only handle the quantifiable. Roszak (1986) argues that data cannot form the substance of thought. Learners invent ideas and derive connections through experience, not by exposure to information alone.

There are constraints imposed by the tabular model. It must be possible to organise data into columns and rows: potential classroom applications are therefore narrowly defined. If information does not fit the structure, it must be modified, thus losing meaning, or even be discarded.

Given its limitations, why is the tabular database used in schools? Complex algorithms involving nodal structures and relational links could not be implemented on early microcomputers. The tabular structure is more easily understood: concrete representation is possible (Paddle, 1984; Heaney, 1986). If the structure is transparent, children may use the database to pursue their own investigations (Ross, 1989).

CHILDREN'S USE OF ELECTRONIC DATABASES IN CRITICAL INQUIRY: AN ACCOUNT OF THE RESEARCH PROCESS

I undertook an observational study of groups of 8–11-year-olds engaged in data handling, in classroom settings (Smith, 1994). My aims were to investigate the processes of critical inquiry supported through database use, and the challenges presented to pupils. The issues of teacher support and appropriate expectations of pupils at this level were addressed.

My approach involved close observation in guided situations. I also needed to observe children working independently. Given the nature of the highly regulated, constrained environment posing a high degree of cognitive conflict, I had to find or create situations in which pupils could acquire adequate mastery in order to use IT to support investigation. Group sizes of three or four were found to optimise interaction.

Whilst it was important to intervene when difficulties arose, I needed to stand back and allow the children to direct the activity. Investigations were usually drawn from children's ideas. They gained the confidence to tackle problems for themselves, knowing that help was not far away. I aimed to develop a non-directive style of questioning, prompting suggestions or developing reflection through offering possible interpretations of pupils' actions.

Initially, I was fortunate to be invited into classrooms by teachers whom I had met through in-service courses. In different settings, common issues began to emerge. These included the nature of children's database questions, and the processes by which they retrieved information.

In order to investigate in greater depth, I worked periodically with one group throughout two years. The pupils (Year 5 members of a mixed Year 5 and 6 class) had previously created and used a data file of birds they had seen. I considered it important that they had already handled their own data, since I wished to begin by introducing *Mammals*, a published database. This file of 561 records is intended to be a representative sample of the world's species. Even though the pupils had not created the file, there was no lack of enthused interest: some had considerable knowledge in this area.

The *Mammals* database offered possibilities for hypothesising, as there exist potential links between fields such as *habitat* and *diet*, or *distribution* and *overall length*. Children quickly found that the file could not provide answers to many questions, since the scope of the information about individual species is limited. Its value, as with tabular databases in general, is in analysis and comparison of groups. As pupils gained experience through exploring the file, it became evident that their questions were designed for particular retrieval strategies, such as searching followed by a frequency graph: 'What is the commonest food that deer eat?'

Work with the *Mammals* database provided much evidence of the processes in which children engage in retrieving information. Other published databases may profitably be used, provided that, as in this case, pupils have motivating interests and, most importantly, possess personal frameworks of knowledge to which database facts can be related.

Subsequently, the same pupils undertook an investigation of prices in other countries, following newspaper reports of unfavourable pricing in Britain. Children suggested a 'shopping list' of six staple items, and wrote letters to overseas contacts to ask for details. Database structure was determined by the pupils.

In entering data, there was much incidental mathematics: calculators were used to deal with conversions from other currencies. Sometimes, the price of a pack had been given: what was the cost of one item? Some pupils, now in Year 6, had difficulties in rounding values, or in estimating the order of calculator (or spreadsheet) results. They gained valuable experience through organising the data prior to entry: many teaching opportunities arose. Children became fully aware that data had to be organised in a form which would enable comparison.

Interrogation was a straightforward matter, making much use of cumulative bar displays showing total shopping basket prices. *DataKing* was used, since direct data plots, in addition to frequency charts, are available. A spreadsheet was also employed, but it was found that without the database search facility we could not, for example, compare prices in one continent with those in another.

These experienced database users were able to suggest potential applications, file structures and questions that might be asked. However, they could not create a data file without help at hand, nor embark on multistep inquiries. They did not have the insight to rectify faulty strategies and operational errors.

CHILDREN'S INFORMATION PROCESSING: WHAT THE STUDY HAS SHOWN

The processes of file creation, manipulation through searching and graphical display, and the nature of children's inquiries are considered in this section. While they may generally encounter the stages in this order, pupils do not progress irreversibly from creation to interrogation. It is of benefit to introduce retrieval strategies at an early stage. Exploration of the incomplete file aids understanding of structure. Errors become apparent, especially where graphs have an unexpected appearance. Searching may be prompted to trace faulty entries.

Getting started

Before data can be entered, the structure must be established. Fields may arise from questions posed in a survey. However, where a collection of similar objects is to be investigated, children must first identify criteria for organising the collection. The structure must permit connections to be sought later: the aims of the investigation must be borne in mind. A data file of stones may be created to investigate whether smooth, flat pebbles tend to come from the same type of location. Categories will need to be carefully established: what are the 'types of location'? It should be noted that children find higher-order attributes such as 'location' harder to attain (Markham, 1989).

Prior to creating a database, pupils may need to plan a questionnaire: will their questions obtain the information needed? A group of 8–9-year-olds, when prompted, rejected the question 'Do your friends take you to school?' in favour of 'Who takes you to school?' since this would yield fuller information. Importantly, involvement at this stage also led children to speculate about possible relationships between fields.

In constructing a database, broad categories may be needed: language may have to be constrained, risking loss of detail. Pupils who had entered free descriptions discovered that each record gave rise to a unique bar on a frequency chart, thus preventing comparison of groups. The file was edited, and advice passed on to others. One ten-year-old pointed out that something 'comparable' should be entered.

Likewise, children discovered the need for accuracy. Graphs were of value, since errors could clearly be seen. A display for *birth month* featured bars for

'February' and 'Febuary'. Year 6 pupils attempted to explain the presence of two bars, before the error was noticed:

James: There's one [bar] for 1 to 14 in the date, and [the second bar] is from 14 to something like 30, in the date.
Fiona: Some Februaries are leap years!
Hannah: Oh, someone's made a mistake!

Can pupils at this level attain an abstract model of database structure? Where details of each country's cheapest fruit needed to be added to the 'Shopping' file, one child suggested 'pears' as the heading (field), since her letter gave pears as the cheapest fruit. Others disagreed:

Josephine: When we do the other ones, it might not be pears, say in Spain or somewhere [. . .]
Nicola: 'Cos that's what we want to try and compare. [. . .] We want to keep the pears there [as the data entry; cheapest fruit] can be the heading for the next one.

These experienced Year 6 pupils, generally of above-average ability, had formed concepts of database fields, derived not from any reflection upon an abstract model but from their knowledge of the instrumental role of the field in enabling data entry and subsequent comparison. Other children were inclined to confuse *field* and *data*, as found by Galpin and Schilling (1988).

Initial inquiries involved searching one field. Little difficulty was experienced with mathematical relations in numeric searches. However, retrieval of a range of values using *less than* or *greater than* demanded careful thought. In text searches, pupils discovered that *includes*, rather than exact matching, is more likely to achieve results. Scaffolding provided through group interaction was critical as pupils acquired these conventions. Indeed, less was achieved when teachers intervened to direct searches!

Here, ten-year-olds wished to find children with dogs. They were not tempted to complete 'Pets includes . . . ' with the plural form. They were becoming aware of the need for a reasoned response at each step:

Fiona: If we write dogs on here, if they've put dog, they won't be counted, will they?
Neil: [Dogs has] got dog in it.

Can pupils cope with multipart inquiries involving Boolean logic? I observed few difficulties with logical AND, provided that the language of the question matched that of the query: 'Find people who swim and play football.' Inclusive OR, which widens a sample, is harder, since it maps to 'and' in natural language: 'Find swimmers and footballers.' OR was rarely suggested, yet was used correctly by a ten-year-old who had been present on an earlier occasion when OR was applied. She had not reasoned the action of the search, but had recognized the context. Context-bound reasoning (Walkerdine, 1982) may take place as conventions, rules and expectations are established through classroom interactions.

Data retrieval supports the development, in the context of familiar examples, of ten- to eleven-year-olds' emergent formal thinking: they are beginning to think in terms of exclusive and inclusive categories. Neil, a ten-year-old of below-average attainment, reasoned that a search for people with brown eyes and brown hair would yield fewer records than a search for brown hair alone. The problem 'Who has a dog and a cat?' was successfully solved by a group of ten- to eleven-year-olds. Laura urged others not to enter the search '*pets* includes dog and cat', although she could not explain why. She supported another child's suggestion: '*pets* includes dog AND *pets* includes cat'.

Working with graphs

Graphs are widely used in pupils' inquiry. Frequency bar charts, histograms and pie charts are standard in current applications. Computer graphs save time and effort, thus shifting emphasis from creation to interpretation (Phillips, 1982). Their value lies in answering questions such as 'Which is the most popular?', 'Which happens least often?' Patterns and tendencies within the data may become evident through graphical display.

The ease of production causes teachers to overlook difficulties in interpretation. There is a widely held view that children are merely dealing with formats familiar from infants school, giving little cognitive challenge (Alderson, 1992). Whilst I found pupils of low ability able to interpret displays in which each bar represents a single category, difficulties arose with numeric data. Although the chart is constructed from a frequency count in exactly the same way, potent representational models, acquired in other contexts, distract pupils from correct interpretation.

Ten- to eleven-year-olds of high ability were convinced that the tallest bar showed 'the hottest day'. They showed no concern that the mode was roughly central, not situated at either extreme. Five highly capable ten-year-olds looked at a histogram of people's ages: only one was able to say that the mode showed 'most of the same age'. These eleven-year-olds believed that the mode showed the strongest person:

Michelle: We thought [the tallest bar] meant who was the stronger, 'cos it sort of goes right up there.
Jenny: The stronger you are, the higher it goes.

From their earliest experiences with number, children become accustomed to representation by rods or rows of cubes. The longer the rod, the greater is the value. Experiences of practical measurement reinforce children's representational models. Similar ideas which interfere in graphical interpretation have been called 'visual distractors' (Kerslake, 1977).

There appeared to be no age or ability differentiation. When the structure of the graph was explained, pupils adjusted their view. Ryan, a seven-year-old in a low-ability group, thought that the chart in Figure 4.1 showed that one person had lost three teeth, which must be more than anyone else. As I began to explain, he pointed to the third bar: 'Oh, that's me then, I've lost three teeth.' In many cases, the closeness of personal data has enabled less able pupils to anchor their thinking in a familiar context.

Histograms, which are usually automatically constructed for numeric fields containing a wide range of values, present the same problem. In one case, children's theory that the tallest bar represented the longest journey to school was supported by their teacher! She thought that Figure 4.2 shows that someone takes thirty-two minutes to travel to school.

The nature of the *x*-axis, which represents a continuum, adds to difficulties in interpretation. Discrete values may be used as labels; children must learn that they encompass higher values. It should not be assumed that children who have drawn frequency plots can interpret histograms. Pupils who had charted outcomes of probability experiments had great difficulty with a computer histogram of children's heights, despite efforts by their teacher to help them make connections. They had plotted discrete instances, not continuous, grouped data.

Phillips (1982) argued that manual construction should precede computer use, to enable sound models for interpretation. However, primary pupils lack experience of arithmetic progressions, and find it difficult to determine *x*-axis groupings (which the computer does automatically). Indeed, manual construction of histograms is now part of the mathematics curriculum for Key Stage 3 (broadly speaking, eleven- to fourteen-year-olds, see SCAA, 1994). It is nevertheless difficult to avoid histograms in primary database work, since there are many contexts where continuous data may be encountered. Even if the teacher supplies the axes, it would still be beneficial as a preliminary exercise for pupils to work through the data, counting occurrences and plotting by hand, thus enacting what the computer does.

Communicating what frequency graphs show is not always straightforward. In class, children gain experience of charts about which they can make correct statements such as 'chips are our favourite food'. It may not be true that *most* people said they preferred chips! Describing what the mode shows in the case of Figure 4.1 is harder. It does not show that most children have lost six teeth! Words such as 'favourite' or even 'commonest' are inappropriate here. The language used by the teacher is important, since it provides a model. It is helpful in such instances to explain that the tallest bar represents the largest set (or group), thus reinforcing the important idea that the bar represents a set of records which conform to a particular criterion. It is easiest to say: 'The largest set is the set of children who have lost six teeth.'

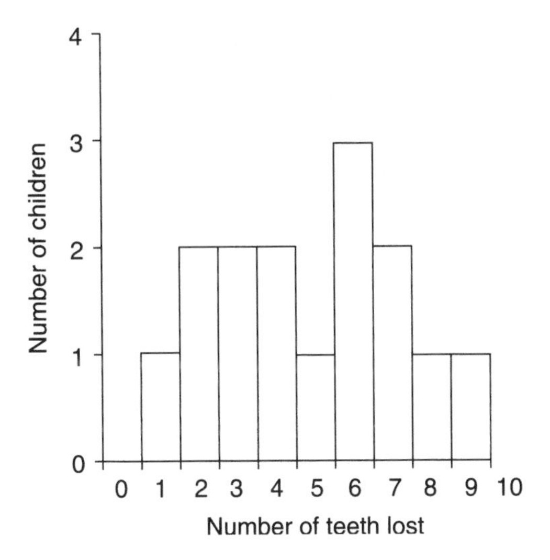

Figure 4.1 Graph of children in Year 3

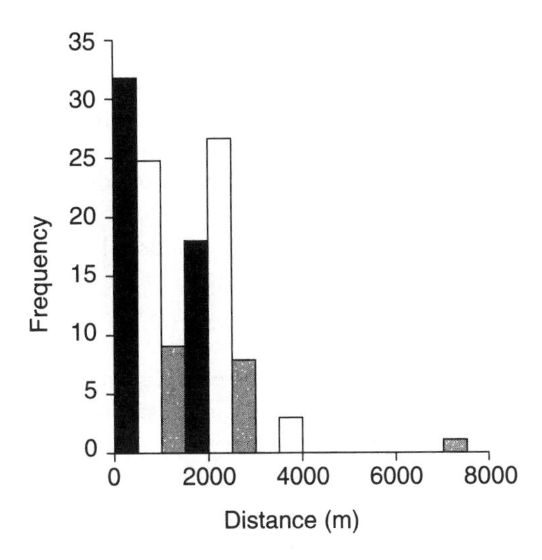

Figure 4.2 Graph of distance travelled to school

Frequency counts may also be shown as pie charts. While pupils were able to identify and compare sectors, quantitative interpretation was rarely correct. While eight-year-olds had no difficulty in relating to 'the biggest slice', capable eleven-year-olds were unable to say *how many* records were represented. Children who had recently covered fractions in mathematics were more successful, especially when interrogating small files of eight, ten or twelve records. Some programs display percentages, which present great difficulties at this level.

To summarise their advantages, computer graphs save the effort of manual construction: rapid production places emphasis on interpretation. Pupils must recall past learning in mathematics in order to interpret graphs. Most importantly, they need sound conceptual frameworks. Numeric fields present special difficulties. It is important to be able to articulate what the graph shows: even older pupils may need models.

Children's approaches to questioning a database

Retrieval tools allow the manipulation of a large body of data. In some earlier research Ross (1989) looked at how pupils interrogated databases to test their theories, and Spavold (1989) and Quee (1991) found that pupils rarely ventured higher-order questions. I wanted to probe more deeply. What kind of questions do children ask, and what is their function? Is there a progression? May even simple referencing inquiries involve higher-order thinking? As we have seen, exploration leads pupils to appreciate that they can only ask questions about what is in the file. There is a deterministic relationship between question and answer.

Pupils rated the database highly as a reference source. If the inquirer understands the structure and has outline knowledge of file contents, there is a high chance that the desired information will be located. I observed a child with a finger on the screen where the search result would appear! Pupils criticised the 'mass of detail' in information books. This had much to do with their finding it easier to list facts from a database than transcribe from a text source.

During a period of activity with the *Mammals* file, only five of twenty-six recorded pupil-driven inquiries inferred connections. Most searches simply made reference, in the first instance, to names of species. Pupils usually progressed to searching for a subset: 'Let's look at whales.' This is an important step, reflecting their growing awareness that the computer can identify and extract groups.

Questioning developed even more closure: 'What do bears eat?' 'Which is the longest bat?' Children were concerned not only to master retrieval skills but also to satisfy perceived expectations. They were therefore receptive to teacher models, for queries and for strategies. Frequently, questions with known answers were entered. This was done to test a strategy or to confirm what is in the file.

After a week, with daily opportunities to explore the file, most children (including some of below-average ability) were able to undertake searches involving two fields: 'Which North American mammals are endangered?' Since the system is menu- rather than query-driven (Spavold, 1989) the need to frame a query using logical AND was avoided. Nevertheless, AND had to be correctly selected from a menu.

While no child suggested using the computer to test a hypothesis, speculation did occur. Pupils ventured explanations in virtually the same breath. There was no intention to test the following idea (not all the information is in the file). Nevertheless, the question is influenced by the language of the computer query:

'Will the animal with the biggest body length and width be the one that spends the most time eating, because it needs a vast amount of food to keep its body going?'

Marc, aged ten, repeatedly speculated that larger species were more likely to be endangered, due to being hunted for meat. I had to intervene to prompt a test. With my support, a demanding multipart inquiry was pursued. Marc first opted for a histogram of length. He knew that this tool provides a profile of the data as a whole, showing groupings. Criteria for searching subgroups of largest and smallest mammals were thus obtained. While the idea was ultimately verified, the suggested reason (hunting) could not be investigated, given the limited scope of the data and lack of elaboration of individual cases.

In other cases, children have been more prepared to suggest connections. Having collected sports timings, ten- to eleven-year-olds suggested relationships between height, weight and aspects of performance. These were investigated through scattergraphs, where one numeric field is plotted against another.

Year 6 pupils studied Ethiopia's record from the *World Development* database. They needed no prompting to suggest connections, relating high infant mortality to the scarcity of doctors and other factors. Other ten- to eleven-year-olds recalled similar details over a week later. Subsequent comparison with other countries contributed to pupils' understanding of a crisis which they had seen reported on television.

In the case of *Mammals*, the lack of hypothesising may have been due to the difficulty of perceiving connections. In other instances, relationships have been more evident to pupils, particularly where they have been involved from the start in planning the inquiry and gathering data, as MAPE (1989) has advocated. Where connections are transparent, pupils may suggest viable investigations. The process skill of using evidence to raise the status of an idea from the merely speculative needs to be developed. The teacher may well need to intervene to encourage pupils to shape questions in a testable form.

SUPPORTING CHILDREN'S USE OF DATABASES: ISSUES FOR TEACHERS

The success of IT in supporting learning depends on careful planning and sensitive, informed teacher intervention: data handling is no exception. In planning for database use, limitations of the tabular model need to be understood. Data, whether arising from surveys, science experiments or other research by pupils, must be checked to ensure that they can be mapped to the column–row structure. The status of outcomes should also be appreciated. Generalisations cannot be made from a limited sample. Findings about an ad hoc collection do not represent a wider truth.

To use a database effectively, teachers must engage in thorough preparation. Pupils expect to be taught data-handling skills (Butt, 1989): these 'are almost impossible to discover' (Quee, 1991). The teacher may wish to devise tasks as vehicles for the teaching of technical skills, and set 'framing tasks' relating to work away from the computer (Somekh and Davies, 1991).

Teachers should be aware of appropriate retrieval strategies, and likely areas of difficulty. For example, sorting is a straightforward procedure and teachers should encourage its use. Otherwise, queries best solved by sorting data into ordered lists may be handled inappropriately. To pupils, an instruction such as 'find the tallest person' may imply a search.

The teacher's role is not limited to the introductory, but must develop to become akin to the role of the expert in providing experience of the environment and patterns for pupil-directed inquiry (Bruner, 1966). We have seen, for example, that pupils need to acquire models of the sorts of questions that can be asked. Discussion contributes to the shaping of pupils' questions into testable form. Teachers should not feel that it is wrong to initiate and direct inquiry in the first instance, but should be receptive to pupils' ideas.

Pupils have an important role in passing on knowledge: the teacher continues to act as orchestrator of individual and collaborative work, judging when to intervene (Somekh and Davies, 1991). The teacher needs to understand the cognitive demands imposed by the data-handling environment. While pupils need opportunities to acquire further skills and strategies through independent exploration, the teacher should aim to keep in touch, judging when and how to support without assuming control of the inquiry. At Key Stage 2 (broadly speaking, seven to eleven years), few pupils will be able to pursue an investigation entirely unsupported. They lack the experience and insight to recognise and rectify operational mistakes and faulty strategies.

The group setting positively enhances pupils' learning through interaction with databases. Individuals' reasoning processes are supported through interactions within the group. Strategies, models and conventions are passed on: there is frequently a positive effect on the contribution of lesser achievers. However, I found that the most confident and skilled pupils were those who took advantage of time for individual practice. Teachers need to consider how to intervene when dominant pupils threaten group processes. Compensatory action is needed when individuals (usually girls or less-able pupils) are excluded from dominant peer groups where IT capability carries high status, and within which expertise is shared.

SUMMARY

In summary, we may consider the outcomes of pupils' database activity both in terms of process and product. While the tabular structure limits the potential field of application, it is sufficiently transparent to enable Key Stage 2 pupils to grasp retrieval skills and strategies, and thus engage in information processing. The process requires concentrated cognitive effort at all stages, and may draw significantly on pupils' present understandings of mathematics and language.

Products of inquiry are less tangible since, due to the limited information on individual cases which the system can sustain, data file interrogation cannot yield all we need to know to pursue a question in depth. However, patterns and connections discovered by children may, through teacher intervention, give rise to further research or launch new areas of inquiry.

Teachers of Key Stage 2 pupils are faced with the challenge of developing curriculum contexts for database use in supporting pupils' critical inquiry. Context is essential, even if the objective is purely to teach database skills. Data handling should not be seen as a discrete content area, but as embedded within research and inquiries which are the focus of curriculum work – for example in science, history or geography. Even if skills need to be identified and taught at specific points they should not be taught in an isolated, piecemeal way. Electronic databases, appropriately planned for and supported through well-informed, sensitive teacher intervention, may inspire and facilitate investigatory work in a number of curriculum areas.

REFERENCES

Alderson, G. (1992) 'Information handling and the development of statistical understanding in primary children', in J. Lodge (ed.), *Computer Data Handling in the Primary School.* London: David Fulton.

Bruner, J.S. (1966) *Toward a Theory of Instruction.* Cambridge, Mass.: Harvard University Press.

Butt, P.J. (1989) 'An educational database: but what about the questions?', *Information Technology and Learning,* 12, 2, 51–2.

Chandler, D. (1990) 'The educational ideology of the computer', *British Journal of Educational Technology,* 1, 3, 165–74.

Galpin, B. and Schilling, M. (1988) '*Computers, Topic Work and Young Children: Learning to Use Information in the Primary Classroom*', Library and Information Research Report 68. London: British Library Board.

Heaney, P. (1986) 'Information skills in the primary school', *Greater Manchester Primary Contact,* 4, 1, 68–78.

Kerslake, D. (1977) 'The concept of graphs in secondary school pupils aged 12–14 years', unpublished MPhil thesis, Chelsea College, University of London.

Kist, J. (1989) 'Electronic publishing', in M. Eraut (ed.), *International Encyclopaedia of Educational Technology.* Oxford: Pergamon Press.

MAPE (Micros and Primary Education) (1989) 'Evidence from MAPE to the National Curriculum Council in response to the design and technology proposals', *Microscope,* 28, 1–8.

Markham, E.M. (1989) *Categorization and Naming in Children.* Cambridge, Mass.: MIT Press.

Paddle, A. (1984) 'Observation, identification and information retrieval', in J. Stewart (ed.), *Micros and Project Work.* London: Microelectronics Education Programme.

Phillips, R.J. (1982) 'An investigation of the microcomputer as a mathematics teaching aid', *Computers and Education,* 6, 1.

Quee, J. (1991) *Park Mead County Middle School Database Project,* Groupwork with Computers Project Report. Brighton: University of Sussex.

Ross, A. (1989) 'Fossils, conkers and parachutes: children's data from science experiments', *Primary Teaching Studies,* 4, 2.

Roszak, T. (1986) *The Cult of Information: The Folklore of Computers and the True Art of Thinking*. Cambridge: Lutterworth.
SCAA (School Curriculum and Assessment Authority) (1994) *Mathematics in the National Curriculum: Draft Proposals*. London: School Curriculum and Assessment Authority/Central Office of Information.
Smith, H.M. (1994) 'The use of computerized databases in critical inquiry by pupils aged 8 to 11 years', unpublished DPhil thesis, University of Sussex.
Somekh, B. and Davies, R. (1991) 'Towards a pedagogy for information technology', *Curriculum Journal*, 2, 2, 153–67.
Spavold, J. (1989) 'Children and databases: an analysis of data entry and query formulation', *Journal of Computer Assisted Learning*, 5, 145–60.
Underwood, J. and Underwood, G. (1990) *Computers and Learning*. Oxford: Blackwell.
Walkerdine, V. (1982) 'From context to text: a psychosemiotic approach to abstract thought', in M. Beveridge (ed.), *Children Thinking Through Language*. London: Edward Arnold.

SOFTWARE

Junior Pinpoint: Longman Logotron, 124 Cambridge Science Park, Milton Road, Cambridge CB4 4ZS.
DataKing: Shenley Software, 5 Coombefield Close, New Malden, Surrey KT3 5QF.
Mammals of the World: a Key Datafile. Anglia Television Ltd, Norwich NR1 3JG.
World Development Database. Centre for World Development Education, 1 Catton Street, London WC1R 4AB.

Chapter 5

Does data logging change the nature of children's thinking in experimental work in science?

Roy Barton

This chapter sets out the teaching and learning opportunities which are available when computers are used to assist in the collection and processing of data during practical work in science. This includes a brief outline of the main constituents of a data logging system. Comparisons are made between computer-aided and conventional practical work, in particular highlighting the different ways in which pupils interact with each other and the equipment. Teaching with the aid of computers also requires changes to the ways in which teachers interact with pupils. These areas are explored by looking at evidence obtained by closely observing pupils working on practical science tasks whilst using a computer.

BACKGROUND

My own interest in this area stems from my background as a science teacher over a number of years. I have always been interested in new ideas and developments to improve the effectiveness of science teaching. For example, in the early 1980s I was excited by the prospect of using computer simulation for the first time, only to be disappointed along with many of my colleagues at the quality of the early software. In 1988 I was seconded from my teaching post to work on curriculum developments to support the use of computers for practical work in science. It was at that time that I became convinced that this particular application of IT was not simply another development but one which had the potential to make a fundamental change to the quality of pupils' practical work in science. Since that time my experiences with pupils and teachers and the results of my research work in this area have served to strengthen this conviction. I will explore the reasons for my views in this chapter.

DATA LOGGING

Before considering teaching and learning, I wish to identify what data logging is and why it currently has such a high profile in school science. Almost every science teacher would agree that practical work enjoys a central place in school science for all age groups. It follows that the possibility of using computers during practical work has the potential to fit naturally into mainstream science activities. This has been given added impetus by the IT requirement set out in the National Curriculum for Science. It is clear that as in other areas of the curriculum IT in science is here to stay.

So what is involved when pupils use computers during practical work? The term data logging is usually used to describe the activity by which measurements are collected during an experiment by sensors and then sent to a computer for processing. The main elements of a data logging system are sensors to collect the measurements, an interface or data logger, a computer and a computer program to control the process. I will deal with each of these four elements in turn.

The sensors simply respond to the physical quantities which are to be measured, such as temperature, light level, sound level, oxygen concentration, etc. These measurements are then converted into an electrical signal which is passed on to the interface or data logger. Data loggers can collect information from several sensors simultaneously and then either pass the information directly to a computer or store the information so that it can be passed on later. When the information is sent to the computer it is often displayed on the computer screen in the form of a graph. However, the software also offers other facilities such as changing the ways in which the data are displayed or allowing further analysis of the data.

Data loggers can be used in two different ways. In real-time logging the graph is presented on the computer screen at the same time as the experiment is in progress, whereas in remote data logging data are collected and stored in the data logger and then transferred later to a computer. Remote logging extends practical activities beyond the school laboratory, for example to woods and sea shores, and also allows experiments to last for longer than a single science lesson, e.g. several days.

A significant recent development has been the growing availability of affordable and powerful portable computers. These computers have a number of advantages for data logging over desktop computers. For example, they can be distributed and stored easily, they have a small 'footprint' on limited laboratory bench space and their hard disk gives pupils quick access to software and the possibility of building up a library of files during their science lessons. The potential of portable computers was confirmed in the recent Portable Computers in Schools project which involved the use of portable computers in 118 primary and secondary schools in all curriculum areas. The evaluation summary (Stradling *et al.*, 1994) suggested that in science the portables provided increased opportunities for active learning particularly in relation to scientific investigations.

We have now reached a stage at which all the elements for laboratory-based data logging are in place: a wide and growing range of sensors, sophisticated and easy to use data loggers, portable computers for easy access and storage and powerful software for the presentation and analysis of data.

CONVENTIONAL PRACTICAL SCIENCE IN SCHOOLS

Before considering the benefits of computer-mediated practical work, I will first briefly consider conventional practical work in science. What is the purpose of practical work in science and what is normally done during this type of activity? Practical work can be either illustrative or investigative. Illustrative practical work is used to demonstrate scientific principles, ideas or concepts whereas investigative practical work is an opportunity for pupils to explore their own ideas and develop scientific understanding. Practical work usually involves planning, collecting and analysing experimental data.

Why is practical work done? There are many reasons put forward but it centres around the belief that pupils will gain a greater insight into scientific ideas and concepts by having 'hands-on' experience. However, this will only be effective if pupils have the time and opportunity to reflect on what was done and, most importantly, have guidance and help from a skilful science teacher. The teacher is needed to provide a framework and to help pupils understand the wider significance of their observations. It is at this point that I believe conventional practical work runs into difficulties. Far too often pupils spend most of the lesson simply collecting and processing data with far too little time available for the crucial analysis and discussion of those data which is so important for an effective scientific understanding. Unfortunately, many pupils see practical work as isolated and unconnected episodes.

PRACTICAL SCIENCE WITH COMPUTERS

What are the advantages of using computer-aided practical work? Can data logging assist in achieving the aims of practical science? It is clear that presenting the results of investigations in a graphical form at the same time as the activity is in progress will save time: time which can be used for the purposes discussed above. However, a number of other benefits are claimed for data logging beyond the time-saving aspect. These benefits centre on the fact that data can be presented in a graphical form on the computer screen as the experiment is in progress. The advantages suggested for data logging include:

- an immediate link between the investigation and the result, rather than the usual long delay between 'the experiment' and 'the graph', which are often seen as separate entities by pupils. This immediacy can lead to an increase in pupil motivation;
- time for the pupils to think and to watch, rather than spend all their time recording data (often taking little notice of their experimental set-up);
- enabling pupils to look at trends and gradients on the graph;
- making the first experience qualitative – numbers are available later if they are required. This contrasts with the conventional approach which requires numerical data to be collected and a graph to be plotted before any kind of analysis is possible;
- encouragement of pupils to predict and to test their predictions.

To what extent are we able to back these claims with evidence obtained from the classroom? Are the research findings providing ideas for how to get the most from this new educational tool?

EVIDENCE FROM RESEARCH WORK WITH PUPILS

I wish to discuss the results of research in the following areas:

- simultaneous collection and presentation of data;
- focus effect of the computer screen;
- graphing skills;
- pupil/teacher interactions.

Simultaneous collection and presentation of data

A three-month study carried out by Mokros and Tinker (1987) making use of computer-aided practical work in several areas of the science syllabus noted significant gains in terms of pupils' graphing skills. They suggested that there may be four reasons for the success of such work: 'it uses multiple modalities, it pairs real time events with their symbolic representation, it provides a genuine scientific experience and it eliminates the drudgery of graph production'.

Manipulating the equipment, experiencing the activity and seeing the physical phenomena change are among the benefits claimed for practical work in general. However, as suggested above, in the case of computer-aided practical work, pupils have the added benefit of seeing the graphical representation at the same time. An example of this was demonstrated by Brasell (1985) using a motion sensor. The motion sensor is a range-finding device which is placed on the edge of a bench and is connected to a computer. As pupils move in front of the device they can see a distance against time graph forming on the computer screen in response to their movement. Brasell worked with three groups of pupils who were taught about motion graphs. In the post-tests those who had used the motion sensor performed much better than those who had been taught conventionally. However, most significantly, the group who had used the motion sensor but who were only allowed to see the motion graph after a delay of twenty to thirty seconds performed as badly as those using conventional methods. It seemed that only a very short delay was enough to lose all the benefit evident when the graph is presented at the same time as the pupils' movements.

I have carried out small-scale studies involving pupils working on the same task but using different methods. This work confirmed the time-saving aspects of data logging but was less conclusive in relation to the benefits of real-time logging. Some pupils used computer-aided practical work whilst others employed conventional methods. The pupils were exploring the relationship between electrical power and current in a resistor. Some pupils did this using a current/voltage module connected to a computer (for a description of this device, see Barton, 1990), whilst others carried out a conventional practical investigation using ammeters and voltmeters. The computer-assisted activity was completed in about half the time needed for the conventional work in spite of the fact that the computer group needed to be instructed in the use of the software prior to the activity. However, the immediate presentation of data did not seem to be significant in affecting the pupils' understanding of those data.

Focus effect of the computer screen

A feature reported by other researchers is the focusing effect the computer screen seems to have. For example, Nakhleh and Krajcik (1993), when comparing pupils' performance on acid-base titrations whilst using different levels of technology (from microcomputer to chemical indicators), suggested that a key factor was the way new technology can have the effect of narrowing the focus of the pupil's attention to the evolving graph on the screen.

In an attempt to obtain more detailed data on this effect I have videotaped sessions of two pupils working at the computer. The transcript, which included pupils' actions, confirmed the way in which the screen was used as the focus point for the whole activity. Pupils used the screen to provide the basis for a shared experience. The videotape shows that pupils watched and frequently pointed to the screen throughout the activity. Comments were often made by the pupils as soon as data started to appear on the screen, particularly if the data did not coincide with their expectations.

Typical action from the collected data included:

Teacher: Take it nice and steady for the bulbs. [Pupil 1 points to the gap between the two types of trace]

Pupil 2: Oooh! [Both smile . . . both pupils pay close attention to the screen . . . conspiratorial discussion]

[Pupil 1 turns the potentiometer up and then down – not systematically; both pupils look closely at the screen]

Pupils use the screen when trying to explain their interpretations and ideas. In this case the answer to a question was given by the pupil pointing along the traces with her finger. At its simplest, pupils made use of the screen as a sort of notebook. Once they had been asked to use a marker pen to label an on-screen graph they chose to mark the screen on other occasions.

Graphing skills

Practical work in science involves not only the use of equipment but also the development of data analysis skills. This has been re-emphasised in the recent changes to the Science National Curriculum which requires pupils to use graphs to identify relationships between variables and to be able to identify trends and patterns in results.

Nachmias and Linn (1987) have reported a number of problems associated with the use of a computer to present graphical information. They reported that pupils tend to view computer-generated graphs uncritically, in much the same way as they are uncritical of graphical information presented in textbooks. They contrast this with the way pupils are willing to question graphs they draw themselves. My experience is that pupils tend to be uncritical of graphical data no matter how they are produced. I feel there is an important role here for the teacher in encouraging a questioning and sceptical view of computer-generated graphical data.

From my own research it is clear that computers can avoid the serious problems pupils face when trying to produce manual plots of moderately difficult data. For example, in the work on electrical power discussed earlier, half of the pupils who were described by their teachers as most able could not produce a plot of power against current using values such as 400 mW and 0.25 A. The use of the computer avoids these problems.

However, no matter how the data are plotted, many pupils find data analysis and interpretation difficult. A closer look at the ways in which pupils analyse data on the computer screen indicates that their graphical analysis skills are in a very dynamic state, with evidence of rapid progress being observed over the period of one session whilst using the computer. Perhaps by giving time to focus on these skills rather than those of data processing, data logging will be a major factor in improving pupils' skills in this area. The problems noted mainly related to the origin and to the scale of the graph. In several sessions pupils misinterpreted the position of the origin or assumed that data would always pass through it. When looking for patterns some pupils saw small fluctuations due to experimental error as quite different numbers; in some cases this was further complicated by pupils reading eight significant figures from their calculator screen.

Pupil/teacher interactions

Potentially the most significant contribution is the effect this new technology may have on the ways in which pupils interact with each other and the teacher during practical work. Teachers will need to identify ways in which they can support pupils to make the most effective use of the software tools available to them. This will involve moving the focus of classroom attention away from activities which involve the collection and processing of data to activities in which pupils use software tools to make predictions and explore relationships between variables.

A number of studies looking at other aspects of IT have identified the central role the teacher plays in making effective use of the technology. The SLANT (Spoken Language and New Technology) project (Mercer, 1994) suggests that the way in which teachers organise their classrooms, the precise instructions they give and the relationships established influence the course of computer-based activities and the quality of the talk generated by them. Amongst their conclusions they noted the importance of the influence of teacher intervention and suggested that more research was needed in this area. In the report on the ImpacT (Impact of Information Technology on Children's Achievements in Primary and Secondary Schools) project, Watson *et al.* (1993) found that the use of IT increased the importance of the teacher's role and their interactions with pupils.

It is very difficult to investigate pupil–pupil and pupil–teacher interactions during the course of normal classroom-based practical science activities; the data discussed below came from closely observing and videotaping pairs of pupils extracted from their normal science sessions. This has provided a detailed insight into these interactions even though the situation is rather artificial.

During my many years as a science teacher it became apparent that pupils do not often have extended discussions about the science activities they are engaged in during practical science sessions. The discussions which do take place tend to be procedural and relate to carrying out rather than analysing the task. The videotaped sessions when pupils are using computer-mediated practical work also show that the majority of the interactions involve pupils and teachers rather than being between pupils themselves. This is not surprising in single one-hour sessions in the unusual setting of one pair of pupils and one teacher. However, there were exceptions to this; for example, when pupils identified with the problem, the exchanges became animated and rapid. The following exchange took place between two Year 10 pupils in a period of only two minutes. They were using a component concealed from them and trying to identify what it was:

Pupil 2: Yes we can test bulb three say, and if it's similar to that it's that and if it isn't then it must be bulb two.
Teacher: OK.
Pupil 2: 'Cos it isn't bulb one. [Pupil 2 sketches the trace from the black box]
Pupil 1: Bulb . . . which one should we do? Bulb two?
Pupil 2: How quick did you do it?
Pupil 1: Wait, wait a sec. [Adjusts the software]
Pupil 2: How quick did you do it?
Pupil 1: Quite quickly. [Pupil 2 adjusts the voltage]
Pupil 1: Yes it does. That doesn't, no way. It might be.
Pupil 2: No I think this is bulb two, I think the other one is bulb three.
Pupil 2: [Turns to teacher] Is it bulb three?
Pupil 1: Let's try bulb three. [Sets up software and starts to collect]

However, most of the sequences show a close and continual interaction between the pair of pupils and the 'teacher'. The form of interaction which proved to be most effective in stimulating pupils to get involved were mainly general questions which required the pupils to link the results collected with broader scientific ideas, for example:

Teacher: Still doing it, isn't it? OK. Any ideas why it should be a different line going up and going down?
Pupil 2: Because when the electricity is coming out it goes this way and when the voltage is coming out it goes down.
Teacher: And why do you think it, I can see it's coming down quicker but why? What do you think is happening to the bulb?
[Pause]
Pupil 1: It's cooling down. [Laughs – unsure of what she has just said]
Teacher: It's cooling down. It's a reasonable suggestion.
[Pause; pupil 1 looks back at the screen]
Teacher: Yes it is something to do with its temperature.

It would seem that, as with other situations, probing questions are a very effective teaching aid. In these situations there is also the added benefit that the investigation is still very fresh in the pupils' minds.

However, there were times when the interaction caused problems, with the teacher thinking more about the next step than taking time to probe the pupils' understanding. For example, pupils were asked to use the data they had collected to predict the shape of a new graph and then immediately collect the data using the computer to compare the screen graph with their predictions (Figure 5.1).

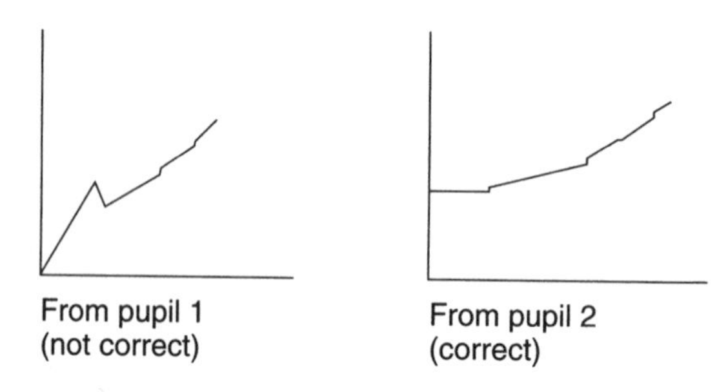

Figure 5.1 Predicting graph shapes

Teacher: Well, how does it compare?
Pupil 2: Up, then down a bit, then up.
Pupil 1: I have done mine wrong.
Teacher: You were able to predict it. That's OK. Have we got time? Yes we have got time to do one more thing.

This was a major opportunity lost to probe with pupil 1 the reasons for her error.

In some cases half-formed ideas were not followed up, for example:

Pupil 2: When it's there . . . the bulb [points to the screen] it sort of goes round. Turning it off it goes . . . it turns off quicker.
Teacher: Right.

The pupil was trying to understand why the bulb behaved differently when they were reducing the voltage. This would have been an ideal situation for the teacher to provide some 'scaffolding' with the aid of the data on the screen.

It must be remembered that all these exchanges took place with a teacher and only one pair of pupils. However, the exchanges do provide some indications of the opportunities and pitfalls. The best use of data logging requires re-evaluation of the ways in which teachers interact with pupils.

SUMMARY OF FINDINGS

The question posed at the start of this chapter related to whether data logging could change the nature of children's thinking in experimental work in science. I think that the data presented in this chapter not only suggest that this is the case but that data logging can change the whole nature and emphasis of school practical work. Practical work in science usually involves the four main stages of planning, obtaining data, analysing data and evaluating evidence. Data logging can make data gathering simply a means to an end and provide the opportunity for much more analysis and evaluation. However, I believe there is growing evidence that a more fundamental change is possible which centres on the way in which data on the computer screen can provide a shared focus for the practical activity. Working in this way does seem to encourage pupils to spend more time on tasks and to interact much more with the activity. This interaction is not often verbal but it is evident by watching pupils' expressions and actions. Perhaps this opens up the prospect of pupils becoming more independent during practical work. Even so, the ways in which teachers interact with pupils is a crucial area. The data on the computer screen and the facilities available in the software have provided powerful tools which teachers can use to develop ideas and to probe pupils' understanding. However, it will take time for science teachers to develop the most effective ways of using this shift in emphasis towards interpretation and evaluation.

Few pupils have had the opportunity of having extended use of data loggers during their science lessons. The Portable Computers in Schools project (Stradling *et al.*, 1994) reported that pupils who were able to use the portable computers most often were much more likely to take the initiative in deciding *when* to use them. My experience within this project confirms this finding. It is remarkable how proficient Year 7 pupils can become in exploring the potential of data logging software after only two or three weeks of regular use. This leads to the next point in terms of the development of expertise for both teachers and pupils. What sort of analysis will these Year 7 pupils be able to achieve in Year

10 or 11 if they continue to have regular access to data loggers? Will they be able to compare their data to preset functions in the software? Will they be able to use curve-fitting functions to identify the mathematical relationship between variables? Will they be able to plot functions derived from data they have collected to look for relationships between variables? At the moment this type of work is the province of A-level and beyond, yet current data logging software can do all of these things. What will happen when we unleash pupils from the drudgery of spending science lessons struggling to plot manual graphs? What will happen when pupils are able to make full use of this new tool to explore scientific ideas for themselves and teachers exploit to the full this powerful new teaching aid?

REFERENCES

Barton, R. (1990) 'Data logging in physics teaching', *Physics Education*, 25, 4, 223–8.

Brasell, H. (1985) 'The effect of real-time lab. graphing on learning graphic representation of distance and time', *Journal of Research in Science Teaching*, 24, 4, 385–95.

DES (Department of Education and Science) and Welsh Office (1991) *Science in the National Curriculum*. London: HMSO.

Mercer, N. (1994) 'The quality of talk in children's joint activity at the computer', *Journal of Computer Assisted Learning*, 10, 24–32.

Mokros, J.R. and Tinker, R. (1987) 'The impact of microcomputer based labs on children's ability to interpret graphs', *Journal of Research in Science Teaching*, 24, 4, 369–83.

Nachmias, R. and Linn, M. (1987) 'Evaluations of science lab. data: the role of computer presented information', *Journal of Research in Science Teaching*, 24, 5, 491–506.

Nakhleh, M.B. and Krajcik, J.S. (1993) 'A protocol analysis of the influence of technology on students' actions, verbal commentary, and thought processes during the performance of acid-base titrations', *Journal of Research in Science Teaching*, 30, 9, 1149–68.

Stradling, B., Sims, D. and Jamison, J. (1994) *Portable Computers Pilot Evaluation Summary*. Coventry: National Council for Educational Technology.

Watson, D. (ed.) (1993) *The ImpacT Report*. London: King's College.

Chapter 6

Can design software make a useful contribution to the art curriculum?

The experience of one school

John McGowan

Progress in education doesn't travel in straight lines. This chapter looks at the progress one secondary school has made in the development of IT art and design activity as an entitlement for all pupils. It looks at this within the constraints of the secondary curriculum, and in particular the successive changes resulting from the implementation of the National Curriculum and its revisions during the five year period 1989–94. It reviews early experimentation with IT in the art department, during 1988–91, when the school was participating in the Pupil Autonomy in Learning with Microcomputers (PALM) Project (for a fuller discussion of PALM, see Chapter 9); and it shows how those ideas have been used as the basis for further development of IT use in art during 1992–4, particularly with eleven- to fourteen-year-olds (Key Stage 3).

Arthur Mellows Village College (AMVC) is a seven-form entry, eleven to eighteen comprehensive school of some 1,200 pupils. It is situated in the Cambridgeshire Fens six miles to the north of Peterborough. The school has a large catchment area which extends from Wittering in the west to Thorney in the east. A large proportion of the pupils are bussed into the College.

The art department has always, since the school's foundation in 1949, had its own identity and a continuous share of curriculum time. It is now part of a creative arts faculty, and at the time of involvement with PALM was part of a design faculty. The faculty structure, in both instances, has been concerned with administrative rather than curriculum integration. The art department now has three fifty-minute periods per fortnight of curriculum time, whereas previously it had one seventy-minute period per week. The changes came about with the school's response to the National Curriculum. The department grew from three to four full-time specialists. Pressures from the NC at Key Stage 4 (broadly speaking, fourteen- to sixteen-year-olds) led to a reduction in the number of full art options offered as General Certificate of Secondary Education examination courses, and the introduction of GCSE art/technology 'slim' course options. Art staff teach art-related aspects of technology – in graphics, textiles and materials study.

PALM was funded by the National Council of Educational Technology in association with Cambridgeshire, Essex and Norfolk LEAs. PALM worked in partnership with teachers to research the role of IT in developing pupil autonomy in learning. It was led by a central team consisting of co-ordinator (Bridget Somekh), secretary and three project officers. In Cambridgeshire Jon Pratt was seconded from his teaching post to take on this role. The core of the PALM project's research was carried out by around one hundred teachers in twenty-four schools. Thirty-six research reports written by teachers were published in the Teachers' Voices series. The research material for this chapter is drawn from one such report (McGowan, 1991).

Although the project was intended for whole school initiatives, the directors kindly accepted a bid from the English and art departments at AMVC. This resulted in my working closely in partnership with Juliet Godber from the English department. There were carrots (computers) and cream cakes (cream cakes) and a considerable number of meetings and discussions with Jon Pratt and Bridget Somekh to set the project underway. We were encouraged to plan our own programme of research and development activities. Our self-designed brief was to introduce IT skills into the normal classrooms at AMVC, and to discover ways in which our pupils could take ownership of the benefits. The formal project lasted two years (1988–90) with a further extension of a year to 1991.

STARTING POINTS

AMVC has had a long history of IT activity. A dedicated staff in the first IT department had introduced eleven- to twelve-year-old pupils to the primitive charms of the BBC Master, but the game didn't really get underway until the new generation of computers became available in the late 1980s. PALM surfed on that wave. Cambridgeshire Education had decided to align its schools with Acorn computers, to which all of its INSET and advisory service was dedicated. This decision produced its benefits and frustrations: initial software developments were painfully slow and unstandardised to other industrial/commercial systems; but there was an impressive network of support.

When we joined PALM, in 1988, the IT inspector for Cambridgeshire provided the art department with one stand-alone Archimedes machine. We had an instruction book and introduced ourselves to programs and systems that were as new to our school IT 'experts' as they were to us. Few of the pupils had had a significant IT experience before reaching the College, and those who had, through summer schools at the College, were most familiar with the relatively unsophisticated BBC Master.

At the start of the PALM project the art curriculum at AMVC was becoming more clearly defined. All teachers shared a common syllabus for Key Stage 3 (broadly speaking, eleven- to fourteen-year-olds) in which pupils would be introduced to a common range of art media and themes. We were aware of the importance of building up the pupils' skills and concepts incrementally.

If I had been asked to describe the general approach of the department towards art and design tasks at this time I would have used words like: sequenced, structured, designed, instructed, objective. I would not have used words like: imaginative, exploratory, open-ended, intuitive. This is not to say that the latter qualities were not employed by teachers and pupils in their work in the department. However, our pedagogic skills were and still are focussed on teaching the framework that can liberate those qualities.

The 1988–90 art curriculum at AMVC

Year	*Medium*	*Project*
7	Paint	Still life jar of one-colour objects
	Clay	Our house
	Paper sculpture and drawing	Shoes
	Card print	Junk still life/plant forms
8	Lino print	Figure in costume
	Graphics/paint	Carrier bag project
	Draw/paint	Figure studies
9	Textile design	Food
	Graphics	Lettering project
	Screenprint	Village studies

Each project was planned to start with a research element through direct drawing, or via the use of found elements (collage). Sometimes photography might be employed (village project and figure studies). Many of the projects would develop the forms and images gathered in this way through a design towards a particular end. Information about the technical process to be employed would also be taught at this time, so that appropriate forms and images could be used by the pupils.

Projects that were aimed at specific design tasks (the carrier bag project and the textile design) usually involved considerable repetition of design, lettering and colour work as pupils worked through a variety of ideas from the original design brief. The skill requirements and strictures of the design process, with their elements of repetition and patient filling in of detail, were typical of the tasks that all designers faced in their work before the advent of electronic designing.

FINDING A ROLE FOR THE COMPUTER IN THE ART CLASS

In the autumn term of 1988 our first Archimedes computer arrived in the art department. It soon departed to my home so that I could begin to explore the machine and the program ARTISAN. We had to find a way in which the computer would help us to achieve our aims within the art and design sphere. However, without personal experience of using a computer and an art package to design and create, it was quite difficult to know what we would use it for and how we could use it in the art room.

All the art teachers at AMVC had completed their initial training long before computers entered art colleges. How should we know how to work the machines or what they could do? On one of the first training days after the computer arrived we discovered that we could turn it on and load the program. The instruction book that arrived with ARTISAN had clear instructions for each different function – but there were so many of them! How could we get our pupils engaged with a computer design process without throwing the book at them?

After general discussion we focused our first intended development on a graphics/poster project for Year 9 pupils (thirteen- to fourteen-year-olds). The decision to specify a project was not founded on our desire as teachers to control process and outcome: it was the result of observing a number of our pupils, largely sixth form students, who were given open access to the machine and allowed to play. Observation revealed that they were entranced with the machine's ability to generate colour/line/texture/colour fill, and so on, but they all ended up drawing with the mouse and vying to see who could make the best-toned drawing. All admitted, at the end, that although it was a challenge to do so, traditional drawing media were more satisfactory, largely because the traditional media are more responsive to touch. Few investigated the program's ability to transform design and image because they did not know how to and were determined to *do something* rather than read the manual and try out effects.

To prepare for the project, we decided that I should create a help file for pupils to find their way through this particular program for the first time. We hoped that the experience of working through a specific task would teach them more about the computer's use in the design process than an open-ended invitation to 'explore'. I designed the booklet using the computer and the ARTISAN program which provided me with a mental map of its functions.

The help file was a ring binder that contained a music poster project and graphic guidance to achieve that outcome. Its aim was clearly stated, 'To introduce you to the ARTISAN program' and 'To help you use the program in a controlled way'. Each page contained two frames which resembled the screen display at different stages of the project. ARTISAN had, at this time, a system of 'pop-up' menus comprising a main menu that led, in turn, to a series of submenus. Each of the submenus dealt with facilities like paint, copy, sprite, toolkit, rubberband, save and help. The help file established a sequence of activity, a guided tour through a selection of the program's facilities, with specific instructions on how to handle the tools available and guidance on the design elements needed to complete the task. Pupils were instructed to create a coloured background for the poster, then place a number of geometric, coloured shapes within that frame. Subsequently, they were shown how to select, create and place text for the message of the poster. The file also contained explanations of the functions of the facilities, advice on how to deal with possible difficulties, such as 'Text does not appear – Try changing colour'. Finally, pupils were asked to complete a self-assessment sheet on the ease or difficulty with which they had handled the program and whether they found the instructions clear. The assessment was on a three-point scale: 1 – easily; 2 – took some time; 3 – needed help. The help file was gradually revised and improved in response to pupil comment.

STRUCTURE OF THE INITIAL COMPUTER ART EXPERIENCE

ARTISAN is an art program with a wide range of functions, including seven submenus: Draw/paint, Geometric shape, Sprite menu, Toolbox/text, Repeat shape, File-store and Help. Each submenu contains from six to fourteen different functions. At this stage of the program's development the on-screen menus disappeared when work began. We trialled other programs but stuck with ARTISAN.

It is important here to distinguish between guidance aimed at the novice user and providing support for the more experienced user. At that time we were concerned with the former. Research during the initial period of introducing the computer and the poster help file revealed much that was to influence later developments.

Our computer was placed adjacent to an art class conventionally engaged in the Year 9 lettering project. Pairs of pupils were invited to trial the poster file. In order to let a wide range of pupils gain experience, each pair's session was limited to one seventy-minute period, although many extended their time by using school breaks. Some seventy pupils in self-selected pairs worked through the file. These were drawn from the full ability range at the school.

Trying to monitor use of the computer proved complex whilst teaching, as there were twenty-three other pupils to attend to. We found we tended to turn our attention to the computer only when the pairs came to a full stop; and so, to enable us to analyse what was happening, we set up a video camera to record a whole session. This provided some invaluable information and led to further modification of the help file (McGowan, 1991, pp. 10–11).

Each operation that the pupils had to carry out within the program – e.g. drawing a rectangle, changing a colour area, selecting a font – required a sequence of actions carried out by clicking one of three mouse buttons on a number of facilities in the pop-up menus. Sometimes the sequence could only be completed in one order, while other sequences were more variable. The pupils showed that they were often able to learn those sequences quickly, once they had seen how they worked. However, my own experience as a computer novice, and that of other adults and children I have worked with since, has confirmed that much time was wasted on learning from a book when a *slow demonstration* would have been the best method of teaching.

We had tried to make the whole learning sequence individualised. Looking back on those early experiments it now seems obvious that the tasks set were too complex and involved too much movement between different parts of the program. There was too little time given for exploration. A closely defined design task needs very specific computer art skills. How could we promote a more imaginative investigation of the program's potential? Perhaps we needed much simpler design briefs but we also wanted to extend our pupils' ability to cope with more demanding tasks.

DEVELOPING AN IT COMPONENT IN AN ART CURRICULUM

We decided, in 1990, to introduce an IT element into each year's art programme. This was achieved by adapting various elements of the existing scheme of work and finding out where the art/design facility of a computer program could have the most effect. This was not because PALM told us we had to, or out of a dandified trendiness. Our ex-students coming back to College after a year on a graphics or fashion/textiles course told us of the work they had been doing using computers. They were learning to create and design with text in a fluent way using Apple Macs; they were seeing the way in which pattern and design could be flooded into a computer model of a dress. The big world of design and commerce was pushing us on. In discussions that took place following the initial experiments, the staff rejected the idea of projects which used only computers. Instead, we decided to try to link traditional media with a computer-aided project and find ways that the computer could help pupils in their design work. The elements of the work scheme that used computers are shown in the box.

In previous years the paint project – with brushes and paint – had concentrated on controlled colour mixing, revising colour theory often learnt in previous years, where the three main colours are red, yellow and blue – the paint primary colours. Our computer-aided project crashed right into the middle of some complex

Year	Project description	Medium	Curriculum objective
7	*Sweet jar/still life* A collection of same-coloured objects fill a sweet jar. Pupils are asked to make studies of a selected area using a card view-finder. At the same	Opaque/transparent water-colour. Different brushes, fine, thick, soft, stiff. ARTISAN program: using draw, brush scale, shape spray, colour palette change	Colour-mixing skills are taught in both additive (light primaries: red, blue and green) and subtractive (paint primaries: red blue and yellow) mixing.[a] Pupils experience the

continued . . .

Year	Project description	Medium	Curriculum objective
	time some of the class take their jars to the computer trolleys and set up to do the same using the paint menu on the ARTISAN programme. The resulting image tends to look quite abstract, as the edges of the shapes are cut off by the view-finder. The groups exchange places on completion		contrasts of working in a traditional art medium and an electronic medium. Comparisons are made. Develops colour awareness and sensitivity. Pupils learn the routes to colour mixtures: what reds make good brown? Translation of image to conventional medium
8	*Carrier bag project* Pupils are shown a collection of carrier bags and consider them from a graphic design point of view. The teacher sets a design brief concerned with balancing text, image and frame. Choice of typeface appropriate for image is also explored	Pencil and paper. ARTISAN paint/draw and font selector. Paint/brushes/paper	Develop a variety of ideas from a design brief. Explore composition and layout skills. Become aware of lettering styles. Use the computer to achieve a variation in font style and movement of the text in relation to the image
9	*Textile design/repeat pattern* Using diverse starting points, abstract a fragment of designand use as the basis of a repeat design. Design brief includes looking at tessellation and colourways for design. Computer allows experiments with variety of repeat formats	Pencil/paint designs. Paint/draw ARTISAN menus – then copy/sprite and 'flip' facilities, followed by repeat and drop menu	Find appropriate units for repeat designs, comparing traditional draw/paint with electronic media. Exploring the variety of designs that can be produced through 'flip' and 'drop' facilities

[a] The ARTISAN program that we use operates in Mode 12 on the monitor – that means it can display twelve colours at any one time. All the graphics in the program itself are made from the same palette. The program offers an opportunity to customise the colour range via an alter palette button. Pupils can try to match the colours in their still life jar by, for example, mixing a range of reds and purples and eliminating greens and blues from the palette. They can then paint their design on the computer screen. To mix a colour, pupils have to select a colour with the mouse button and then move three sliders above the palette display; they are labelled R/G/B – red, green, blue.

physics of light and colour mixing: the difference between additive and subtractive colour mixing. We found we were working in light/additive primaries whereas previously with brush and paint we had been working with paint/subtractive primaries. To make matters more complex, the department had a colour-jet printer which used the paint/subtractive primaries to print out a screen display. The pupils often complained that the coloured print didn't have the same colours as the screen display.

The result of the introduction of IT/art elements was to increase the level of involvement of a wide range of pupils with their art tasks. Conversations were reported where pupils would confess their lack of expertise in the traditional media (a familiar crisis of confidence in the early teens) but express their delight at being able to paint/design in the electronic medium. In truth, their art/design ability was often no better in one or the other: ability in art has to do with sensitivity to a range of spatial/formal/colour/tonal/textural relationships – but because the computer is a 'clean zone' the most almighty messes are contained as binary blips and it is always possible to experiment and then change your mind. Also, because the teacher has more opportunity to make a *significant intervention*, the pupils are more willing to persevere with the task. This perseverance pays off in terms of better results in design work and a more positive attitude that may carry over into conventional tasks.

The notion of significant intervention is a critical issue. In an art class the pupils are all engaged in 'doing' for a lot of the time. The inexperienced painter or printer can make marks, mix colours, carve sections of lino that are irredeemable. For the pupil who gets confused, or who constantly makes poor decisions, a complex art task can be a minefield of mistakes. One of the art teacher's most important tasks, having explained the task/design brief and set the class in motion, is to support the pupils who find it difficult to negotiate those tasks. In certain art techniques, such as printmaking and ceramics, there are natural breaks built into the process and these give the teacher an opportunity for intervention; others, like painting and drawing, are seamless activities where intervention is much more problematic.

In computer-aided art/design work it is always possible to save the current state of the work and explore with an individual or group a number of potential courses of action. The pupils can then make a choice and continue. The teacher can create a structure whereby each stage of the process is saved on disk and a review process is charted separately.

CUSTOMISING THE IT ENVIRONMENT

One of the problems we encountered with early users was that they would get lost in the further reaches of the program and either become entranced and side-tracked or simply be unable to get out of wherever they were. This was a problem because we were concerned to keep the pupils on task. A second version of ARTISAN allowed the user to customise the program. Disks could be prepared that allowed the teacher to switch off some of the facilities – these would then appear as a grey ghost graphic rather than a colour symbol. So, for example, if we wanted the pupils to avoid using a 'pattern fill' for the background, that facility could be switched off. Or, if there was no need to use the 'sprite menu' (a device for grabbing a section of the screen display), it too could be made inaccessible.

This seemed like an exciting idea to start with but the practical problems of introducing dedicated program disks for each task proved beyond our organisational capacity. Each year group needed a different set of facilities in the program and in our open-plan department disks do not stay in one place, and disk sets can and do get mixed up. Latterly we have worked from a hard disk to supply programs to the mini-network but this hasn't enough memory to support three versions of the same program. Instead, staff now give an in-depth *slow demonstration* of the particular tools to be used.

The system of customising software could work well in a more controlled or contained IT facility or a much simpler 'one teacher, one machine' arrangement. However, we judge that it is important for all pupils to have an IT/art experience, so we either need a lot of computers or some co-ordinated turn-taking – and in these circumstances customising software has proved impracticable.

ART AND DESIGN, IT AND THE NATIONAL CURRICULUM

The National Curriculum has been a catalyst for further development of the use of IT in art at AMVC, but like all externally imposed changes it has also acted as a constraint upon the development work already in progress. It was introduced, on a subject-by-subject basis, following the Education Reform Act of 1988. At AMVC we began initial planning for the NC in art during 1989–90 (the second year of the PALM project) but its impact was not really felt on the Key Stage 3 curriculum until 1992.

Proposals for Art, 5–14 (DES, 1991, p. 7, para. 2.15) described current use of IT in art:

> Use is made of information technology in art and design in 39 per cent of Primary schools and 50 per cent of Secondary schools. HMI found that they were being used successfully as a tool to aid preparatory work and as a medium for analysis and investigation. They are also proving to be invaluable in the development of a design; for example in experimenting with alternative colour ways for textiles; or, for a poster, speeding up the various stages of a design and helping refine and manipulate graphic images. In a few schools, computers are used to help in teaching about tone and colour and as a medium in painting pictures. Computers are also being used by teachers and their pupils to help record assessments, for word processing and desktop publishing.

Later in the same document the authors suggested some ways in which art and design could contribute to design and technology capability, saying: 'The skilled and sensitive use of information technology . . . provides an opportunity to understand the presentation of ideas in visual form and has increasingly important applications in graphics, in the media and in advertising' (DES, 1991, p. 15, para. 3.41). However, in the general requirements for programmes of study (DES, 1992) where teachers were directed to give pupils opportunities to 'Make appropriate use of information technology', there was only one mention of IT: 'discuss how their research in the community has informed a computer animation sequence about the dangers of smoking'.

In June 1992 the National Curriculum Council published *Art: Non-statutory guidance* (NCC, 1992), which was intended to help teachers understand the statutory requirements and to provide advice and guidance on implementation in the classroom. In this document the authors discuss the relationship between art and technology, and suggest that, at Key Stage 3, there should be effective collaboration between departments (NCC, 1992, section D 12). It goes on to list the strands of IT capability and suggests ways in which these might appear in an art context:

Communicating information	Develop, organise, store ideas in visual form Desktop publishing Extend range of media and techniques Experiment with colour mixing and geometric constructions.
Handling information	Search, view and cross reference works of art Teletext
Modelling	'Walk through' an interior design
Measurement and control	Transfer a design from one medium to another
Applications and effects	Reflect on how the use of IT has influenced the development of an image or design.

(NCC, 1992, section D 15)

The revised proposals for art drawn up by the Schools Curriculum and Assessment Agency (SCAA, 1994, p. 1) again maintained the view that 'Pupils should be given opportunities to apply and develop their IT capability in their study of art where appropriate.' However, a reading of the advice for using IT in the art curriculum at Key Stage 3 gives the impression that the authors were not able to include examples of current practice, such as those listed by HMI in 1991 (DES, 1991), or put them in language that helps to present the idea of art/IT activity in an accessible manner. In fact the whole document moved further away from specificity with regard to all aspects of art activity. There was now a real need for a lengthier exposition of the part that IT could play in art education, suggesting ideas and activities to those engaged at the paintface.

This kind of practical advice on implementing the National Curriculum in art has only gradually become available. In 1995 SCAA published a four-page leaflet entitled *Art and Information Technology – Key Stage 3*, along with the revised programme for information technology (DfE, 1995). This slim document was more specific in describing appropriate activities. It outlined the ways in which art work can be supported by the use of IT and detailed the way in which IT can contribute to work in art. The two centre pages were devoted to case studies that linked the art and IT programmes of study: examples included 'Investigating light and tone', 'Working in two and three dimensions', 'Designing for textiles' and 'Promoting our heritage'. The leaflet concluded with a list of IT facilities and their potential for use in the art class.

In summary, although practical advice and examples were slow in coming, the National Curriculum provided us with considerable stimuli to continue developing the use of IT in art at AMVC.

NATIONAL CURRICULUM ART: OTHER PRESSURES

However, there were other ways in which the National Curriculum impinged on our ability to further develop IT in the art curriculum. In particular, Attainment Target 2: Knowledge and Understanding introduced a new element to the established art curriculum. In the period leading up to the implementation of the NC in art the vast majority of tasks encountered by the pupils in an art class were practical – drawing/painting/printing/modelling/casting – and it was relatively easy to make IT part of that. National Curriculum guidance in 1992 suggested that one-third of curriculum time should be allocated to critical and historical work to develop knowledge and understanding. In 1994, the programme of study for Key Stage 3 within the revised National Curriculum in art (SCAA, 1994, p. 6) stated:

> Pupils should develop the ability to give sustained attention to the works of art, craft and design. Examples should include works in the locality and contemporary work. The Western tradition should be exemplified by work in a variety of genres and styles from Classical and Medieval, renaissance and post-Renaissance periods through to the nineteenth and twentieth centuries. Works taken from non-Western cultures should exemplify a range of traditions from a variety of times and places.

All art departments were faced with a new balancing act.

I have a strong belief in the necessity for the critical and historical studies aspects of art education and was involved in a number of major projects that prefigured its introduction in the National Curriculum (Taylor, 1986, pp. 141–9). Nevertheless, the prescription to deliver such wide-ranging critical and historical studies within seventy-five minutes per week over three years, as well as the practical work which has always been the core of art and design, meant that something had to give. We took the decision to reduce the amount of time given to art/IT projects and to retain the 'fine art' elements of our Key Stage 3 course. The art staff have spent endless hours trying to find a way to wrap up the various curriculum elements into an acceptable parcel. Our decision to use three 'mega-themes' for Key Stage 3 – Still Life, Portraits and Landscape – has helped to keep a large amount of our in-depth approach intact. However, only in Year 9 have we been able to retain the computer/textile design element from our earlier programme. But, at the time of writing, we are not yet at the end of the three-year introductory period and I have no doubt that we shall continue to revise and develop our courses.

I wrote, three years ago, that I expected the computer awareness of our pupils to grow as a result of the curriculum at Key Stages 1 and 2, in the primary school. This has proved true as all pupils in local primary schools are being introduced to simple IT/paint programs. I also commented that soon we would not need to treat our Year 7 pupils as novices. That has also proved true. The rub is that, given the greatly increased content of the National Curriculum in art, we now find it hard to make time to utilise their new skills.

REFERENCES

DES (Department of Education and Science) (1991) *Art for Ages 5–14.* London: HMSO.

—— (1992) *Art in the National Curriculum.* London, HMSO.

DfE (Department for Education) (1995) *Art and Information Technology – Key Stage 3.* London: DfE.

McGowan, John (1991) 'From Lascaux to Archimedes', *PALM – Teachers' Voices,* no. 11, Norwich: CARE, University of East Anglia.

NCC (National Curriculum Council) (1992) *Art: Non-statutory Guidance.* York: National Curriculum Council.

SCAA (Schools Curriculum and Assessment Agency) (1994) *Draft Proposals for Art in the National Curriculum.* London: SCAA.

Taylor, Rod (1986) *Educating for Art.* London: Longman.

Chapter 7

Children exploring the Queen's House in hypertext

Has the hype any educational potential?

John Jessel and Vicky Hurst

Imagine that you are sitting in front of a computer. On the screen there is a picture. It is a view of a very large park. There are no words. You have been told, however, that if you use the mouse to point to some part of this picture and press the button you may then see a new picture. This new picture shows some more of the area. What is shown depends upon where you point; it may be a view slightly further to the right or the left, or it may bring you closer to something, such as a house that was in the distance. You soon find out that you can, in turn, explore the new picture by pointing with the mouse and pressing the button. This will lead to further pictures; each taking you further on in your tour of the area, or allowing you to inspect something more closely and in more detail. You may, for example, wish to try to find a way into the house and examine some of the furnishings inside. There are many possible routes that you can take and it is also possible to retrace your steps; you find out that you can point to a symbol on the screen which takes you back to the previous picture. There are now no further demands upon your computing skills; you are free to explore.

Such an activity is, of course, easily allowable through the use of computer technology that is available today. The hundreds of photographs used to model the house and the park could be stored on a hard disk or a CD-ROM. Links between the photographs to allow a means of travelling from one place to another could be provided through almost any one of a number of commonly available 'hypertext' database applications. Our example could also have included such entities as words, both written and spoken, sequences of moving images, and music, although the method of finding one's way around this type of terrain could have been essentially the same as with pictures alone. Although widely used (see, e.g., McAleese, 1993) the word 'hypertext' is nevertheless problematic. If our understanding of the word 'text' is limited to a body of words in written or printed form then there is, of course, reason to be ill at ease with 'hypertext', unless we apply the prefix 'hyper' rather loosely. Similarly, there are problems with another potentially applicable term, namely 'multimedia' (Heppell, 1994). Although the technology has arrived, a widely agreed vocabulary pertaining to it has not, and so with some reservation we will adopt the term 'hypertext'.

Our model of the house and the park is but one example of a hypertext application. Although perhaps rather basic in terms of facilities offered when compared with some other models, it does, however, share a central feature which is commonly encountered in such applications: it allows one to explore. In this chapter we will pursue our exploration of the house and the park and, on the way, examine the nature of such an exploration and what might be gained from it. To this end we are helped by our explorers Remee and Ashley (five years), Darren and Haylie (seven years), and Caroline and Faye (eleven and ten years), pupils from a south-east London school. The model to be explored was developed by the authors for the purposes of the present work. It was constructed from some 200 colour photographs which were scanned so that they could be recorded and displayed by the computer. The photographs showed views and details of Greenwich Park and the Queen's House, the latter being regarded as a centre of historic interest and frequently visited by groups of children from schools in the locality. The Queen's House was commissioned by Queen Anne of Denmark and designed by Inigo Jones in 1616 and, today, remains furnished in a style believed to be characteristic of seventeenth-century royal apartments. Our explorers would be visiting the Queen's House as it was related to classroom work on the Tudors and the Stuarts. We wondered whether the experience of hypertext provision in the classroom would have any impact on the children's attitude to and experience of the real Queen's House when they visited with the school. We wanted to find out (a) whether, indeed, these pupils would wish to explore our model of the park and the house, and (b) having embarked on their exploration, how long they might wish to continue. We also wanted to discover what approaches and strategies they would adopt spontaneously, so on all occasions a free hand in exploring was given and with a minimum of guidance. Another question concerned the nature of any talk and collaboration that might occur, and so the pupils worked in pairs from each year group and were encouraged to talk to each other about what they saw and their decisions regarding where to go to next. We also thought that we might begin to get some insight into some developmental issues through considering these questions in relation to the children from the different age-groups.

Getting started presented few problems, regardless of age, once the children had been shown the basic manoeuvres with the mouse. Caroline and Faye (eleven and ten) were, within a few minutes, able to gain good control and give attention to the pictures as they appeared, Remee and Ashley (five) took a little longer. In the construction of the model there was an effort to maintain visual continuity. However, some links between pictures were more visually challenging than others by virtue of large variations in direction of view or proximity, and because of minimal interconnecting detail. We found, however, that from an early stage of exploration there was no apparent difficulty in relating one view with another. In one case, Haylie (seven) on her first encounter with a particular scene, spotted a minute fragment of a wrought-iron banister that was just visible at the top of a stair-well: 'OK down there'. This is the quality of attention to information presented visually (and to possible symbolic connotations of items or their relationships in the visual array) that makes young children experts at using picture-books, observing human artefacts and natural objects, and the interpretation of video and cinematic material. One possibility that readily comes to mind is that children are able to come to terms quickly with the qualities and limitations of the medium's inherent visual grammar as a result of their acquaintance with the many conventions adopted in television programmes. Furthermore, we also found that the pupils were amused rather than confused if any inappropriate relationships arose between where they pointed with the mouse and the picture that followed as a result. Unlike television, however, changes in view are not merely presented but occur as a result of physical action on the part of the observer. The importance of this in perceiving the form of the surroundings has for some time been recognised in work such as that reported by Hein (1980).

Each pair of pupils very quickly set themselves the task of finding a way inside the house. 'We'll just go in and then we might find something' (Faye, ten); 'I'm playing next' (Remee, five); 'I'm playing after Remee' (Ashley, five). Imagination and story-telling are two of the most powerful modes of approaching and representing the world. Here, the younger children are constructing an imaginative 'play scenario' of a kind which is noted in all early childhood studies (e.g. Guha, 1987). 'Embedded' learning commonly arising from strong incentives such as these can be effective and long lasting (Donaldson, 1978). Finding a way inside happened not to be easy since the door (which in reality would have been the one used when making a visit) was concealed within a central courtyard and could only be found once a series of moves through a number of pictures had been made. For Faye and Caroline (ten and eleven), initial talk was about how to explore the whole of the house, where different parts of a picture might lead: 'Oh, you want to go back, do you?' (Faye); 'See if we can go up to the landing' (Caroline). Here, the exploratory behaviour shown by these two girls links closely with the initial stages of play behaviour, in which children will investigate and verbally list every item of equipment, furnishing and accommodation they find in an area where they hope to play.

Faye and Caroline's talk concerning the overall mapping can be contrasted with the five-year-olds who tended to frame their talk in terms of what was shown, or in terms of details available in close up: 'The foot, go on press it, you've got to stay on one of these' (Ashley); 'Look at that fence' (Remee). For Haylie and Darren, between the above age-groups, exploration of the whole house featured prominently, but was subject to the occasional diversion, as the following dialogue suggests: 'It's like you're really in a house. Take a close up of that picture there' (Darren); 'See in the door' (Haylie); 'Yes, go in the door, go in the door' (Darren). Here the imaginative experience of moving at will within an unknown environment has become real for the children, who have adopted the computer's functions as their own. From the above dialogues we may also get a sense of the kind of conversation which children engage in with regard to the extent of their collaboration. We can also see that much of the above talk reflects a desire for the child who is not controlling the mouse to direct the other in order to satisfy his or her own curiosities. With the youngest of the children, especially Remee, there was also a tendency to be less attentive when not using the mouse.

We have already noted that Remee and Ashley were slightly slower than the older children in gaining control of where they wished to go. However, within fifteen minutes they had also found their way into the house and to the upstairs rooms. Remee was beginning to become more aware of the potential offered by doors for further large-scale exploration and her actions became very selective in this respect. Like the seven-year-olds, however, exploratory behaviour also took on other dimensions; Ashley, for example, upon discovering a room full of paintings, attempted to gain a close-up view of each painting, and approached this systematically. Exploration on a large scale occurred even though some awareness of detail on the computer screen was clearly there, as may be noted above from Remee and Ashley's interest in the paintings. After some ten minutes Faye and Caroline's mouse movements were quite controlled and selective in terms of the detail that was visible. Small or indistinct areas were explored, but with the intention of gathering fuller information, for example, 'See what's in that picture' (Caroline, eleven); 'What about that, what's that?' (Faye, ten, pointing to railings in the corner of the screen). Much of the talk remained directional: 'Can we go down there?'; 'Find another part – try to get into another part'; 'Shall we go back and try the back of the house?'; 'Try from this end then'; 'Go to the first bit, we should go there.'

They were also recognising scenes that they had come across before, albeit by different routes: 'We can't go in there' (Caroline); and getting a useful sense of layout and general qualities of the house: 'Shall we go out and come in again? You know, the door on the other side of the balcony?' (Caroline). After about twenty minutes Haylie and Darren (seven) had found a way into the house and had also explored the general layout inside as well as outside. They were able to use their knowledge of layout in that they could go back and forth to find particular rooms at will. At this later stage in their exploration an interest in details and features of the rooms was becoming more noticeable. Paintings on the walls became a focus of interest; for example, Darren, on finding that close-up views were obtainable with some paintings, went systematically through some of the rooms to see how many similar close-ups he could find.

In sum, then, mapping out the terrain on a large scale was dominant at early stages of exploration before attention was paid to smaller details. This was particularly noticeable with the older children whose strategies concerned with large-scale mapping also tended to be vocalised. This observation identifies the relationship between physical action and 'knowing' (Piaget, [1951] 1962).

While the above exploring approaches were beginning to emerge, other patterns were also evident, namely that for all children the time spent looking at any one view presented on the screen was relatively short, typically in the order of a few seconds. This meant that the activity was characterised by frequent clicking of the mouse button as different shots came and went. The intention seemed to be to find further views; travelling seemed to be more important than arriving. Each screen display was viewed in terms of where it led, rather than in terms of what it contained. While some of the views within the house would have shown little more than a connecting corridor or doorway, many of the others showed a wealth of potentially interesting detail which could have sustained extended perusal. However, if there were any noticeable variations in viewing time, these seemed to be dictated by the number of possibilities that a given display might present for leading on to others, and the decisions and the trials that would have to be made as a consequence of this. The above pace of exploration was held throughout, even when there was familiarity with overall layout and close-up views of details were being sought. The distinction between exploration and later, more in-depth interaction with materials has been established as a separate stage both in use of tools (Sylva *et al.*, 1975) and in play (Hutt *et al.*, 1985).

In addition to maintaining a rapid pace of exploration, it was apparent that pupils from all age-groups were willing to continue this for extended periods of time. At five years of age, Ashley and Remee were content to explore for nearly half an hour. After thirty minutes Haylie and Darren (seven) were also very much involved and, likewise, Caroline and Faye (eleven and ten) after some forty minutes. That the slightly longer period of activity for Caroline and Faye could simply be attributed to age, however, cannot be assumed since they were working in classroom conditions which were less distracting than those for the younger children. Moreover, in all cases the duration of activity can be regarded as substantial and those interested in any debate on comparative attention spans may view the timings in terms of their similarity rather than their differences.

Although we might regard the children as being naturally disposed to exploration, their continued attempts to find further views may nevertheless bear further consideration. Was this merely a novelty effect, or were other motivational forces at work? Would we have witnessed the same degree of engagement with these, or any other collection of pictures, presented in book form for example? Was the continued activity an attempt to assess the nature and extent of the material? In hypertext this would be less easily apparent than with a book. Were our explorers hoping to find something more special? Might something quite different, or at least, something more dramatic or aesthetically pleasing, be discovered? On talking to the children afterwards this appeared not to be the case. Although some of the screen displays could be regarded as having met the latter criteria, exploration, as we have already noted, continued at a regular pace with any one screen being given roughly the same viewing time as any other.

A question which arises at this stage concerns whether we should view the continued activity in terms of motivation or of inertia. Is our hypertext environment a comfortable one within which one can wander aimlessly and where few mental demands are made? Although the term 'exploration' has been a convenient one to use, it is also a term which carries with it notions concerning purpose and direction. Is it right that we should regard the pupils as 'explorers'? Were these pupils exploring with questions in mind, or was the endeavour disconnected and superficial in nature? Were these pupils simply wasting time? Holt (1989) has argued that when children follow their own curiosity they may go through a vast amount of material but relatively little is retained. With language learning, for example, children are exposed to an enormous amount of verbal information of which comparatively little sticks. Importantly, however, bits which they want are picked out. What is picked out may be picked out subconsciously. However, in view of the sheer volume, this small fraction can become significant. Holt goes on to argue that if any adult attempts to make this process more efficient then they may in effect simply reduce the intake. With hypertext, material can be available in volume and, in turn, what is retained could become significant. Furthermore, Case (1985) has suggested that developmental process is characterised by an innate capability for setting goals and for deriving strategies for attaining these goals. At first no goal is made explicit and the start of any activity may be cued by almost any feature of what is present. A number of initial lines of inquiry may be entertained concurrently, evaluated and modified, if necessary, en route. Case uses the term 'exploration' to describe this process, although, initially, it could be regarded as being driven by what lies without rather that by what lies within. Protagonists of the constructivist school of early childhood education would maintain, however, that the relationship between experience and developing ways of conceptualising is more complex (Athey, 1991; De Vries and Kohlberg, 1990).

A term which has been associated with the use of hypertext is 'browsing' (e.g. McAleese, 1993). As with Case's notion of exploration, a situation is presented where there is no overt target. What lies ahead is unknown. It is up to the individual to enter this situation and see what arises. On its own, this could stand in contrast to the notion of quality in learning put forward in Chapter 1 of this book where the attempt would be to maximise consciousness of learning and the predictive and active role of the learner. However, McAleese (1993) argues that an active atmosphere can be created through hypertext, but this rests on activity being directed. He also points out that consciousness of learning can result from making information needs explicit. If we are to assume that there is an innate capability for setting goals, then, from a teaching point of view, even if we do not wish to set questions for our 'explorers' or give them explicit direction, we could at least try to get them to express their own questions or directions overtly.

If direction can be set either overtly or covertly, what might pupils gain from a hypertext environment, as opposed to any other environment? Other media such as books or film may, of course, contain a large number of items such as pictures or other elements of information. However, these elements are usually locked into a fixed sequence, which consequently restricts any connecting links. One can browse through an encyclopaedia, or a library for that matter, but the mechanisms associated with inbuilt links or cross-references can be cumbersome and a distraction. With hypertext it is relatively easy for an author to create a variety of links and also for a user to follow them. Although the pictures of the Queen's House in themselves can convey information, there is further information to be had from the links between these pictures; each link represents a relationship, and each picture can take on a particular meaning as a result of the mutual context provided. Additionally, however, the same picture, or unit of data, may yield different information and take on a variety of meanings according to the route by which it is approached. For example, if we return to the Queen's House, then an object such as a chair can be seen as a functional entity within a room or, seen in terms of its design, as a statement in terms of wealth and royalty. Importantly, in one sense we can regard our explorers as exploring the links between pictures and gaining information and meaning from this rather than from the pictures themselves. With this in mind, the rapidity with which moves were made from one picture to another and why travelling seemed to be more important than arrival may be understandable.

If we are to seek comparisons between exploration of a hypertext model, such as that of the Queen's House, and exploration in the real world environment, then, although there may be a degree of surface isomorphism between the pictures and the location that they represent, we cannot claim that this is a virtual reality. It is, of course, a construction where there is a choice of elements and links which is influenced by the underlying conceptions, perceptions and intentions of an author, as Faye (ten) indeed reminded us: 'Did you make this program up yourself?' If our construction is likely to influence children's conceptions and perceptions then we may need to plan carefully. At the level of picture composition there could be effects on choices made in the course of exploration. For example, when the starting point was the park, interest quickly focused on the Queen's House which could be seen in the distance. With regard to structure, we might consider the kind of connections we want children to make and whether these would have to represented as interconnections within hypertext. We might ponder whether we are giving our explorers freedom or imposing constraint. Children, however, are constrained in both museum education and in information technology, as with any other medium, because of the limits imposed by its very nature. They cannot be allowed to play freely with valuable artefacts, nor can they create new rules for the operation of a computer program.

Continuing our comparison with a real environment, we have found using hypertext that, although children maintain a rapid pace of exploration, they go back to where they have been before and have another look, and keep looking. That this can open the way for attention to be drawn to a range of viewpoints and detail was evident: Faye liked the close-up facility: 'You can see all the materials'; 'Silky sort of patterns'. When asked to describe the House for a distant friend, Caroline and Faye also identified long alleyways, paintings, beds, lots of windows, and the (spiral) stairs which they associated with going up high and, more creatively, with the experience of turning round 'like the whirlwind'.

Darren (seven) felt that he had 'learnt that you cannot just see things from outside but inside as well, and that it is interesting seeing all the rooms and taking close-ups of the pictures and furniture', while Remee (five), on being asked what she had noticed, replied: 'Everything, the carpet, the door, the house'.

The rapidity of travelling in hypertext may be equated with a common tendency for children, particularly when left to their own devices, in a museum setting such as the Queen's House to rush from one place to another. However, we can also argue that there is an important difference in so far as travelling in our hypertext model was characterised by perseverance; the House was repeatedly revisited and re-viewed from many different angles. An extensive model can also convey a sense that all the limits may have not been reached. With Caroline and Faye (eleven and ten), for example, this was found to be a motivating feature: 'It's nice to have the feeling that there is always a bit more to discover.'

We also found that use of the hypertext model had enhanced enthusiasm for seeing the real house. Caroline and Faye, for example, had clear ideas about what they want to look at, draw and write about, and had followed these up. Here exploration of the model had usefully linked in with subsequent first-hand experience. By way of further comparison with the real world we can, of course, quote situations where a model in hypertext, such as inside a nuclear reactor for example, can be explored with comparative ease and safety. While this may be valid for many educational purposes, models such as these can be regarded as special cases and we should be careful not to overlook the more fundamental and pervasive qualities of hypertext as a medium which can allow a range of viewpoints and details to be presented, resulting in perseverance in exploration, even with everyday objects and environments that may be regarded as ordinary.

The emphasis throughout this description has been on the creation of a new kind of environment for learning; one which, while it restricts children in some ways, has in other ways given them a freedom they would be unlikely to have in an actual museum environment. The children have responded by establishing the environmental repertoire and making links between different items, making use of playful relationships, 'real-world' knowledge and understanding, and imaginative and creative metaphors. Their use has shown hypertext to be capable of providing the setting for a developmentally appropriate curriculum, in which adult experience provides the carefully selected setting while the children make the choices that are appropriate for their experience, interests and understandings of the world. In the present work the focus could be seen in terms of the role of the adult as provider of a given setting. However, in the classroom context this role can be extended towards being the observer who is available to interact according to the needs of individuals. For example, this may include giving whole attention to and social acceptance of the child's initiative together with emotional support while the child is exploring, meeting frustration and trying things out. This can be contrasted with approaches characterised by early versions of 'programmed learning' which aimed to reduce direct involvement of the adult in individualised learning. Blenkin and Kelly (1987, 1994) have concluded that, for children under eight years of age, there is no substitute for the highly educated professional drawing on knowledge of child development and curriculum expertise.

The Queen's House in hypertext has enriched rather than reduced the child–adult relationship, seen in the context of developmental approaches. A further stage might be to see what its relationship could be to a planned course for junior age children in the context of, say, a National Curriculum study unit. Museum educationalists are exploring how they can include opportunities for play in their provision (National Maritime Museum, reported in Hurst, 1991). Is there a parallel development to be looked for in the possibilities inherent in hypertext?

Rather than attempt to examine complex forms of hypertext we have focused on one that is relatively basic. Through this focus, however, we find that a model consisting of no more than a network of items presented in one modality is capable of holding attention for extended periods of time; we have also found, incidentally, that college students have become similarly engaged. In all cases no extrinsic incentive was necessary, nor did the model require any inbuilt tasks or directions or end goals for the user to be stated. Furthermore, it should be noted that the content represented nothing more than that plainly visible at a given location.

It might, of course, be instructive to test the extent to which a hypertext environment lends itself to exploration by replacing the Queen's House with a singular object that could be available for inspection alongside its hypertext representation. Although this may sound rather extreme, there might nevertheless be some useful consequences for classroom application if the outcomes were similar to those for the Queen's House. For example, historical artefacts could be used, and through hypertext pupils could be encouraged to have another look at a variety of details and attributes. Close-up photographs of flowers and minibeasts might usefully lend themselves to this treatment for the purposes of scientific study. A variety of objects could provide a similar focus for study in relation to design and technology. Paintings could lend themselves to this treatment in the context of detailed study in art. Developing resources of this type could be relatively easily accomplished and, no doubt, much could be gained by pupils creating their own models. More ambitious models could, of course, represent such structures as the cardiovascular system, the atom or an oil refinery.

It might also be reasonable to speculate that data in a variety of other forms could be interlinked and hold attention in a similar way. However, simplicity in modelling is, perhaps, an important feature which should not be overlooked. Although the availability of a model in hypertext for open-ended exploration may not in itself necessarily be a formula for classroom activity, there are qualities here which could be drawn on more generally and provide a basis for enriched classroom activity.

ACKNOWLEDGEMENTS

The authors are grateful for the help from the pupils and staff at Myatt Gardens Primary School, New Cross. We would also like to thank the National Maritime Museum for their co-operation, and Acorn Computers Ltd for their generosity in making the necessary equipment available.

REFERENCES

Athey, C. (1991) *Extending Thought in Young Children.* London: Paul Chapman.

Blenkin G.M. and Kelly, A.V. (eds) (1987) *Early Childhood Education: A Developmental Curriculum.* London: Paul Chapman.

—— (1994) 'The death of infancy', *Education 3–13*, Oct: 3–9.

Case, R. (1985) *Intellectual Development: Birth to Adulthood.* New York: Academic Press.

Davis, N., Desforges, C., Jessel, J., Somekh, B., Taylor, C. and Vaughan, G. (1995) 'Can quality in learning be enhanced through the use of IT?'. Chapter 1 in this volume.

De Vries, R. and Kohlberg, L. (1990) *Constructivist Early Education: Overview and Comparison with Other Programs.* Washington, D.C.: National Association for the Education of Young Children.

Donaldson, M. (1978) *Children's Minds.* London: Fontana.

Guha, M. (1987) 'Play in school', in G.M. Blenkin and A.V. Kelly (eds), *Early Childhood Education: A Developmental Curriculum.* London: Paul Chapman.

Hein, A. (1980) 'The development of visually guided behaviour', in C.S. Harris (ed.), *Visual Coding and Adaptability.* Hillsdale, N.J.: Lawrence Erlbaum Associates.

Heppell, S. (1994) 'Multimedia and learning: normal children, normal lives and real change', in J.D.M. Underwood (ed.), *Computer Based Learning: Potential into Practice.* London: David Fulton.

Holt, J. (1989) *Learning All the Time.* Reading, Mass.: Addison-Wesley.

Hurst, V. (1991) *Planning for Early Learning.* London: Paul Chapman.

Hutt, J.J., Hutt, C., Tyler, S.T. and Foy, H. (1985) *A Natural History of the Preschool.* Windsor: NFER/Nelson.

McAleese, R. (1993) 'Navigation and browsing in hypertext', in R. McAleese (ed.), *Hypertext: Theory into Practice.* Oxford: Intellect.

Piaget, J. ([1951] 1962) *Play, Dreams and Imitation in Childhood.* New York: Routledge & Kegan Paul.

Sylva, S., Bruner, J.S. and Genova, P. ([1975] 1985) 'The role of play in the problem-solving of children 3–5 years old', in J.S. Bruner, A. Jolly and K. Sylva, *Play: Its Role in Development and Evolution.* Harmondsworth, Middx: Penguin Books.

Part Two

Learning to use IT as a teaching tool

Strategies for teacher training

Introduction to Part Two

This book recognises that the teacher holds the key to learning in schools. It is the teacher who facilitates and manages the learning process. Therefore the effective use of IT as a learning tool will be dependent on the development of the profession of teaching.

In the opening chapter of Part Two Peter Scrimshaw sets out the challenge and the opportunity for teachers. He recognises that the development of a synergy between teaching and IT will result in a far deeper reappraisal of the teacher's role than is currently recognised. This requires a fundamental and continuous process of rethinking what is taught, how it is taught and why. IT is itself a cause of the radical changes in education which are opening the classroom to the world.

This process of rethinking teaching and learning can be used to inform the development of strategies for the professional development of teachers. We need to find ways of enabling teachers, from nursery schools to higher education, to challenge traditional assumptions about the practice of teaching. IT provides possibilities for organising classrooms in new ways and setting new kinds of learning tasks. The remaining chapters in Part Two provide strategies with which to stimulate and underpin the reflective process of professional development which is essential to make this possible. All these strategies aim to enable teachers – including teachers in training – to develop new and better practices for teaching and learning, with and without IT.

Many practising teachers have a notion that computers *should be* of value to them and their learners. However, most of the early initiatives to provide IT resources and training for teachers did not achieve the expected infusion of technology into classrooms. A large study of the impact of IT in education clarified the need for sustained professional development for teachers (Watson, 1993). One attempt to provide this was the Pupil Autonomy in Learning with Microcomputers (PALM) project described by Bridget Somekh in Chapter 9. The PALM approach ensured that classroom teachers took ownership of their own professional development using action research. The focus of their professional development was to introduce or extend the use of IT in teaching and learning. Bridget describes this successful approach in some detail. She notes that although the teachers all used IT resources, the first stage of the analysis of their research focused on more general issues related to learning. They took time to rethink the teaching and learning in their classrooms before moving on to finding new ways of using IT resources. IT had the effect of helping teachers to reappraise the whole process of teaching and learning within their classrooms and in the wider educational context. IT was the catalyst which helped teachers critically re-examine their pedagogy. To complement this approach, Chapter 11, by Bridget Somekh and Niki Davis, analyses the particular stresses of coming to terms with new technology for the first time. Drawing on well-known theories of the self, they develop strategies to develop the confidence and routine procedures which enable individuals to acquire IT competence through self-teaching.

Beginning teachers are often in a better position than experienced teachers to adopt new methods of teaching and learning. They do not have established routines, nor do they have to take sole responsibility for their classroom at first. They are also exposed, during their training, to a range of opinions and contexts. Two of the chapters in Part Two focus on the development of IT in initial teacher training, recognising the importance of three partner groups in the process:

- the teacher educators in higher education;
- the teachers in schools; and
- the student teachers.

Colin Biott and Malcolm Bell describe in Chapter 10 a strategy in which all three partners work together to use IT effectively in the classroom. University staff prepare student teachers to deploy IT in primary school classrooms, working with practising teachers who also find this an opportunity for professional development. Colin and Malcolm analyse some of the problems in establishing an effective working relationship between these partners, but they also show how such co-learning partnerships can lead to new insights into the teaching and learning process. The development of a new kind of partnership between universities and schools is also Graham Byrne Hill's theme in Chapter 12. He describes the evolution of a partnership between college- and school-based tutors responsible for developing a postgraduate course to train secondary teachers. This development was informed by a careful process of information-gathering and negotiation in the partner schools, and led to agreed statements of student entitlement in IT across a wide range of subjects. Both these chapters demonstrate the value of using action research to inform course development.

The developing Information Superhighway for education offers new strategies for professional development: IT can support the process of professional development as well as providing a stimulus to rethinking the teaching process. Niki Davis describes in Chapter 13 the application of electronic communications in the classroom and links this to the professional development of teachers. This IT tool is challenging and innovative, providing new channels and new modes for the most fundamental part of education: communication itself. Its potential is immense, although it is not yet fully understood. It appears to enable teachers across the world to contribute to the development of their profession, and to provide new possibilities for education. IT can be seen as a stimulus to radical change in education, but it is critically important to ensure that this change leads to improved educational opportunities for learners. Everything depends upon effective professional development for teachers, who are currently under extra-ordinary pressures that are stimulated, in part, by new technologies themselves.

REFERENCE

Watson, D. (ed.) (1993) *The ImpacT Report: An Evaluation of the Impact of Information Technology on Children's Achievements in Primary and Secondary Schools.* London: King's College, Centre for Educational Studies.

Chapter 8

Computers and the teacher's role

Peter Scrimshaw

INTRODUCTION

Teaching is one of the most demanding social activities in our society, involving the presentation of a sophisticated cultural inheritance to a large group of learners while working within the constraints of a heavily bureaucratised National Curriculum. Compulsory computer use can easily be experienced as an extra burden rather than a potential aid. Nevertheless, while teachers have little choice over whether to use computers, they retain a great deal of control over how and when they use them.

However, the computer is not simply another curriculum innovation; it is also arguably the most important technical aid to teachers wishing to explore their own practice. This is because it is an immensely flexible (albeit often infuriating) device for generating and modifying curriculum innovations to enable learners and teachers to try out for themselves new approaches to teaching and learning. As the contributions to Part One of this book demonstrate, the nature of the computer radically changes when the teacher replaces one piece of software with another; in choosing which software to use the teacher is making a first approximation at specifying what kinds of learning they are hoping to promote. Once chosen, most forms of software allow teachers and learners a great deal of freedom in how they make use of it. Thus the detailed formulation and implementation of computer-based classroom activities allows for a closer approximation to what kinds of learning can be achieved. But this requires teachers to see the computer not as an exotic extra, but as a responsive and integral element in a classroom curriculum that has been rethought to include a view of what computers might do. To ask how teachers need to use computers is in large part to ask how the computer might be used to support and explore the theoretical and practical implications of their own philosophy of education, with a view to its improvement.

The first part of this chapter offers a model of the curricular elements in the pre-computer classroom and then considers how different kinds of software relate to this framework. The later part of the chapter discusses the changes that the computer is bringing to the school and the world beyond, and considers some of the implications of all this for the professional development of teachers.

THE STRUCTURE OF THE PRE-COMPUTER CLASSROOM CURRICULUM

The accounts of classroom events given in Part One clearly reveal that there are various ways in which teachers can conceptualise classroom life. Behind the diversity of experiences explored in those chapters lie a range of views that the contributors take of learners, curriculum materials, adult knowledge and the pattern of relationships between these and the teacher's role (see Figure 8.1).

How teachers regard each individual in a class varies greatly, but behind those variations it may be possible to distinguish a general disposition. One position is to consider that learners should be encouraged and enabled to become alert receivers and sensitive appreciators of externally generated knowledge; another that they are interested explorers of such knowledge; a third that they are active and imaginative creators of their own understanding. Many intermediate positions are possible here, but nevertheless many educational controversies are presented in terms of these underlying distinctions, such as debates about the relative importance of spelling, grammar, imagination and originality in writing.

There is again a choice to make when teachers consider how each individual should relate to other class members. A teacher may wish to promote a view of

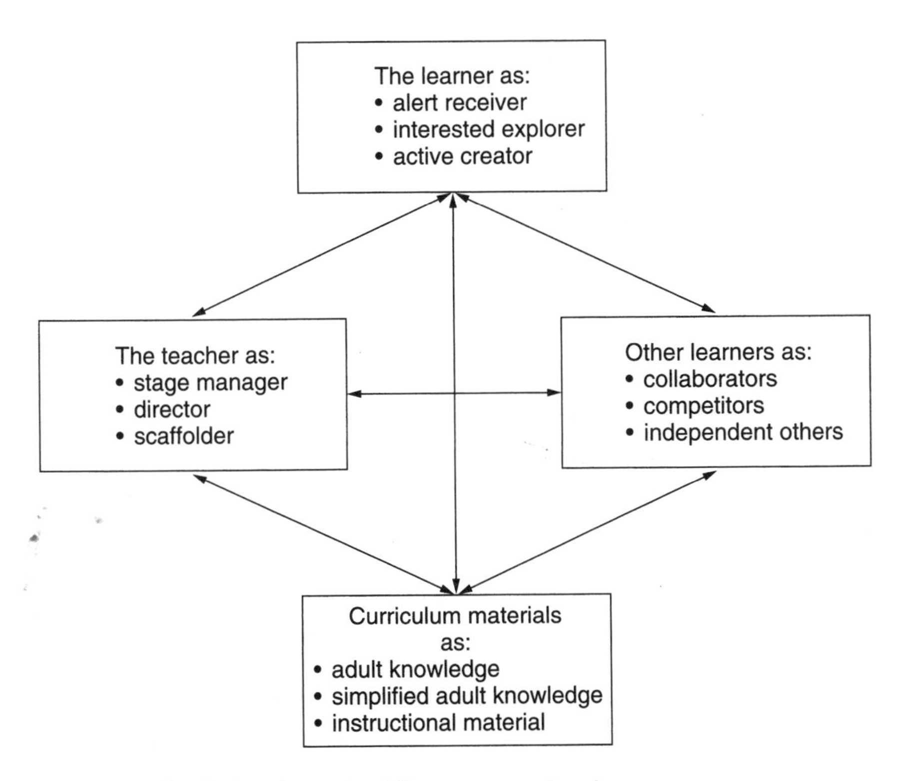

Figure 8.1 Curricular elements of the pre-computer classroom

others as potential collaborators with whom the individual must learn to work, or as competitors to be related to in a pattern of healthy and good-natured conflict for fairly earned success. In contrast to both these perspectives stands the view that others in a class are irrelevant distractions and that ideally the individual should pursue his or her own activities independently. Here too intermediate possibilities are present, but simply to say that gets us little further forward unless some rationale can be offered for why a particular balance is favoured.

Our views on the characteristics of individual learners and their relationship to the group are in turn affected by how we think of classroom knowledge, and the connections between that and what we may call adult knowledge, i.e. the immense body of conflicting beliefs, values, skills and capabilities that form the human resources with which members of a society conduct their affairs and attempt to realise their individual and joint intentions.

One position here could be that classroom knowledge should be an unvarnished selection of the most important adult knowledge, to be confronted by learners with little or no mediation. Whether the learner, the teaching profession, the community, industry and business or the government should define what adult knowledge to present distinguishes several very significant variants within this general position. What they all share is a distrust of the education establishment and of what are seen as its self-interested attempts to interpose itself and its arcane and inefficient procedures between the learner and 'real' knowledge, as embodied in one or other notion of 'real life'. While this approach rightly emphasises the value of schools in helping learners towards increasingly sophisticated conceptions of knowledge, it can allow the logical structure of adult knowledge to dominate unduly how it is best presented, as Gay Vaughan points out at the start of Chapter 3.

Over against this position we can place the belief that it is essential that adult knowledge be carefully and professionally presented to school-age learners in ways that make it easier for them to grasp. One way in which this can be done is to introduce curriculum materials or activities that provide the learner with a series of simplifications of adult knowledge, each presentation progressively closer to the full picture. Some children's fiction, school assemblies, children's encyclopaedias, five-a-side football, Lego blocks and the infants' Wendy house exemplify this approach. Such constructions present unembellished simplifications of adult knowledge but do not of themselves generate learning. For this to emerge, the teacher (or perhaps another learner) must provide some framing, direction or instructional support.

However, a related category of curriculum materials builds in such directions from the start, thus partially filling a role that might otherwise be taken by the teacher. This category includes such things as textbooks, some educational television, worksheets and (as a marginal case) structured reading schemes. Here too teachers face choices: how far to rely upon curriculum material and experiences that have no instructional component, and how far to rely upon materials in which such instruction comes prepackaged.

If we turn now to the conception we might have of the teacher's function in all this, again there are a number of options. Different views on the relationships between learners and knowledge influence the extent to which we see teachers as dominant actors in the classroom directing activities or as stage managers of what are seen as largely self-generated learning activities emanating from learners as individuals or as a group. It is here that decisions on such matters as the ideal balance between instruction and support, between open and closed questions, between direction and enabling come into focus. We will return to the role of the teacher later, but first we need to consider how the use of computers might fit into this general framework.

THE COMPUTER AS A MORE EFFECTIVE CURRICULUM RESOURCE

So how can we most usefully characterise the ways in which the computer can be used within the diversity of classroom cultures that we find in our schools? Clearly, what computers can do depends substantially upon what software they are running at any time; and there are many kinds of software. This suggests that we should ask instead what sorts of computer packages are best suited to supporting particular kinds of learning, and how far each kind of software is amenable to use within a different pedagogic framework from that for which it appears to have been designed. Here we could envisage a range of possibilities: at one end of the range the chosen software would completely determine the sort of activities needed to accompany its effective use; at the other end of the scale some kinds of software might be relatively neutral, being highly malleable and responsive to many different teaching approaches. Table 8.1 classifies (albeit in a simplified and debatable form) many commonly available kinds of software in these terms.

Some types of software (the 'open-ended' or 'tool' packages) assume that the learner is predominantly an active creator of knowledge. Productivity tools, such as presentation packages, word processors, outliners, ideas processors, spreadsheets, graphics packages, music composers and database packages, all allow users to collect and enter their own data and so are in this category because they all leave the initiative to the user. Programming languages and modelling packages, too, require the user to take the lead in defining the purpose of the activity and in evaluating the results of his or her own choices as they are in effect devices for enabling users to externalise and evolve their own conceptualisation of some process. Gay Vaughan's account of the use of LOGO with four- and five-year-olds in Chapter 3 is a good example of this process of externalisation in action, while other kinds of open-ended software are discussed in Scrimshaw (1993a), Straker (1989) and Underwood (1994).

While open-ended packages assume an active learner, as far as other dimensions of the classroom curriculum framework are concerned they are much more flexible. To start with, they all allow a variety of kinds of group relationships

Table 8.1 Types of software and their educational characteristics

Software type	*Learner seen as*	*Group relationships encouraged*	*Knowledge embodied is*
Word processors	Creator	Neutral	Adult/simplified
Desktop publishing packages	Creator	Neutral	Adult/simplified
Presentation packages	Creator	Neutral	Adult/simplified
Spreadsheets	Creator	Neutral	Adult/simplified
Graphics packages	Creator	Neutral	Adult/simplified
Music composers	Creator	Neutral	Adult/simplified
Ideas processors	Creator	Neutral	Adult/simplified
Database packages	Creator	Neutral	Adult/simplified
Modelling packages	Creator	Neutral	Adult/simplified
Programming languages	Creator	Neutral	Adult/simplified
E-mail	Creator	Collaborative	Adult
Computer conferencing	Creator/receiver	Collaborative	Adult
Remote databases	Explorer	Neutral	Adult
Filled read-only tools	Explorer	Neutral	Adult/simplified
Text disclosure	Explorer	Neutral	Adult/simplified
Simulations	Explorer	Neutral	Simplified
Adventure games	Explorer	Neutral	Simplified
Instructional hypertexts	Explorer	Neutral	Instructionalised
Encyclopaedias	Explorer/receiver	Neutral	Adult/simplified
Talking books	Explorer/receiver	Neutral	Adult/simplified
Intelligent tutors	Explorer/receiver	Independent	Instructionalised
Video games	Explorer/receiver	Independent	Simplified
Data logging	Receiver	Neutral	Adult
Drill and practice programs	Receiver	Independent	Instructionalised

when they are being used; individual use, collaborative work by a group with a shared task or competitive working are all possible. They also have some capacity for what we might call self-adjustment to their users. As they are essentially empty shells into which users place and manipulate content of their own choosing (text, pictures, numbers, formulae or whatever), users can choose for themselves the level of complexity of that content, and the level of sophistication of the manipulation of it. This encourages learning, by reducing the risk of frustration and failure that more rigid packages are prone to (here again pp. 44–5 in Chapter 3 offers a good illustration). However, in other contexts this openness can discourage learning for precisely the same reason; namely, that it does not make demands upon the user that they do not themselves choose to accept. In Chapter 2, for example, Jon Jessel notes how children using word processors may not engage in discussion of their collaboratively written text without teacher intervention. This is presumably in part because the software does not require such activities of them or indicate the need for them. In addition open-ended packages, like any others, may create obstacles to learning simply through their lack of user friendliness in the sheer mechanics of operating them, rather than any intrinsic difficulty in the content they are used to order and modify.

However, not all types of open-ended packages are neutral as between different modes of use. Electronic mail and computer conferencing are (like the telephone and the postal service) impossible to use except in collaboration with others willing to act as recipients and initiators of messages too (see Davis, 1994, for a detailed consideration of this matter). Bernadette Robinson (1993) has also discussed this point at some length. As she notes, computer conferencing may be used not only for the transmission of factual information but also as a powerful tool for creative writing, a point supported and expanded elsewhere by Brent Robinson (1993). What we have in this sort of software, then, are learning media that are at least as flexible in most respects as other kinds of open-ended software, but which have a built-in requirement for shared use.

In the second main category of software types the emphasis swings from the learner as knowledge creator to the learner as interested explorer. Here either the software designer or the teacher provides a structured body of content that learners then explore (an approach well exemplified by the hypertext package discussed by Jon Jessel and Vicky Hurst in Chapter 7). This category includes what we might call the 'filled' versions of the tool packages discussed above, i.e. those in which the database, spreadsheet or whatever is presented to the learners with some content already in place. Related types of software include text disclosure packages (Scrimshaw, 1993c), talking books for young children, video games, adventure games (Underwood and Underwood, 1990), simulations and the hypermèdia simulations and encyclopaedias now appearing on CD-ROM. Finally, data logging devices (as Roy Barton demonstrates in Chapter 5) are another rather different form of tool package. Here, however, the filling is provided through the ongoing collection of data from the environment itself. Thus these packages offer a distinctive mix of active data collection by the learner and close control over what kinds of data are collected by the program designer and by the nature of the environment in which the equipment is used.

These sorts of package are all neutral as between individual and collaborative use, but they differ not only in what knowledge they embody but also in the form that it takes. Many databases (for example most of those that can be accessed remotely) are designed for adult use, and to that extent can claim to be direct introductions to some aspect of the adult world. Conversely simulations, video games and adventure games (which can be seen as a rather exotic form of non-real-life 'simulation') are by definition simplifications, and thus potentially easier for younger learners to understand, although the underlying complexity of such popular simulations as *SimCity* and *Civilization* suggest that this point can be overstated. So too are many forms of control technology devices (see, for instance, Whalley, 1994), such as LOGO-based floor turtles. Between these two subgroups are packages that may take either adult or simplified forms, such as electronic encyclopaedias and all the filled tool packages, which may be presented with content that makes greater or lesser concessions to the relative lack of experience of younger users.

Another subgroup within these more exploratory kinds of software are instructional hypertexts, in which some teaching material is included to help the learner deal with the substantive content provided. Here too there can be wide variations in the level of complexity of the instruction provided. Related to these are the drill and practice programs in which learners reinforce and/or test their knowledge (for a discussion of one example, see Jones and Mercer, 1993). Such programs may have some form of branching (a simple hypertext structure) built in, through which the user is channelled from activity to activity according to the responses made. This kind of program has developed over the past fifteen years into intelligent tutor packages, which respond with a much greater degree of relevance and flexibility to the learner's inputs to the computer. These packages may have an explicit didactic element or may be designed in a more exploratory and occasionally collaborative mode. These programs assume an alert user who is willing to make choices, but one who reacts to the program's initiatives and definition of the task, rather than creating such a definition for him or herself, or exploring in a more or less open-ended way the information provided; they thus stand on the borderline between exploratory and receiver models of the learner.

CD-ROMs are becoming increasingly widespread in schools and homes. CD-ROM disks are simply another device for storing information, operating on the same general principles as audio CD disks. CD-ROM disks, however, store and play back a much wider variety of kinds of information; text, diagrams, photographs, animations and computer programs can all be included as well as sound.

The reason that CD-ROMs need separate discussion from an educational point of view is that they store far more material than floppies. This allows the designer to include around a quarter of a million pages of text on each disk, or to include items such as good-quality sound and animations (including short video clips) that take up so much space that only a CD-ROM can hold enough of them to make up an effective presentation. Consequently CD-ROM titles range from text-only designs, through multimedia encyclopaedias (where the text is leavened with many pictures and some sound and video clips) to CD-ROMs whose most obvious characteristic is a great deal of animation and sound. Thus far more complex software packages can be provided through this medium, such as general and special-interest encyclopaedias, annotated databases of pictures and a variety of 'talking books', in which learners follow an animated story with access to both a printed text and a spoken reading. Something of the potential of CD-ROMs in schools are beginning to be reported (Steadman *et al.*, 1992; Collins *et al.*, 1996) and first indications are positive.

What emerges from all this is that the distinctions drawn earlier between kinds of curriculum materials reappear in rather similar form when we look at computer packages. While there are also many differences in convenience and speed (not all favouring the computer), software packages can be grouped in the same ways as conventional materials as far as their potential roles in classroom teaching and learning are concerned.

THE COMPUTER AS CATALYST FOR RADICAL EDUCATIONAL CHANGE

The previous section assumes that the importance of computers lies in their capacity to help us pursue our current conceptions of education more effectively than we could do with traditional kinds of resource. It also assumes that the wider place of the school and teachers within society will remain the same. Can these assumptions be sustained? I think not, which means that the account so far, while plausible within its limits, seriously underestimates the impact that computers will have upon schools and therefore of the opportunities that they will offer for teachers.

If we look beyond the classroom and the school we see a world in which changes are continuous and diverse. Historically schools have been partly sheltered from these processes, because in their location, staffing and to some extent in the knowledge they were expected to transmit they were physically and organisationally separate from the society around them. But as the millennium approaches, all these three screens between schools and society are, for good or ill, disintegrating, making schools far more open to external influences. This opens up another route by which computers will influence teaching and learning, because society itself is being powerfully and directly changed by the ways in which computers are being employed.

As we have seen earlier, electronic networking involves the connection of individuals to each other via the computer and to massive databases of stored information. This facility is already available to, and in some cases used by, schools but the fastest growth is in the electronic interconnection of companies, universities, government bodies and individual homes through computers. This is evolving into a vast network, precursor to an eventual 'Information Superhighway'. This is currently estimated to link over 20 million people worldwide. All of them have, in principle, access to each other and to the databases that each is prepared to make available to others, either free or for a small charge.

Schools can choose to link into this network, and to the extent that they do, they redefine both what constitutes learning groups for their pupils and the role of teachers. When the group includes other children and adults from all round the world, the teacher's contribution to the group's discussion is quite different from that which is possible and required when everyone involved is present face to face in the classroom.

This development also raises questions about how children themselves might use information available on the network. For instance, in Chapter 4 Helen Smith points out some of the conceptual difficulties of primary age children in carrying out complex searches on databases chosen by their teacher. How then will teachers help children deal with databases they encounter through the Internet, designed for adult specialists to use?

THE REDEFINITION OF PUBLIC KNOWLEDGE

So far I have discussed these issues as if the notion of adult knowledge itself was unproblematic; as if this was, if not a static entity, at least something that was evolving and changing slowly through time; but in fact adult knowledge and its mode of dissemination are both changing rapidly, and the computer is at the heart of this process, as the spread of computers through the wider world forces a reconceptualisation of one human activity after another. In business management and commercial practice massive changes have already taken place and are already partially reflected in schools. But computers are also altering how, for instance, English, art and history are conducted and conceived of as academic and creative activities. In consequence the option of simply seeing computers as a better means of transmitting the traditional curriculum is already dissolving, especially for students now preparing for teaching.

First, in many areas the form and substance of what constitutes knowledge is being modified by the introduction of the computer, even in areas in which the motive for this change was simply to provide some improvement in ways of accessing or generating kinds of knowledge whose nature was assumed to be impervious to the effects of such changes. In many cases this was indeed so, but in others it was not. Novels written in hypertext format are not simply equivalents of the linear novels published on paper (see Scrimshaw, 1993b; and, for more detailed discussion, Bolter, 1991, and Landow, 1992). Art packages do not simply reproduce in a more convenient way the artwork produced with traditional media (although some of them to some extent can), and the same is true of computer-based musical composition and performance.

If we turn to more practical activities and the sorts of craft knowledge and skills that define them, the changes are, if anything, even greater. This is nicely illustrated in Chapter 6, where John McGowan points out how his school's use of computers for design work was in part a response to the message that school-leavers were sending back from their workplaces in which the use of computers to support design was becoming commonplace. Today computer-aided design is changing the ways in which all kinds of objects from dresses to aircraft are being created, while electronically generated simulated news studios now replace the images of real studios behind the (so far still real) news reader. Occupations such as accountancy, stockbroking, product development and marketing have been significantly altered in many firms by the introduction of spreadsheets and computer databases to identify, for instance, the quantitative aspects of possible future developments, and to locate patterns and problems in current practices.

More generally, electronic communications within companies are changing the balance between individual and group activity on a massive scale, with the development of such interesting devices as electronically shared personal diaries that allow members of a team to see at once when a suitable time for a group meeting is available, to set up that meeting and to have it recorded in everyone's diary automatically. In the same way shared files that several people can access and change, even if they are in offices in different countries, are transforming what can be meant by co-authoring.

Whether people are working at a checkout counter, stocktaking in a warehouse or producing a parish newsletter, computers are redefining what capabilities their tasks require, and in ways that cannot but feed back eventually into the school curriculum. These changes are not only in individual techniques and skills, but are also altering the whole balance in thought and action between the intuitive and the explicit, and between the rationally simplified and the qualitatively complex. These are changes that teachers not only should not, but in practice cannot, ignore.

THE TEACHER'S ROLE

What are the consequences of such changes for the way in which teachers do their work? This is best approached by again looking separately at computers and software that can be seen as improving the effectiveness of current kinds of teaching and learning, and then turning to the more radical demands made by those new technologies that are beginning to require a wholesale rethinking of the teacher's role.

There is something to learn about any new piece of software of a straightforwardly technical kind, although perhaps less than might often be feared. I have argued earlier that teachers also need to see how different kinds of software relate to various views of learners, their relationship with each other, and the view of knowledge that the design of the software assumes. Below these more general considerations is the need to become familiar with the distinctive features of specific software packages, for as much of the educational potential of a program lies in the detailed structure as in its more general character.

How teachers use a particular program has to take account of all these aspects, but it is not completely determined by them, although both programs and more frequently the accompanying advice for teachers suggest that the designer favours a given approach. In practice teachers can employ software in ways that fit their own educational philosophies, rather than automatically taking up the particular educational stance that the designer may favour. In that sense virtually all software packages are, as far as the teacher's role is concerned, open to at least a fair degree of interpretation, as a variety of studies have shown (see, for instance, Olsen, 1988, and Cochran-Smith *et al.*, 1991). Open-ended packages can, as we have seen, be closed down by the teacher pre-specifying content for them that sets limits on the range of ways that children then use them. These limits can subsequently be selectively loosened or tightened as the activity progresses. On the other hand, the teacher may instead want to open up the ways in which a learner uses an open-ended package, because the learner has too restricted a conception of the possibilities it offers to use it to best effect. This strategy is exemplified by John McGowan's creation of a help file for his students (Chapter 6). Even where the package provides prestructured material that the teacher cannot change (as in adventure games, for example), the teacher can still use the package in various ways by presenting it to learners within a different framework of instructions and suggestions.

In practice, therefore, teachers are faced with very similar choices when using computer packages as they are when using any other kind of curriculum materials, namely how to adapt and interpret them to fit their own philosophy of education and the best interests of the learners they work for. But neither the full implications of what we each take our philosophy of education to be or what constitutes the best interests of learners are ever fully obvious to us, for our understanding of both evolves and changes continually in the light of experience. This is especially obvious when we face a new situation (such as that created by the introduction of a different kind of software package) which itself offers more possibilities and limitations than are immediately obvious. This implies the teacher's role too cannot be rigidly prespecified and then applied in every situation. For instance, to ask if the teacher should be an unobtrusive stage manager or a hands-on director of classroom activities is to miss the point; sometimes one is appropriate and sometimes the other. The problem is to know which strategy to use when.

One approach to this problem has been to look to the notion of scaffolding. The term refers to the actions that a helper (usually an adult) takes to reduce the demands of some task on a learner so that he or she can concentrate on gaining the particular skill or understanding that the task requires. This concept is clearly relevant to classroom learning (although it is by no means restricted to that arena). However, it needs a fuller definition if it is to be of practical use to teachers. Maybin *et al.* (1992, pp. 188–9) offer the following provisional formulation:

> ['Scaffolding'] is help which will enable a learner to accomplish a task which they would not have been quite able to manage on their own, and it is help which is intended to bring the learner closer to a state of competence which will enable them eventually to complete such a task on their own . . . To know whether or not some help counts as 'scaffolding', we would need to have at the very least some evidence of a teacher wishing to enable a learner to develop a specific skill, grasp a particular concept or achieve a particular level of understanding. A more stringent criterion would be to require some evidence of a learner successfully accomplishing the task with the teacher's help. An even more stringent interpretation would be to require some evidence of a learner having achieved some greater level of independent competence as a result of the scaffolding experience (that is, demonstrating their increased competence or improved level of understanding in dealing independently with some subsequent problem).

Scaffolding in this sense does indeed get us beyond thinking about what teachers do in terms of a single kind of approach, as the form that scaffolding might need to take would clearly differ from context to context. It also emphasises the role both of the teacher's intentions and the learner's subsequent achievements in deciding whether scaffolding has been successfully accomplished. Finally, it makes very clear that such a view of the teacher's role requires a great deal of careful observation and reflection by the teacher, so that the links between what the teacher attempts and the subsequent learning can be identified with some confidence.

However, the concept of scaffolding is not by itself sufficient, for it makes no distinction in terms of the relative value of different kinds of learning; or, indeed, between ethical and unethical (as distinct from effective and ineffective) methods of scaffolding learning. It needs therefore to be set within a wider conception of education based upon a thought-through philosophy. This is even more clearly the case when we turn to those forms of software and delivery systems (such as CD-ROMs and electronic networking) which demand a radical rethinking of their role by teachers.

The first difference that these two technologies introduce is to increase greatly the range of knowledge available to learners. This alone changes the teacher's role. How, for instance, does the teacher respond to a situation where different pupils have based individual project work not upon the information contained in books in the classroom or school library, but upon data gathered from an encyclopaedia on CD-ROM or electronically from outside sources that, in total, are too many and diverse for the teacher to check directly for accuracy?

Electronic networking also widens the range of learners in a group far beyond the classroom walls, through computer conferences and e-mail. But when the group with which a learner interacts includes other learners and adults from all around the world, the teacher's contribution to the group's discussion is quite different from that which is possible and required when everyone involved is present face-to-face in the classroom.

Such networking also expands the range of 'teachers' available to children. These include not only those fellow learners elsewhere who can advise their peers on a particular topic, but adult experts. This raises the question of how, for instance, the teacher contributes to a discussion on science between pupils and a working scientist whom they have contacted for advice, or how two teachers in different countries jointly organise and support a shared project involving both their classes.

So how can schools and teachers respond to these new possibilities? One option is simply to view the wider resources as something to be closely controlled by the teacher by setting closed tasks that require only materials which the teacher already knows to be available on the CD-ROM or in the national database that the learner is to use. While such tightly focused activities have their place, they hardly make full use of the potential available and will not, if used exclusively, help learners develop their own capacity for independent study. Such closed tasks therefore need to be supplemented with activities and instruction that enables learners to benefit from both the wider range of knowledge available and from their interactions with learners and teachers outside their own school.

The implication of the first requirement is that teachers need to teach the processes of learning rather than its products. The conventional learning skills, such as locating, collating and summarising information, and identifying connections and contradictions within a body of information, all need to be explicitly moved to the centre of the classroom curriculum. The development of such skills also needs to be done in ways that then enable learners to develop them further for themselves through using appropriate forms of software.

Another major contribution from the teacher is to assist learners to find out how to collaborate with and learn from others. This requires the explicit teaching and learning of ways of organising co-operative activities involving computers, whether in face-to-face groups round a single machine or through co-operation at a distance via a conferencing or e-mail system.

In order to do this, teachers themselves need more opportunities and support in using the new technologies in collaborative contexts, so that they can both identify the problems and possibilities for themselves and find ways to model these activities in their own practice with learners. Finally, when introducing these newer technologies teachers too need time to reflect upon and research what is happening.

What all this suggests is that the ever-increasing influence of the computer in schools and in the wider community will demand a far deeper reappraisal of the teacher's role than is commonly recognised, requiring a fundamental and continual process of rethinking what is taught, how it is taught, and why. If this change is not to be externally imposed, teachers themselves will need to develop forms of reflective classroom practice that enable them to make the best use of the educational and professional opportunities as they open up. Some of the detailed implications of this, and ways in which the problem is already being addressed, are the central concern of this part of the book.

REFERENCES

Bolter, J. (1991) *Writing Space: The Computer, Hypertext and the History of Writing.* Hillsdale, N.J.: Lawrence Erlbaum Associates.

Cochran-Smith, M., Paris, C.L. and Kahan, J.L. (1991) *Learning to Write Differently: Beginning Writers and Word Processing.* Norwood, N.J.: Ablex.

Collins, J., Longman, J., Littleton, K., Mercer, N., Scrimshaw, P. and Wegerif, R. (1996) *CD-ROMs in Primary Schools: An Independent Evaluation.* Coventry: National Council for Education Technology.

Davis, N. (1994) 'Electronic communication', in J. Underwood, *Computer Based Learning: Potential into Practice.* London: David Fulton.

Jones, A. and Mercer, N. (1993) 'Theories of learning and information technology', in P. Scrimshaw, *Language, Classrooms and Computers.* London and New York: Routledge.

Landow, G. P. (1992) *Hypertext: The Convergence of Contemporary Critical Theory and Technology.* Baltimore, Md: Johns Hopkins University Press.

Maybin, J., Mercer, N. and Stierer, B. (1992) 'Scaffolding learning', in K. Norman (ed.), *Thinking Voices: The Work of the National Oracy Project.* London: Hodder & Stoughton.

Monteith, M. (ed.) (1993) *Computers and Language.* Oxford: Intellect Books.

Olsen, J. (1988) *Schoolworlds/Microworlds: Computers and the Culture of the Classroom.* Oxford: Pergamon Press.

Robinson, Bernadette (1993) 'Communicating through computers in the classroom', in P. Scrimshaw, *Language, Classrooms and Computers.* London and New York: Routledge.

Robinson, Brent (1993) 'Collaborative writing using distanced electronic communications', in M. Monteith, *Computers and Language.* Oxford: Intellect Books.

Scrimshaw, P. (ed.) (1993a) *Language, Classrooms and Computers.* London and New York: Routledge.

—— (1993b) 'Reading, writing and hypertext', in P. Scrimshaw, *Language, Classrooms and Computers.* London and New York: Routledge.

—— (1993c) 'Text completion programs', in P. Scrimshaw, *Language, Classrooms and Computers.* London and New York: Routledge.

Steadman, S., Nash, C. and Eraut, M. (1992) *CD-ROMs in Schools: Evaluation Report.* Coventry: National Council for Educational Technology.

Straker, A. (1989) *Children Using Computers.* Oxford: Blackwell.

Underwood, J. (ed.) (1994) *Computer Based Learning: Potential into Practice.* London: David Fulton.

Underwood, J. M. and Underwood, G. (1990) *Computers and Learning: Helping Children Acquire Thinking Skills.* Oxford: Blackwell.

Whalley P. (1994) 'Control technology', in J. Underwood, *Computer Based Learning: Potential into Practice.* London: David Fulton.

Chapter 9

Classroom investigations

Exploring and evaluating how IT can support learning[1]

Bridget Somekh

ACTION RESEARCH AS A STRATEGY FOR TEACHER PROFESSIONAL DEVELOPMENT WITH IT

Classroom investigations using an action research approach are a particularly effective means of bringing about teachers' professional development in information technology. This chapter draws on the research of the Pupil Autonomy in Learning with Microcomputers Project (PALM)[2] which adopted this approach in twenty-four primary and secondary schools in East Anglia during 1988–90. Similar approaches have been used very successfully in teacher training, both with tutors (see Chapter 18) and student teachers (see Chapter 10).

The chapters in Part One of this book give examples of ways in which the use of IT *can* provide innovative learning experiences, but in all cases a great deal depends upon the teacher to provide the context which makes this possible. Teachers need to be competent and confident users of the hardware and software, but this in itself is not enough. They need, also, to understand how to organise the classroom and to structure learning tasks so that IT resources become a necessary and integral part of learning rather than an add-on technical aid. Unfortunately, many courses in IT concentrate on technical matters such as how to operate particular software packages. Consideration of how to use this software in teaching is often squeezed into whatever time is left at the end of sessions. Teaching of this kind – almost literally key press by key press – is very time-consuming and has the disadvantage that it concentrates upon the area of teachers' weakness rather than building upon their existing professional knowledge. Even when courses of this kind are perceived by participants as useful and enjoyable, some research by Ridgway and Passey (1991) suggests that they often do not result in any changes in teaching practice.

Action research involves participants in any social situation (such as a classroom, a hospital ward or a small business) investigating their own practice with the aim of improving it. The term action research indicates that there is not the usual separation between research and the application of its outcomes to practice at a later stage. Instead, research and action are integrated in a cyclical process of collecting evidence (data), examining it very closely (analysis), deciding if there are any implications (interpretation), planning a course of action on the basis of this evidence, putting this into practice, and evaluating it by collecting data, analysing it and interpreting it, and so on.

Action research is close to what good teachers do on a daily basis in the ordinary course of their work, with the very significant addition of data collection. Teachers reflect continuously upon what they are doing and adapt their practice to achieve the best possible outcomes in the classroom (or the staff meeting, or the parents' consultation evening). The crucial difference between action research and what Donald Schön in his book *The Reflective Practitioner* (1983) calls 'reflection-in-action' lies in the collection of data, or evidence. Even if a busy teacher is only able to collect a small amount of data, this can be considered much more carefully in a quiet moment away from the classroom than is ever possible at the time when events are rushing past at speed. Data also help to overcome the normal human problem that we interpret things mainly from our own point of view – experiencing them of necessity through our own senses and making quick judgements on this basis. In the PALM project teachers referred to their data (e.g. a child's opinion given in an interview) as giving them 'an extra eye' because their data often showed them things they otherwise would have missed.

For an innovation to be effective, those responsible for implementing it need to feel a sense of ownership. It is always difficult for established professionals to introduce change because it means abandoning some of the tried and trusted strategies built up from years of experience. In addition, an innovation is often threatening to those who have to introduce it, because they subconsciously experience it as a criticism of their own past achievements. A further problem is that no change is entirely for the better – there is always some trade-off between the advantages and the disadvantages of the innovation by comparison with retaining the status quo. All this means that unless teachers believe in an innovation it is very unlikely that they will introduce it effectively. Under coercion they may introduce some elements at a minimal level, but they will perceive it to be either impractical or educationally indefensible to make major changes if they cannot see any real benefit. In the case of IT, it is particularly important to convince teachers of its value because many perceive themselves to be technologically incompetent and feel deskilled and demoralised when they first begin to use computers in the classroom.

As a result of the high level of 'ownership' and depth of understanding of the innovation which action research can engender in teachers, it is recognised as one of the most effective ways of bringing about educational change (see Elliott, 1991; and Fullan, 1982, who cites Elliott's work in the Ford Teaching Project as an example of successful support for innovation). Of course, since it is carried out alongside their normal full-time work, teachers are seldom able to meet the ideal and carry out the whole action research process. However, the power of action research lies in their involvement as researchers while *at the same time* the main focus of their energy continues to be teaching and learning.

The remainder of this chapter focuses upon what we learned from the PALM project about the effectiveness of the action research approach to teachers' professional development in IT.

THE PUPIL AUTONOMY IN LEARNING WITH MICROCOMPUTERS (PALM) PROJECT

The Pupil Autonomy in Learning with Microcomputers project (PALM) sought to combine computer-mediated curriculum development and teacher professional development in a single action research process. It had two aims:

- to work in partnership with teachers to research the role of IT in developing pupil autonomy in learning;
- to investigate the effectiveness of action research as a means of teacher professional development in the IT innovation.

The project was led by a central team of which I was the co-ordinator, with three teachers acting as full-time project officers (Jon Pratt, Cambridgeshire: Erica Brown, Essex; and Bob Davison, Norfolk) and a secretary (Laura Tickner). In the three LEAs PALM worked under the auspices of the Adviser or Inspector for IT, who set the broad framework of county policy for IT. There were altogether twenty-four PALM schools ranging in size from a large secondary school with 1,422 pupils to a small primary school with fifty-nine pupils and drawing upon a mixture of rural and urban catchment areas.

PALM provided no funding for the purchase of computers. Most of the schools, however, acquired some new hardware as an indirect result of being in PALM, because the project raised the profile of IT with senior management, or gave the school a higher priority with the LEA IT inspector. Nevertheless, none of the schools had sufficient hardware to provide an environment in which there was immediate access on demand for teachers or pupils. The general level of equipment varied considerably. The ratio of computers to pupils in each secondary school ranged from 1:167 to 1:22 at the beginning of the project in September 1988, and from 1:43 to 1:8 at the end of the project in June 1990. In the primary schools it ranged from 1:230 to 1:31 in 1988, and from 1:115 to 1:24 in 1990. These appeared to be typical ratios for schools in East Anglia at that time; the improvement over a two-year period reflected a general improvement in the level of equipment in all schools, although participation in the project was a contributory factor. The size of the schools varied considerably (secondary from 1,420 to 427; primary from 459 to 54) but this was often not the crucial factor in determining the number of computers per pupil. Access to computers for teaching was far from ideal. In primary schools computers were usually shared between several classes on either a daily or a weekly basis. In secondary schools they were normally located in a specialist computer room which had to be booked in advance, although in a few cases departments had one or two computers permanently allocated to their rooms (see Chapter 6 of this book).

It was a priority for PALM that the participating schools should benefit from working with the project in two ways:

- through teachers developing more effective strategies for using computers to enable pupil autonomy in learning; and
- through headteachers and IT co-ordinators developing more effective strategies for in-school support for teachers using IT.

The project did not offer what most headteachers and teachers at first assumed (funding for computers and traditional style in-service training in its use for teachers). Therefore, the aims and working methods of the project had to be fully explained and the terms of participation negotiated. This had to be done in such a way that the participant teachers would be given control over their own action research, while the overall aims and working methods of the project retained coherence and integrity.

PALM was itself an innovation, and there is a danger that innovations can undergo significant changes at the point of entry to a school (House, 1974, pp. 77–81). The action research methodology had to be established and expectations of more traditional kinds of working methods had to be resisted. For example, we needed to resist the request to 'Tell us what we have to do'. Instead, we explained that PALM would be looking at the impact of computer use on children's learning. We suggested that computers cost a lot of money and it was important to evaluate their usefulness. We said we were asking teachers to use computers in the normal course of their teaching and to look closely at the learning which took place; and that, in order to ensure that the project's work had practical outcomes, we wanted individual teachers to decide on the exact focus of their investigations.

Most heads and teachers became interested when we explained PALM in this way, although the teachers' degree of enthusiasm was strongly related to their feelings about computers (in many cases apprehension and anxiety). The teachers' role as action researchers was difficult for us to explain and their response developed gradually as they practised the role with our support. In each school there was a teacher with overall responsibility for IT, and nearly always these teachers were the key contacts for the project; we encouraged them to undertake research into their own role in supporting colleagues as managers of change, but although many developed and extended their roles, only one undertook sustained action research of this kind (Griffin, 1990).

Of the one hundred teachers who undertook substantial research and development work in PALM, fifty-one were in primary (or middle designated primary) schools and sixty-seven in secondary schools; forty were men and seventy-eight women. The primary school teachers taught across the whole curriculum. The specialisms of the secondary teachers are set out in Table 9.1 (although it should be remembered that a small number consciously directed their work towards cross-curricular projects). It is of interest that considerably more teachers of arts-based subjects worked with PALM than did teachers of science-based subjects. It should be noted that six teachers taught more than one subject and so have been counted twice.

Table 9.1 Subject disciplines of the secondary teachers who carried out action research in PALM

English	18
Humanities (geography/history)	17
Art	6
Modern languages	5
Special needs	5
IT	5
Maths	5
Science	4
Home economics	4
Music	2
Business studies	1
CDT	1

PALM was set up with the assumption that, because of the length of time since computers had been introduced into schools, we would be working with teachers who already had some experience in computer use. However, schools were not selected on the basis of high levels of equipment or a reputation for good computer use (the methods of selection were different in the three LEAs but in none was this a factor). Whether for this reason, or because the level of competence in schools generally was lower than expected, or because the project unintentionally attracted teachers selectively, PALM actually worked with very few teachers who already had computer experience. At the end of the two years the project officers estimated retrospectively the level of computer experience of each teacher at the time of joining the project. This is set out in Table 9.2.

Table 9.2 The project officers' retrospective assessment of teachers' level of competence with computers at the time of joining the PALM project

Novices or near novices	67
Already using a computer fairly regularly in teaching	34
Very experienced user of computers in teaching	17

It is not the purpose of this chapter to report the outcomes of the PALM action research. Chapter 6 gives an account of the work in one school, and a full account can be found in PALM (1990–1); Somekh and Davies (1991); see also Somekh (1990a, 1990b, 1991a, 1991b, 1993, 1994a, 1994b); Pratt (1993).

ACTION RESEARCH IN PRACTICE IN THE PALM PROJECT

Although the overall research focus of the project on 'pupil autonomy in learning with microcomputers' had been chosen by me, and was specified in the contract I had signed with the sponsors, the PALM teachers had as much control as possible over their own research. This was done by developing a style of working within the project which centred on the teachers while protecting and supporting them. Specifically,

- teachers decided on their own specific research questions within the overall framework of autonomy in learning;
- they decided what data they needed and collected them;
- they analysed their data;
- they wrote up their research;
- their writing was published;
- they contributed to the meta-analysis of their own and each other's writing in order to generate theories from the work of the project as a whole;
- they presented their work at local teachers' meetings and, in some cases, at national conferences;
- they and their schools were named in both oral presentations and written publications by the university-led team, unless they wished to remain anonymous;
- in the writing of the university-led team, teachers' publications were fully referenced.

The working relationship between the teachers and the project team was governed by a written code of confidentiality. This protected their rights and was essential to ensure that they could discuss problems honestly and openly, rather than guarding against any possible criticism of their professional competence by concentrating only on what was going well. The code contained the following clauses:

1 It is understood that the use of any evidence or data collected by teachers will be fully negotiated with the individuals concerned.
2 It is also understood that the discussions of formal or informal meetings remain confidential to participants in the meeting until they have given permission for more general release (but see 3 below).
3 It is understood that pupils will have the same rights as teachers to refuse access to data that they have provided (e.g. notes taken of interviews with them).
4 Pupils' anonymity will normally be safeguarded at all stages of the research. Individuals will be mentioned by name only with their prior agreement or, where appropriate, with that of their parents.

. . .

9 Wherever possible PALM teachers will share the outcomes of their

investigations, first with their school and cluster teams and with the central team, then across the participating LEAs, and finally more widely where appropriate.

10 All reports produced by teachers will be published under their names in order to give full credit to them for their work. All such reports will be subject to negotiation with the sponsor and the three LEAs. The central team will assist teachers with this work as and when required.

The PALM teachers collected data relating to their classroom using methods such as: making regular notes in a research diary; interviewing (e.g. pupils, colleagues, the head teacher or parents); taking photographs or videorecordings; photocopying pupils' work; collecting computer print-outs; collecting documents (e.g. school policy statements, government circulars, publicity materials). Where possible they worked in pairs so that there was the possibility of occasionally observing each other teaching.

The teachers were given in-school support, either by a PALM project co-ordinator or the head teacher or deputy head teacher. This was in the form of continuing interest and encouragement; more specifically it might include assistance with classroom research, special allocation of rooms or equipment, refreshments at after-school meetings, and occasional release from teaching. Although external support from the project team was obviously important (e.g. classroom observation or interviews carried out at the teacher's request, transcribing of tapes), this internal support was often what sustained teachers' research activities on a day-to-day basis. In many cases the schools made available funds for small amounts of supply cover, and in secondary schools the time-tabler often played a crucial role in sharing out this non-teaching time to enable as many partnerships as possible to work together.

The biggest barrier to the teachers carrying out classroom investigations was time. To help to overcome this, the PALM team suggested to teachers that they should think in terms of periods of 'bounded time'. Almond (1982) suggests that teachers should go through the diary of the school year and identify periods of greater and lesser stress. Research should then be fitted into the periods when there are fewer extra demands, such as assessments and report-writing, upon their time. So in PALM we asked teachers to plan their research activities, setting aside specific periods of time in advance and then sticking to the plan. We suggested that they should fit their research into periods of lesser stress. We also suggested that they should collect data in 'concentrated bursts', whenever possible collecting three or four different kinds of data bearing on the same event. This had the advantage of preventing them collecting too much. A further advantage of working in this way was that resources could be targeted to support teachers at key moments. Thus whenever possible PALM teachers collected a significant, but manageable, quantity of data which could be cross-referenced to enable greater validity in the analysis. This might be traditional triangulation (Somekh, 1983), allowing comparison between the opinions and interpretations of the teacher, an observer and the pupils, or it might put together one or more of these viewpoints with documentary evidence such as computer print-out and work sheets, photographs, audio or videorecordings.

Whenever possible the analysis was also planned in advance to take place in a set time, often as a session involving a close colleague or small group working with the project officer. Frequently this led to planning a follow-up session to complete the analysis, but the key factor was that no further data should be collected until the analysis was complete and any necessary action steps had been planned.

Data analysis proved to be the most difficult part of the research process for the teachers but ultimately the most interesting. At first it can be difficult to see any significance in data. This is particularly true of extracts from a research diary which you have written yourself, but it can also be true of data with which you are not so familiar – e.g. transcribed extracts from a tape-recording of pupils' talk while they are working together at a computer. However, PALM developed a simple approach to data analysis which enabled teachers to examine their data closely and learn to distinguish what was significant from what was not. The key was to examine the data with a specific question in mind, such as: 'Are there any indications in the pupils' language that learning is taking place?'; or 'Is there anything here which you find unexpected or surprising?'. This worked best if three or four teachers were able to meet and examine a piece of data together (of course, by invitation of the teacher who 'owned' it). The normal procedure would then be for individuals to spend ten minutes highlighting what they saw as significant and to follow this with a group discussion. It was common for this kind of session to generate a very high quality of professional debate about teaching and learning. There was always a strong sense of revelation typified by one teacher's comment: 'I never would have believed there was so much in that three-page transcript. That was the best professional discussion I've had with colleagues for years.'

The PALM team developed a number of 'practical materials' which the project officers or in-school PALM co-ordinators could use as handouts to teachers. These were usually given out at the end of a meeting as an *aide-mémoire* to what had been discussed or a framework to help structure the work to be undertaken next. They included: 'Finding a research partner'; 'Notes on observing'; 'An action research planning sheet'; and various sheets on analysing data including 'Looking for the unexpected'; 'Content analysis'; 'Pattern analysis'; and 'Dilemma analysis'. All the 'practical materials' were later published in a pack, *Supporting Teacher Development Through Action Research* (PALM, 1990).

THE VALUE OF ACTION RESEARCH IN SUPPORTING TEACHERS WHO BEGIN TO USE IT

The value of the inquiry-based methodology of action research adopted by the PALM project lies in its ability to support the IT innovation from its introduction until it is firmly established. (See Chapter 14, p. 191 for an account of Fullan's theory of the four stages of an innovation.) Innovations often seem to fail because initial support is not followed up, and teachers who have experienced its partial implementation become disappointed and lose the conviction to continue their efforts to develop it further (Fullan, 1982, pp. 81–6; House, 1974, pp. 1–5).

By inviting teachers to evaluate the impact of IT use on children's learning, PALM was able to support teachers during the initial stages of adoption of the innovation, in such a way that they continued to develop and refine their use of IT rather than establishing habits of use too quickly. By this means teachers could develop the competence and confidence to try out a range of uses of IT and evaluate their relative effectiveness, rather than falling into the common trap of being too easily satisfied with low-level use. Action research, consisting as it does of a continuing process of inquiry, self-monitoring and development of teaching strategies, is effective in allowing teachers to develop understanding of the educational potential of IT, during a period of experimentation. In this way action research enables and consolidates full institutionalisation of the IT innovation.

This process can be explained more clearly by reference to the stages of development of PALM action research. An unexpected and uncomfortable phenomenon which occurred during the first year of PALM was that, apparently as a result of concentrating teachers' attention on carrying out action research into children's learning, interest in computers began to recede into the background. We called it the phenomenon of 'the disappearing micro'. It was not that teachers were not using computers since, with the exception of some preparatory work in one school, every single piece of PALM data related to pupils' learning in computer-related contexts. Rather, it was that their interest was on learning *per se*, irrespective of context. During the second year of the project, however, the focus of the teachers' action research shifted more specifically to how learning might sometimes be of a different kind in a computer-mediated context.

TEACHERS' APPROACHES TO USING COMPUTERS IN THEIR TEACHING

The work of PALM provides insights into the way in which teachers adopt the use of computers in teaching and learning. It seems that there are three broad approaches which teachers can take to computer use:

- the computer as tutor;
- the computer as neutral tool;
- the computer as cognitive tool.

These approaches demand different kinds of competencies of teachers and have major implications for the nature of the learning which results. Action research appeared to be an effective method of ensuring that teachers did not limit themselves to one or other of the first two approaches, but in time went on to make a real attempt to adopt the third, higher-level approach.

The computer as tutor

Many teachers who have only recently begun to use a computer assume that its role will be to replace the teacher as a kind of machine-tutor. An example of this was a history teacher in PALM who told us that he had bought a piece of software and been very disappointed with it because, when he watched his pupils using it, they didn't learn anything of value. It had not occurred to this teacher that he should play any active role in the pupils' learning with this software – instead, he saw it as a complete package which he could load and then stand back and watch while it 'taught' his pupils. In reality, software is not able to fulfil this role unless it is highly sophisticated (and very expensive to develop) – an example would be an expert system flight simulator from which a trainee pilot can acquire experience of flying an aeroplane and in some senses 'learn to fly'. Teachers normally need to play an important part in their pupils' computer-mediated learning: in drawing out points for discussion, planning follow-up work, and (once they are familiar with the software) providing lead-in activities to maximise its impact.

The computer as neutral tool

Other teachers who have begun to be familiar with using a computer often make a different assumption – that its role is similar to that of a pencil: they see the computer as a tool which is virtually neutral and can be used to carry out the same learning tasks their pupils would have undertaken previously with pen or pencil. This is sometimes mistakenly the outcome of advice to make sure that computer activities are 'education led' and not 'technology led'. Arguably, if there is no change in the nature of the tasks pupils undertake when they are using a computer, they might just as well not have used it in the first place. Teachers who adopt this approach often place a high value on the computer's capacity as a presentational tool, because this enhances what was already being achieved rather than changing the nature of the tasks. For example, they may encourage pupils to use a word processor to type out what they have already written by hand and print 'best' copies for display or publication, but deny them the opportunity to write direct on screen and use the power of the word processor to change the nature of the writing process.

The computer as cognitive tool

Those teachers best able to use computers to enhance their pupils' learning are those who have come to understand that computers are powerful cognitive tools which enable them to set new kinds of learning tasks that their pupils could not attempt before. Computer use in these classrooms will be varied – and often computers will be used for tasks similar to those which could have been undertaken without them – but the possibilities they have to offer become integrated with the planning, enactment and assessment of learning activities. To use computers in this way requires that teachers change their pedagogy. An example from PALM shows how difficult it is for teachers to begin to think in this new way:

> A history teacher in a secondary school was experimenting with using a computer database of information about the Spanish Armada. In an interview after the lesson, he told the Project Officer that he was unhappy with the program because it 'gave too much information' and this had resulted in the children 'asking trivial questions' so that they didn't learn anything of value about the Armada. He said that he would have preferred to make his own database so that he could have selected a more limited amount of information and in this way guided the pupils to ask important and interesting questions. What this demonstrates is his instinct to use the computer to continue to teach with the pedagogy he has tried and tested over the years. His practice has been shaped in the past by the availability of only a small amount of data, and by the difficulty both he and the pupils have in accessing it – for example finding relevant books in the library. He has been helped by publishers who have produced packages of selected source materials (e.g. Jackdaw Files) and he has gradually built up his own packs which he has been able to use and re-use again and again. Suddenly the computer database on the Armada has disrupted this pattern and provides easy access to a large amount of much less carefully selected information. It is moving towards overcoming the long-standing problem in accessing information (although it is still far from providing all that is available). But, in offering more open access to information, it demands that he sets his pupils a different kind of learning task. Instead of setting them to explore the information provided – in a more or less random way – he must now help them to distinguish what might be an important and interesting question worth pursuing from one which is by comparison trivial and likely to waste their time. They are no longer faced with the artificial situation of information selected to enable them to answer questions apparently of their own choosing, but in reality largely predetermined by their teacher. Instead, they are faced with the more normal situation – particularly in the modern world – of information overload, comprising a very large assortment of disparate information 'to make sense of'.

This is a good example of how the computer often provides both the opportunity of teaching a more difficult and ultimately much more useful skill, and the challenge of having to rethink the purpose of the lesson, the nature of the task which should be set, and the method of assessing how pupils carry it out (should they perhaps be asked to evaluate the questions they have chosen to ask?).

What appeared to happen in PALM was that teachers began with a concept of 'the computer as a tutor' but moved fairly rapidly to one of 'the computer as a neutral tool'. During the first year of the project they gained familiarity and confidence in using computers with their pupils but did not use them in any way which altered the nature of their pupils' learning – hence, when they carried out research into learning related to computer use they found nothing to remark on which was specific to the computer-related nature of the task. This learning looked very much like any other learning in their classrooms. It was only during the second year of PALM, when their confidence and competence with computers was established, that they could begin to look at the implications of computer use for changing the nature of learning. Even then, sadly, the limited access to the computers available to them made it difficult to bring about radical changes in pedagogy.

CONCLUSIONS

In 1989 the Department of Education and Science included in its criteria for accrediting courses in initial teacher education that newly qualified teachers 'should be trained to be able to evaluate the ways in which the use of information technology changes the nature of teaching and learning'. Although there was always doubt about whether even experienced teachers could meet this criterion, I believe it is extremely important that all teachers, including students, should be asked to make the attempt.

The purpose of asking the question lies as much in the process of seeking the answer as in coming to any conclusion. What is important is not the precision with which teachers evaluate their pupils' learning, but that, from their first steps in joining the profession, teachers should begin to acquire the habit of questioning the value of the educational experiences they offer to pupils.

The work of the PALM project suggests that action research is a practical and effective methodology for promoting effective, long-term use of IT in education. Such an inquiry-based approach ensures that teachers, student teachers and teacher educators do not merely bow to the command to use computers and slip into habits of using them as 'tutors' or 'neutral tools', but collaborate together to develop their use as 'cognitive tools'.

ACKNOWLEDGEMENTS

I should like to thank Jon Pratt, Bob Davison, Erica Brown, Laura Tickner, Richard Davies and John Elliott who worked with me on the PALM project. Special thanks go to the National Council for Educational Technology and to Cambridgeshire, Essex and Norfolk Education Committees, who provided the funding which made this work possible. I should also like to thank all the schools that worked with PALM and in particular the large number of teachers who undertook the core action research upon which this chapter draws.

NOTES

1 An extended version of this chapter was first published in *Journal of Teaching and Teacher Education*, 3(2/3): 227–50.
2 PALM was funded by the National Council for Educational Technology, in conjunction with Cambridgeshire, Essex and Norfolk Local Education Authorities.

REFERENCES

Almond, L. (1982) 'Containable time', appendix in *Institutional Self-evaluation*, Block 2, Part 2 of Course E364: *Curriculum Evaluation and Assessment in Educational Institutions*. Milton Keynes, Bucks.: Open University Press.

Elliott, John (1991) *Action Research for Educational Change*. Milton Keynes, Bucks.: Open University Press.

Fullan, Michael G. (1982) *The Meaning of Educational Change*. Toronto: OISE Press (Ontario Institute for Studies in Education).

Griffin, Elaine (1990) *By Hook or by Crook: Putting IT into the Curriculum*. Norwich: PALM Publications, CARE, University of East Anglia.

House, Ernest R. (1974) *The Politics of Educational Innovation*. Berkeley, Cal.: McCutchan Publishing Co.

PALM (1990) *Supporting Teacher Development Through Action Research: A PALM Resource for Advisory Teachers*. Norwich: PALM Publications, CARE, University of East Anglia.

—— (1990–1) *Teachers' Voices* series (40 titles). Norwich: PALM Project, CARE, University of East Anglia.

Pratt, Jon (1993) 'Beyond the metaphor: breakdown and realignment', in M. Monteith (ed.), *Computers and Language*. Oxford: Intellect Books.

Ridgway, J. and Passey, D. (1991) *Effective In-service Education for Teachers in Information Technology*, STAC Project, University of Lancaster. Coventry: National Council for Educational Technology.

Schön, Donald A. (1983) *The Reflective Practitioner*. New York: Basic Books.

Somekh, Bridget (1983) 'Triangulation methods in action: a practical example', *Cambridge Journal of Education*, 13(2): 31–7.

—— (1990a) 'Learning autonomy', *Educational Computing and Technology*, June: 19–22.

—— (1990b) 'Palmistry', *TheTimes Educational Supplement*, 15 June, p. B18.

—— (1991a) 'Pupil autonomy in learning with microcomputers: rhetoric or reality? An action research study', *Cambridge Journal of Education*, 21(1): 47–64.

—— (1991b) 'Teachers becoming researchers: an exploration in dynamic collaboration', *RUCCUS Occasional Papers* (University of Western Ontario), 2: 97–144.

—— (1993) 'Flies on their classroom walls', *The Times Educational Supplement*, 20 July.

—— (1994a) 'Inhabiting each other's castles: towards knowledge and mutual growth through collaboration', *Educational Action Research*, 2(3): 357–82.

—— (1994b) 'Teaching writing, writing research: an analysis of the role of computer-supported writing in action research', *Computers and Composition*, 11(3): 293–309.

—— and Davies, Richard (1991) 'Towards a pedagogy for information technology', *Curriculum Journal*, 2(2): 153–70.

Chapter 10

Using IT in classrooms

Experienced teachers and students as co-learners

Malcolm Bell and Colin Biott

With increasing emphasis on school-based teacher education it is timely to consider how, and what, students might learn about using information technology during school placements. In 1992 a directive from the Department for Education (DfE 1992) indicated that courses should contain 'compulsory and clearly identifiable elements' for students to gain practical experience of using IT in classrooms, and that these opportunities should 'provide a sound basis for their subsequent development in this field'. It may be relatively straightforward to make arrangements for students to work in school classrooms, but it is more difficult to establish favourable contexts in which they can learn that IT could be more than a supplementary activity in a school curriculum.

INSTITUTIONAL CONTEXT

At the University of Northumbria, school-based provision has grown from various *ad hoc* initiatives in different schools and subject areas, towards more elaborate partnership arrangements across whole programmes. Since the early 1980s, and especially since the introduction of 'serial school experience', tutors have looked, with varying degrees of success, for pockets of good practice in all subject areas in primary schools. Cornish *et al.* (1994) have recently described how inquiry-based school experience for teaching English has evolved in our institution, and at the same time they have noted the different characteristics of primary school-based provision across subjects:

> The range of 'confident' contexts for science and technology was (predictably) much smaller than for maths and English, and this led to a narrower spread of contexts and experiences in the former than the latter.
>
> (Cornish *et al.*, 1994, p. 82)

Despite these difficulties some colleagues in other subject areas have been able to adapt to circumstances, as in the case of expressive arts where a full cohort of specialists works in one or two schools with a strong commitment to arts education.

One consequence of the uneven history of placement practices is that tutors have been opportunistic and resourceful in seeking educative school contexts for students. Action research and classroom inquiry projects are woven throughout initial teacher education programmes, and they also form a major part of post-qualifying provision. In English, for example, a research-based approach to classroom work has been acknowledged as 'the strongest vehicle for the development of partnership activities' (Cornish *et al.*, 1994, p. 84), and there have been many notable examples of experienced teachers from our post-qualifying progamme working on teaching and learning issues with student teachers as part of their courses.

PARTICULAR PROBLEM OF IT IN PLACEMENTS

If the task of locating and using teachers' expertise has been found to be so problematic in key subject areas, it is not surprising that difficulties arise in finding favourable classroom contexts for observing and using IT in classrooms and then matching these with students' own stages of development. Amongst experienced teachers, distinctions between those with or without expertise and confidence in IT are not simply related to factors such as designated status for supporting students, subject knowledge or length of teaching experience. What is particularly important is a teacher's willingness and openness to work and learn with students who are using IT. We have found that some teachers who are allocated students still avoid using computers in their classrooms. Sometimes, hestitant students have been placed with reluctant teachers and both have taken advantage of the chance to ignore or sidestep IT in a kind of conspiracy of silence: 'Because I'm not very competent about using IT in the classroom and the teacher wasn't either, we avoided the issue' (interview with student).

Another interrelated factor affecting worthwhile learning opportunities for students in schools is the apparently variable availability of computers in classrooms. We say apparent, because sometimes a teacher might make a computer inaccessible to a student as a strategic way to avoid having to acknowledge his or her own apprehension about using it effectively. As one IT co-ordinator said about the absence of a machine in a student's classroom: 'That's just an excuse for not using IT. There are machines on trolleys so there could easily be one in the classroom. The truth is the teacher's frightened of it and if that wasn't an excuse she'd find another' (interview with primary school IT co-ordinator).

Problems of access and unhelpful organisational arrangements in schools can affect the extent to which IT can be an integral part of central teaching and learning processes rather than a marginal activity in corners of classrooms. One student, placed in a middle school, said:

> The way computers are in the school is that there's a computer lab which you have to book and it's never free when you want it, so it's made difficult for me to use IT in the classroom. The longest period I have with a class is an

hour and ten minutes, which isn't like in primary where you can set something up to take place over the whole day, so I can't apply my knowledge of IT to my teaching.

(Interview with student)

Some students have said that their class teachers apologised for not having the computer available at times when they wanted to use it. For example, one had the use of a computer for only the second and third weeks of a six-week placement; another found that 'all three computers were in Year 2 for SATs'; and one student arrived at a school just after the computer was stolen. Lack of availability of the equipment at critical moments can restrict, and sometimes obstruct, the productive use of IT: 'They did it on a rota system. What they were using had nothing to do with what the lesson was about. It was just their turn'. 'I don't have one to make use of in an integral way. What I am doing is OK to introduce this to all the class, but I really want a small group to use it all week. I can't do that unless I book the room, and it's not available again this week' (interviews with students).

Overall the picture is patchy, but improving. As well as having scheduled classroom IT practice in serial school visits, students are expected to include IT in their block placements. From a survey of our final year primary BEd students in 1992, we found that although 81 per cent had used IT during their final block placement of six weeks, a proportion (40 per cent) had not made any reference to IT in their written evaluations. Furthermore, of those who had used IT, 8 per cent had not mentioned it in their lesson plans. They had continued their class teachers' practice of using IT as a routine, isolated activity, and children took turns to use the computer. Whilst it is important to ensure that IT is used by more and more students, it is also necessary to give serious consideration to how the educative quality of the students' school experiences can be enhanced.

DIMENSIONS OF PLACEMENTS

School-based provision for learning to use IT is variable and, given the current emphasis upon matching subject specialisms of students and teachers, discovering favourable settings for IT development can sometimes be a challenge to tutors and a lottery for students. As part of an overall strategy to evaluate and develop school-based experiences in IT, it is important to identify and describe best practices across a range of subjects and to build a critical review of case studies into university curriculum sessions and mentor meetings.

We suggest that it would be helpful, as a way of clarifying criteria for evaluations, to plot variations in placement characteristics along five interconnected dimensions. These dimensions refer to the willingness of the teachers to use IT with students, arrangements for access to computers, the envisaged potential for IT in the curriculum, the kind of professional learning envisaged and the main strategies class teachers used to support students.

Willingness of teachers to use IT with students

Willing to use IT with students ———————— Avoiding IT with students

This dimension refers to the extent to which class teachers are willing to work with students using IT. We acknowledge that this oversimplifies a subtle and complex range of orientations towards IT, but the extent of teachers' personal confidence to use computers with students, even if uncertain about their own skills, has been seen to be an influential factor in shaping students' opportunities to use them in classrooms. We are aware that teachers' feelings of confidence will be related to the degrees of challenge and risk which they allow themselves to accept. We have evidence that extreme lack of confidence can lead to avoidance or rejection of computers and to students being denied access to equipment.

Problems can arise when the orientations of the student and the teacher are markedly different, such as when the teacher rejects or avoids its use or when an enthusiastic, confident teacher over-challenges an exposed and reluctant student. Circumstances such as these test the negotiating skills of students and the mediating skills of university tutors.

Arrangements for access to computers

Constantly available ———————————————— Inaccessible

Concerns about the availability of equipment have been common amongst students, especially those who seek to integrate IT into the primary school day or to have computers readily available in the classroom during secondary school lessons. The mid-point on this dimension can refer to having to book networks or computer labs in middle schools or secondary schools, or having to 'take your turn' in primaries. Sometimes the use of a rota system can be incorporated into planning, but we have evidence to show that it can also be a limiting and even off-putting factor.

Envisaged potential of IT in the curriculum

Integral/reconstructing ———————— Supplementary or 'add on' activity

This is a key dimension referring to the extent to which the experiences of students in schools enable them to understand more about how children learn through IT and about how National Curriculum programmes of study can be enhanced by IT in a fundamental way. For some students, using IT means merely trying out software, such as an engaging educational game, with a small group of children as a separate clasroom activity. For others, it may mean that children are working at processes which are intrinsic corner-stones of learning within school subjects such as crafting writing, using evidence from databases or creating graphical images.

This dimension is related to teachers' values and their notions of subject integrity. Easdown (1994), for example, has described how secondary school history teachers, mentoring student 'interns' in Oxford, had reservations about using time on IT unless it mirrored what historians do. For example, simulations were sometimes rejected because they presented pupils with simplistic models of historical issues, but databases were acceptable, on the grounds of appropriateness and value, because they enabled children to find and draw conclusions from data.

Nature of professional learning envisaged for student

Transforming understanding ———————— Gaining technical 'know-how'

This dimension, like the previous one, is a key to evaluating what is learned about IT from a period of school placement. In plotting the position of any particular practice it is the main concern of the partners to determine which is to be given most weight. We are not suggesting that transforming understanding and technical 'know-how' are mutually exclusive ends of a continuum. It is necessary to recognise that competence in basic and technical matters can be crucial at a time when students may feel generally vulnerable in classrooms, and many teachers are put off using computers because the machines keep going wrong and they are unable to fix them. The salient issue, however, is the extent to which the placement experience results in the student seeing IT in new ways, and for this reason it should be the focus of systematic inquiry and reflection.

The dimension reflects the nature of the partnership between the teacher and the student. For example, the presence of a student can provide opportunities for teachers to investigate and learn more about their children's learning and how this can be affected by the use of IT. The focus, purposes and methods of working together between the students and the teachers are shaped to a great extent by their assumptions about the kinds of professional learning which might result for both partners.

Main strategy of experienced teacher to support a student

Inquiring/creating new knowledge ———————— Telling, demonstating

This dimension refers to how experienced teachers try to support students, and how their strategies will affect what students will see, practise and talk about. As with the previous dimension, we are not undervaluing the occasions when experienced teachers might simply tell or show students what to do, but are trying to draw attention to the difference between confining support to that and nothing more, compared with aiming to create new knowledge through investigating the use of IT in classrooms. The latter requires, at least, that teachers are willing to learn. Most fruitfully, teachers, as co-learners, will identify dilemmas or feelings of unease about particular aspects of teaching and learning and then try things and talk about them; a mixture of posing questions, making plans, taking provisional action, recording what happens and deliberating from the basis of the evidence available.

Both partners will need to use and combine their prior personal knowledge and technical know-how in order to edge forward through 'wondering if', being watchful, and 'taking stock'. Concerns about success and failure are suspended and the teachers' and students' roles may become blended so that, at times, teachers may be observing in order to record and analyse classroom processes rather than to assess a student's level of competence. Cameron Jones (1987) has shown that, even within the hurly-burly of classrooms, some teachers do have the capacity to attend to simultaneous occurrences in their relationships with student teachers, just as they have learned to do with children. She refers to how the supervising teachers in her study were able to 'sustain this kind of parallel processing as they handled student-related information and pupil-related information simultaneously' (p. 152). By giving on-the-spot comments on what was happening, their students gained 'live, episodic, insider commentary on the fine grain of classroom practice as it actually unfolds' (p. 153).

USING THE DIMENSIONS TO PLOT CHARACTERISTICS OF PLACEMENTS

The dimensions can be used to plot the pattern of particular placement characteristics and to show the actual nature of any variations. Example 1 plots the experience of a student placed with a teacher who is willing to help the student with IT, uses the computer regularly as supplementary activity for groups of children, demonstrates its use and tells the student what works well and what won't be successful, as though the teacher's knowledge was objective and predictive.

Example 1

Teacher willing	•			Teacher avoids
Computers available	•			Computers inaccessible
IT integral			•	IT supplementary
Transforming			•	Technical know-how
Inquiring			•	Telling, showing

Example 2 plots the case of a dutiful but sceptical teacher who for some time has used IT activities as disembodied, routine events, and has only just become willing to explore the use of databases as an integral part of a history project. This teacher sets up an inquiry with a student into how children use a database in relation to other documentary source materials they have been given. The teacher and student inquire together: the student starts the children's project work, then conducts and records focused conversations with the children about what they have been doing whilst the teacher oversees the whole class. The student then categorises themes from the children's conversations along with the teacher's observation notes, samples of children's work and her own lesson evaluation notes. She returns to the school and together they identify key issues and plan a set of new discussion activities for the children with a more concentrated focus on one feature of the database. They also discuss what evidence they will collect at the next stage as their partnership deepens.

Example 2

Teacher willing		•		Teacher avoids
Computers available	•			Computers inaccessible
IT integral		•		IT supplementary
Transforming	•			Technical know-how
Inquiring	•			Telling, showing

CO-LEARNING PARTNERSHIPS

The main purpose of this chapter is to outline and discuss a set of principles that characterise favourable relationships, which we have called co-learning partnerships, between students and experienced teachers. The kind of co-learning partnerships we have in mind are characterised by:

- teachers being willing to try IT with students in their classroom, even if this means allowing students to do things about which they are uncertain or unfamiliar;
- teachers and students building on their existing knowledge and competence and combining their roles to try out new practices or explore the familiar in more depth;
- shared inquiry and created knowledge, rather than experienced teachers merely telling or showing what they already know or can do;
- seeing potential for IT to affect teaching and learning in fundamental ways;
- seeing professional learning as a process of transforming meanings and of gaining new understandings, in addition to getting more technical 'know-how' and acquiring new computer skills.

The critical task for university and school partners is to create educative events and frameworks to enable teachers and students to engage in co-learning. Such co-learning is likely to take place over an extended period, with students revisiting the school for different purposes and teachers getting to know what is happening in university sessions and, where possible, participating in them. Given favourable contexts and using a combination of serial school experiences of, say, half days over a set period and blocks of full-time placements, students have scope to achieve both breadth and depth in learning to use IT in classrooms.

It is important to give students some modest experience of co-learning with teachers as early as possible in the course. For example, a group of first-year students was asked to explore data collection and presentation with Year 2 children at a first school during a period of serial school experience. The students were expected to outline a provisional plan and identify the potential for IT use; and the class teachers, some of whom had no prior experience of this aspect of IT, were asked to provide a framework, within the school's curriculum requirements, for trying out the students' ideas. The starting point for students was their own college work on data handling. During the course they had considered its potential for IT use in classrooms, but at that stage they were unfamiliar with the practical demands of classrooms and they did not know what software and hardware would be available in specific schools.

They were challenged to find out what was both practicable and worthwhile given the time-scale and contextual factors in the schools. In effect, they had to consult and negotiate with class teachers, and in the process apply their own recently acquired knowledge as well as discover what the teachers' experience and knowledge could offer to them. This could not be achieved instantly at the outset, as is sometimes implied in preparation meetings which are scheduled to cover basic tips and pointers. Over time, ideas were revisited and unanticipated things were learnt as an integral part of working together. The teachers were asked to identify data handling activities which were directly related to their current teaching topics and which should be able to continue after the designated period of serial practice had ended.

The challenge of the task meant that most students did make additional visits to the school to meet the teachers outside the formally timetabled sessions. The early visits were mainly used for further hints and fact-finding as the students thought about how they could create a framework database to which children could add data. Between their visits the children worked on the data. The teachers observed what was happening and gave guidance where necessary. This established some continuity, and during subsequent visits students tried to explore the data in greater depth with the children. In some cases, students were able to see some progression in children's work and teachers had the opportunity to integrate data handling into their normal curriculum. As two of the teachers said in subsequent interviews: 'They've worked hard and really made it possible for me to do this with the children. If they weren't in I don't think I'd have the time'; 'I'll be able to do this with all the children now because the framework's there.'

Another group of students was working with Year 3 children. They were exploring a topic 'Shops and shopping'. They approached this in a cross-curricular way and discussed possible approaches with the teacher. The teacher wanted students to include aspects of technology, mathematics and science in their IT project with the children. The class teacher had already worked with the children to explore how historical and geographical factors had affected the location and functions of shops in the area and was currently undertaking a range of creative language and art work with the children. After observing and discussing, the students set out to create a model shopping centre and to explore the mathematics of shape and money with children. The students worked with children to explore networks, shapes and artefacts which were then built into a shopping centre.The university tutor was also involved in the preparatory discussions and suggested that floor turtles might be used to build in the use of shopping lists. In the project the turtle was sent, by the children, around the appropriate shops to locate and buy items on shopping lists.

The teacher and the students saw how the floor turtle had helped the children to conceptualise the shopping centre spatially and how it made the whole project seem real to them. The students had seen the legitimacy, practicability and impact of using IT in cross-curricular work: 'We've talked about how we could do this for other topics . . . the cross-curricular thing . . . and we wouldn't like to try it without support. This teacher's great. She's really helpful.'

In our model of co-learning partnerships we have emphasised learning which is about transforming understanding and advocated that partners should find a focus in which an attempt is being made to reconstruct the curriculum through IT. Translating this aspiration into action is essentially about setting about concrete tasks which are defined in manageable and meaningful ways. It requires a willingness to try things out and to talk about what is happening; a mixture of provisional thinking, action and deliberation. Both partners use and combine their prior personal knowledge and technical know-how and then try to create new knowledge by 'wondering-if', observing, talking and questioning.

In another example, a third-year student introduced LOGO to a Year 3 class as part of a mathematics project. He used floor turtles and then moved some children on to screen LOGO. Even though the class teacher had never used LOGO with children and knew nothing about it, she was willing to learn. Her prior knowledge of the children was used extensively, however, as she and the student observed what was happening. The children were asked if they could draw a square on the screen, which they did with ease. Then they were asked to draw a triangle. The children struggled at first and made some headway as they started to talk about angles. Despite having no direct teaching about angles, and to their class teacher's surprise, they showed that they understood the importance of degrees as a unit of measure. The student was interested that children could use a concept which they had not been taught formally, and the teacher had experienced some surprise admidst the familiarity of her own classroom. As she said: 'I'm going to have to think about how I can use this with more children because they're doing something which I thought was way beyond them.'

Together the teacher and student planned ways to fit this kind of activity into the regular curriculum for all children. They spent time after school finding ways to arrange for other children to explore angles through LOGO. They also discussed how the student's original plans could now be developed. The teacher's intention was to use the ideas with other children after the student's placement had ended, and the student took this learning forward into subsequent serial school placements. The experience had so much impact upon the student that he has designed an extended investigation into the role of LOGO in mathematics learning, and this is the focus of his final-year project.

CONCLUSION

The main purposes of this chapter have been to suggest a number of dimensions which can be used to review students' opportunities to learn to use IT in classrooms and to define and outline the advantages of co-learning partnerships between teachers and students. In our own institution, school-based work takes many forms and purposes. As a consequence, students learn about IT cumulatively and, to some extent, opportunistically. Over the whole course, they work on IT in designated components as well as in subject-specific and age-range-specific contexts. This gives them different kinds of opportunities to become familiar with a range of software and applications and to try them out in schools. This has led to a variety of relationships with practising teachers. Sometimes students have arranged to use applications with which teachers are unfamiliar, and in some cases they have been commissioned by schools to develop packages of materials and to introduce IT ideas to teachers, as in a recent example of physics students in secondary schools. At best, it has generated classroom investigations into how IT can bring about fundamental changes in teaching and learning. It has resulted in students and teachers working as co-researchers and co-learners.

The next step is to use the dimensions as a heuristic framework to help students to review their own experiences in various school contexts; especially, to describe their working relationships with teachers and to reflect on their own learning. This will be done both individually and collectively. A selection of case studies across subject areas can then be used as a focus for discussion in course reviews and in mentors' meetings, about how school-based provision can best contribute to students' practice and understanding of IT in classooms.

REFERENCES

Cameron Jones, M. (1987) 'Professional practice in the primary school', in S. Delamont (ed.), *The Primary School Teacher*. London: Falmer Press.

Cornish, M., Hamer, A. and Reed, B. (1994) 'Undergraduate teacher education for primary teachers', in M. McCulloch and B. Fidler (eds), *Improving Initial Teacher Training: New Roles for Teachers, Schools and HE*. London: Longman.
DfE (Department for Education) (1992) *Circular 9/92: Guidance Notes.* London: DfE.
Easdown, G. (1994) 'Student teachers, mentors and information technology', *Journal of Information Technology for Teacher Education,* 3(1): 63–79.

Chapter 11

Getting teachers started with IT and transferable skills[1]

Bridget Somekh and Niki Davis

This chapter considers teaching and learning strategies suited to teachers who are taking their first steps with IT. It recognises the particular challenge that this poses for such adults and provides a framework which maximises their capacity to continue their own independent learning and to apply this learning in new situations – that is, with maximum transferability. The strategies are derived from over ten years' experience of supporting practising school teachers, student teachers and higher education staff in their acquisition of information technology skills. We explain our approach by focusing on the attitudes and feelings of these teachers and the contexts in which they are placed. The illustrative examples are drawn from our own experience with teachers, family and other colleagues. They have been verified through the experience of others involved in professional development. We have found considerable evidence that the problem of acquiring computer skills is a generic one which manifests itself in all phases of education. The key variables which distinguish all those engaged in any form of teaching from other computer users are:

- their need to maintain their professional status with students and colleagues;
- their need to demonstrate newly acquired computer skills publicly before they have sufficient time to consolidate them.

The most challenging and memorable episode for teachers is often in the first stages of their acquaintance with a computer. Below is a description, personal to Bridget Somekh, of events which occurred over ten years ago. It relates to a personal computer of that time, the BBC 'B' manufactured by Acorn Ltd. Despite the changes in the technology, similar strong emotions are felt by teachers new to technology today.

Skilled performance and the self

In 1985 I was seconded from my job as Head of English and Drama at a Cambridge comprehensive school to the post of Curriculum Development Officer with the Netherhall group of software developers. At the time I had been using a BBC

'B' computer for word processing for about a year, and during the previous three months had used it in teaching writing to a mixed-ability class of eleven-year-olds.

On my first day at Netherhall I was asked by the Director, Rod Mulvey, to fit a Wordwise word processing chip into a BBC computer. I can still remember my strong feeling of incapacity. I knew that this required me to take the top off the machine. I had in my hand an open box with a small rectangular piece of metal sitting on a bed of foam. If I had not known it was delicate, its packing would have made this obvious. My hands seemed to hang by my sides without any functionality. I had to think through what to do first . . . and what next . . . there were no routines of action to call on from previous experience. Of course, I needed knowledge of the right location for the chip in the machine. It had two rows of little metal 'legs' down each side of the base and I needed knowledge that the tips of one whole row should be inserted in one row of tiny holes, just far enough to enable me to bend them slightly inwards, bringing the other row of legs to a position where their tips could also be inserted. I was told these things and left to try them out. My sense of physical incapacity in simply using a screwdriver and turning the machine over to find the screws stills lingers in my mind. I was literally sweating as I got the chip into place and pressed it carefully home into the two rows of holes. In the next eighteen months I was to repeat this operation many times, sometimes taking chips in and out of machines several times in a day. I only broke off one leg in that whole time, and that was in my final week of the job. I suppose I had become overconfident.

This story from personal experience illustrates the problem we want to address. A great deal of what we do in our daily lives is highly routinised so that we scarcely have to think in order to transfer intention into action. That bit of our 'thinking' which governs body movement becomes automatic, freeing up our intellects to concentrate on other things. We can literally 'do two things at once'. Once we have acquired a skill like fitting a chip into a BBC computer we are able to carry out the job while simultaneously chatting to a teacher or children standing by our side. There may just be a moment or two, at the tricky point of bending those little legs, when we have to stop talking and give the job our full attention. For the rest of the time we perform the task confidently, and we look confident performing it, and our sense of looking confident and knowing exactly what to do, quickly and without fuss, builds up our own *sense of our worth in the eyes of others.*

Routines of unconscious thought directly transferred into action are a central part of carrying out skills. When we lack those routines there are two incapacitating consequences: first, we have to use up intellectual energy on thinking what to do; and second, we experience a sense of loss of personal worth both in our own eyes and in the eyes of others. The seriousness of the second of these consequences can be understood in terms of Mead's theory of the individual. Only through 'engagement' of the 'I' and the 'me' with the 'generalised other', according to Mead, does the individual 'develop a complete self':

> It is in the form of the generalized other that the social process influences the behavior of the individuals involved in it and carrying it on, i.e., that the community exercises control over the conduct of its individual members; for it is in this form that the social process or community enters as a determining factor in the individual's thinking.
>
> (Mead, 1934, p. 155)

Translated into crude terms, what this means is that when we are called upon to use a skill which we do not possess, the actor and problem-solver which is the 'I' is undermined by both loss of self-esteem through self-criticism of the 'me' and a perceived negative response from those around us (the 'generalised other').

COMPUTER SKILLS FOR EDUCATIONAL PURPOSES

Our particular interest over the past decade has been in the acquisition of computer skills for educational purposes. These have included skills at two levels:

- the *technical-level skills* of being able to use a machine and software effectively;
- what might be called the *higher-level skills* of being able to use a computer as a tool to support either one's own learning or the learning of students.

The former are crucially important because without them there is no possibility whatsoever of acquiring the higher-level skills. But they often pose so many problems for the learner that their acquisition comes to appear as an end in itself. It is vital that teachers acquire the higher-level skills, and one way of helping them to do so is to make the acquisition of the technical skills much less daunting and time-consuming.

A major problem in teaching technical-level computer skills is that people's perceived needs are immediate and specific. ('How do I use this particular computer, this particular printer, or this particular piece of software?') Many children and most teachers or student teachers expect to receive instruction of this specific kind. It is very time-consuming. At present levels of resources in schools and higher education institutions, instruction in how to use a substantial word-processing package, such as MS Word, can easily fill up the computer slots in a course for half a term. And all the evidence suggests that learners who receive specific instruction in MS Word only acquire specific skills in that one piece of software, with very little or no transfer of skills to other kinds of software or even other word processors, and certainly not to other machines. It would appear that a quite different approach to teaching computer skills is essential if computers are to be used cost-effectively in education, at least in the short term.

SELF-TEACHING AS A STRATEGY FOR TRANSFERABLE SKILLS ACQUISITION AND SITUATED LEARNING

Bridget Somekh takes up the story again

In my early work I attempted to tackle the problem of transferability of computer skills as a motivational problem and a problem of self-image. My theory was that if you begin by exciting the interest of a teacher or student in the educationally interesting things which a computer can do, they will learn the basic technical skills easily because they perceive a need for them. Partly this will be because their interest will help to overcome any emotional blocks they may have to using technology, what Pirsig (1974, pp. 298–306) calls 'internal gumption traps' or 'hangups' of which he identifies the most difficult as the 'value traps' which 'block affective understanding'. In my experience of working with teachers during 1984–5 such emotional blocks were often obvious. Sometimes they were exhibited through body language (awkward sitting postures, starts and jerks in response to 'bleeps'), sometimes through the repeated efforts of individuals to distance themselves from computer use by incorporating their lack of computer skills into their projected self-image ('I'm no good at computers . . . don't ask me, ask the children'). The latter phenomenon exactly matched the 'I'm no good at maths' syndrome. It is a peculiarity of British culture that many people feel very comfortable constructing themselves as non-technological or non-mathematical people, whereas they would not dream of claiming: 'I'm no good at reading.'

My growing understanding of the barriers to the computer innovation (Lewis, 1990) led me to adopt strategies which would increase teachers' professional motivation and reduce their sense of cultural alienation ('hangups'). I worked experimentally, basing my strategies on the hypothesis that once I had gained teachers' interest in the potential of computers as learning tools they would not only acquire computer skills easily, but be able to transfer these skills easily from the use of one specific computer or software application to another. There is a lot of evidence to support the view that a high level of motivation can have this effect, not least in the fact that almost all highly skilled computer users profess to be largely self-taught.

In the Pupil Autonomy in Learning with Microcomputers (PALM) project I used action research as a strategy for creating and sustaining teachers' motivation, and thereby supporting their development of both technical and higher-level computer skills (Somekh, 1991). Teachers were asked to experiment with computer use in their classrooms, in order to research their educational potential. Their misgivings about any possible harmful effects of computer use were reconstructed as research questions which could best be investigated by teachers using computers in their teaching and evaluating the impact of their use on pupils' learning. My hope was that by diverting the focus of teachers' attention away from the acquisition of technical skills, and towards issues which were of the highest professional concern, we would enable them to acquire technical skills easily: I believed that the perceived difficulty of acquiring technical computer skills was created by fear and a sense of alienation from machines (because, in their appearance and the discourse or 'jargon' which surrounded their use, computers carried the cultural stamp of Science and Technology). Once teachers started experimenting with their use and researching their value, I believed they would not find computers difficult.

In short, PALM used action research as a strategy for motivating teachers to acquire computer skills through self-teaching. This may sound naive, but to an extent the strategy proved very successful. The majority of teachers who worked with PALM had few computer skills when they joined the project and by the end counted themselves as confident, if not highly proficient, users. Of course, this was not unsupported self-teaching. PALM provided a considerable amount of on-the-job support through the three full-time project officers. Once motivated to self-teach, participating teachers were provided with both educational and technical backup. They also had access to low-level financial resources: this meant that they were not blocked for lack of computer paper, printer ink or backup disks – the kind of disincentives which Pirsig calls 'setbacks' or 'gumption traps in which you're thrown off the Quality track by conditions that arise from external circumstances' (Pirsig, 1974, p. 299). From the point of view of research there was a price to pay, in that the teachers' action research into pupils' learning in PALM progressed much more slowly than similar work in other projects (see, for example, the work of the TIQL project, in Ebbutt and Elliott, 1985). Nevertheless, their research still generated a considerable amount of knowledge and understanding of the higher-level computer skills needed to realise some of the potential of computers as learning tools. And because their research was carried out in ordinary – rather poorly equipped – classrooms in England in 1988–90, it provides a meaningful knowledge base for other teachers wishing to acquire these higher-level skills (see Somekh and Davies, 1991).

Bigum (1990) suggests a much simpler strategy for promoting self-teaching in student teachers, by providing them with 24-hour, open-access computer facilities and a good technician constantly on hand to provide help if needed. Learning computer skills is then the responsibility of the student, with the help of manuals. According to Bigum the success of this approach lies in providing a context where 'situated learning' is possible. The theory of situated cognition has been most clearly stated by Brown *et al.* (1989). They argue that learning is easiest and most productive when it takes place in an authentic situation, alongside experienced practitioners of the discipline. This obviates the need for teachers to develop unnecessary abstractions – instead, part of the cognitive task is 'off-loaded . . . onto the environment' (ibid., p. 35):

> The context of activity is an extraordinarily complex network from which practitioners draw essential support. The source of such support is often only tacitly recognized by practitioners, or even by teachers or designers of simulations. Classroom tasks, therefore, can completely fail to provide the contextual features that allow authentic activity.
>
> (ibid., p. 34)

The theory of 'situated cognition' also helps to explain the usefulness of action research as a strategy for teachers' learning in PALM, since they acquired most of their higher-level computer skills and many of their technical skills in the classroom working alongside their pupils.

ENABLING SKILLS: CREATING CONFIDENCE THROUGH ROUTINE PROCEDURES

Despite the success of these approaches, with their emphasis on self-teaching, there still remains a problem with the acquisition of *transferable* technical-level computer skills. Increased motivation and a decrease in the sense of cultural alienation together remove many of the barriers to teachers' development of these skills. But the story with which this chapter begins illustrates a continuing and more basic problem which must also be addressed. Conceptual inquisitiveness on its own cannot confirm and maintain the kind of positive self-image which seasoned computer-users bring to the learning of new skills. Conceptual inquisitiveness must be matched by a set of practical routines which *enable* exploration and both promote *self-confidence* and ensure that *confidence is reflected back to the learner from peers and observers.* In terms of Mead's theory of the self, only in this way can the 'I' embark on exploratory learning without being undermined by self-criticism of the 'me' exacerbated by apparent loss of esteem from the 'generalised other'.

If you watch an expert computer user tackling a new piece of software or a new machine, you are likely to notice a high level of exploratory key pressing, often accompanied by mutterings and exclamations: 'Ah, yes! . . . Hey, WHAT!? . . . I see!' You are unlikely to notice very lengthy perusal of the manual, though it will be to hand and may be searched for the answer to some specific questions. The key-pressing may appear almost random, but will actually incorporate systematic elements. It will partly be governed by knowledge of how computers and software designers tend to work (drawing on past personal experience), and partly entail a set of routine procedures which are informative because they elicit responses from the machine.

In October 1990 one of the authors was lucky enough to watch Leon Shuker of ILECC (Inner London Educational Computing Centre) working with post-graduate primary students at Goldsmiths' College. Instead of setting out to teach them how to use a particular piece of software he taught them a set of procedures for handling any software on a BBC machine. If they ran into problems, he told them, there were three keys they could press to try to sort things out: Escape, Return and Space Bar. After they had tried these two or three times they should assume that there was something wrong with the computer – rather than themselves – and give up. We are probably oversimplifying, but what impresses us about this approach is the simplicity of the message. The students were clearly reassured and had no difficulty in beginning to explore the software. He had enabled them to approach the computer in the style of an expert user – and this brought with it a sense of confidence.

There are two elements which make up a skill:

- an element of knowledge and understanding (Bridget could not have learnt to fit a Wordwise chip without being told its correct location in the BBC computer and given a strategy for inserting the legs without breaking them);
- an element of routinised action (which Bridget lacked, with the result that she experienced a strong sense of disfunctionality and actual physical discomfort).

When an expert computer user approaches a new piece of software or a new machine, he or she draws upon *transferable* technical skills in computer use. These rely upon two essential and interdependent ingredients:

- personal confidence;
- a set of routine exploratory procedures.

They might more accurately be called 'enabling skills' since they are not skills in the ordinary sense. Nevertheless, there is a connection between them and more specific computer skills – since confidence and a form of routinised action are common to both.

Observing ourselves and others, over the years, has enabled us to develop a set of routine exploratory procedures for tackling a new piece of hardware or software. It is not a definitive list. Many of them are rather obvious. In an important sense the routines amount to a style and an approach rather than a definite set of answers. To some extent each individual can develop his or her own personal set of routines. But they can also be taught, and it is best to be prescriptive for the sake of simplicity, knowing that as technical skills develop the routines will be naturally extended. We have begun the list below and left plenty of gaps to be filled by readers:

- Read the manual to find out how to load the software. If the manual isn't clear, ask someone to load it for you.
- Experiment with pressing keys and reading what it says on the screen.
- When in doubt, press Return, Enter, Tab or Space Bar (or Escape if the computer has this key).
- Keep a paper and pen beside you and make a note of any instructions which you think might come in useful later.
- Keep the manual to hand for occasional consultation. Sometimes it is useful to work your way through manuals systematically. If they are not clear it's best to abandon them.
- When you are learning how to use a generic package (word processor, database, etc.) try using it to carry out a particular job of work which is simple, but which you have a real need to do.
- When you are learning how to use a generic package, work on a 'need to know' basis rather than trying to learn how to use the whole package. There will probably be many facilities which you will never need to learn how to use.
- If the computer won't work, check that it is switched on at the mains, and that the leads to any separate pieces (e.g. monitor, mouse, keyboard) are plugged into the right sockets.
- If the computer is definitely switched on, but won't respond to any key press, switch it off at the mains and reload the software.
- If the printer won't work, switch it off at the mains and then try again.
- If you are still trying unsuccessfully to get the machine or software to work after half an hour, the chances are that they are at fault and not you. It's time for a cup of tea!
- ?
- ?

True skills can be acquired much more easily if the learner can be given these interdependent 'enabling skills' of confidence and a set of routine, exploratory procedures. This seems to be because:

- having a procedure which enables an immediate start instils an initial sense of confidence;
- putting the routines into practice provides immediate feedback which can be interpreted and this contributes directly to the learning process;
- having something practical to do frees the mind to concentrate on understanding the machine's responses.

Through these enabling skills initial confidence is conserved and grows with the sense of developing understanding and facility with the software. Routine procedures also guard against unproductive self-recrimination and time-wasting in trying to make a piece of faulty hardware or software work. They provide a check-list of things to try and a rule of thumb about when to give up and blame the machine.

These routine procedures should only be taken as a short cut to the development of personal strategies which evolve over time. For example, the third point: 'When in doubt, press Return, Enter, Tab or Space Bar' could change with Windows software to:

- Click the mouse on the icon buttons at the top of the screen.
- The way to quit is usually in the top left of a screen.

Those involved with helping others to use computers often draw an analogy with learning to drive a car. There is no need to become a car mechanic, but routines are often emphasised in order to help the new driver. Perhaps you, like us, remember your driving instructor's insistence on looking in the mirror before overtaking: 'Mirror, indicate, mirror, slowly pull out!' This is a bit like the hints above. In addition, while it is unnecessary to become a car mechanic it helps to have some appreciation of how a car works: for example, that the accelerator causes an increase in fuel to the engine and thus the speed of the car increases. Now let us move on to the use of analogies to help the teacher new to IT.

ENABLING SKILLS: A MENTAL FRAMEWORK

Mental models or analogies can help teachers adjust to the ways in which IT works (or doesn't!). We describe two common situations in which teachers new to IT frequently have mental models that disrupt their use of IT: these are with the word processor and the computer local area network.

Teachers new to word processors often bring with them a concept of typing on to sheets of blank paper. This needs to be adjusted to help them appreciate that the 'paper' is more like a continuous scroll which is created as it is written on. The scroll can also be edited and sections can be 'magically' cut and pasted elsewhere without any sign of the join. The word processor can also have additional tools. For example, the text can be analysed by the computer checking for spelling against a long dictionary list or a thesaurus. Other tools are available to enhance layout. Finally, the computer screen is best thought of as a window which can be moved around to look at different parts of a long document. Teachers should therefore be encouraged to change their style of working as they try their first simple tasks using word processors.

When computer systems become complex, analogies are useful to simplify the mental model; and humour can relieve the stress often felt when computers are unreliable. The analogy provides a mental model of the strengths and limitations. It can also help teachers new to these apparently all-powerful machines to appreciate their variations in speed and unreliability.

Niki Davis takes up the story

An analogy I often use for the way in which a local area network functions is that of the comic waiter Manuel in the hotel restaurant in *Fawlty Towers.* Manuel is my analogy with the way in which the file server works. The file server (Manuel, the waiter) serves each work station (restaurant table). He must listen to requests for software and files (the order) which he gives to file store (the kitchen), and the file store then gives him the software (the food) to take to the work station (the table). The file server, like Manuel, can only do one thing at a time. If the order is big it takes longer, and when the network is busy (the restaurant has many tables full), the person giving the later order will have to wait. Although a computer is much faster than a person, teachers will notice that when a class full of students ask for software at the same time there will be a delay in its delivery and work stations will be ready at different times. The larger the software requested, the longer the delay. Teaching should be planned with this in mind.

My analogy of Manuel was chosen because local area networks can become unreliable, so it is good practice to save work regularly. Manuel's restaurant in *Fawlty Towers* frequently went wrong with a consequent humorous uproar. Keeping humour in a difficult situation can be helpful even in a busy classroom! Difficulties can arise in any classroom, so teachers usually have an alternative activity away from the computer for the occasions when the network has crashed. Let's hope that they have also taken a copy to back up work that might be lost, so that they can return to it another day.

In this chapter we have considered teachers who are new to IT and the tremendous challenge that they can face. The saying 'old habits die hard' emphasises the fact that previous experience can be unhelpful. However, teachers new to IT also bring with them a lot of relevant experience. Returning to the analogy with learning to drive a car: a major skill required is road sense and navigation. Most new drivers are already familiar with behaviour on roads, including priority at junctions. They can also read maps. In the same way teachers are familiar with classroom practice, the curriculum and the process of teaching and learning. The introduction of IT in education should focus more on education than IT.

CONCLUSIONS

We would like to note that many of those who have faced the challenge of IT unwillingly have come through and thanked us for helping them face it. Mature teachers and student teachers particularly have appreciated the increase in their professional status that IT has given them personally. They have pride in their increased access to resources and the improved appearance of their self-prepared teaching materials.

This chapter has emphasised approaches which enable teachers to transfer their newly gained skills and confidence to other applications of IT. We noted that the choice of the first task is important. For practising teachers it should be one which they need to do. Relevance is also vital to student teachers, both for their own purposes and that of the curriculum. Teachers who start with word processing, perhaps to produce a report, may need to 'start again' to apply this to other contexts such as word processing in their classroom. Similarly, new approaches will be required in order to adopt other software tools or computer equipment. However, provided the teacher has adopted a transferable learning style, each further development should become an easier step. Other chapters in this book consider IT in relation to teaching and learning and its management, and the book ends with a chapter on strategies for staff and institutional development with information technology. The first memorable and challenging steps with IT, possibly the most important, can be consolidated over time, enabling all teachers to use IT effectively in their teaching and learning.

NOTE

1 Part of this paper was published by Bridget Somekh under the title, 'Making ready for change: acquiring enabling skills', in D. Bridges, *Transferable Skills in Higher Education.* Norwich: ERTEC, University of East Anglia, 1994.

REFERENCES

Bigum, C. (1990) 'Situated computing in pre-service teacher education', in A. McDougall, and C. Dowling (eds), *Proceedings of the IFIP 5th World Conference on Computers in Education,* Sydney, Australia, 9–13 July. Amsterdam: North-Holland.

Brown, J.S., Collins, A. and Duguid, P. (1989) 'Situated cognition and the culture of learning', *Educational Researcher,* 32 (Jan–Feb): 32–42.

Ebbutt, D. and Elliott, J. (eds) (1985) *Issues in Teaching for Understanding.* London: Longman, for Schools Curriculum Development Committee.

Lewis, R. (1990) 'Selected research reviews: teachers', *Journal of Computer Assisted Learning*, 6(3): 217–24.
Mead, G.H. (1934) *The Works of George Herbert Mead*, Vol. 1: *Mind, Self and Society*. Chicago: University of Chicago Press.
Pirsig, R. (1974) *Zen and the Art of Motorcycle Maintenance*. London: Bodley Head; reprinted London: Corgi/Transworld.
Somekh, B. (1991) 'Pupil autonomy in learning with microcomputers: rhetoric or reality? An action research study', *Cambridge Journal of Education*, 21(1): 47–64.
Somekh, B. and Davies, R. (1991) 'Towards a pedagogy for information technology', *Curriculum Journal*, 2(2): 153–70.

Chapter 12

Partnership in initial teacher education

Graham Byrne Hill

INTRODUCTION

This chapter reviews the development of a school–college partnership scheme at Goldsmiths' College, London, during the period 1990–5.

The education of new teachers, in common with most vocational education, involves a complex process of preparation for the job and guided practice on the job. The partnerships between schools and teacher training institutions that have developed in England and Wales during the 1990s bring together experienced teachers, student teachers and college tutors in close working relationships. As a result, what students must achieve to qualify as teachers has had to be made explicit. All parties must understand the new distribution of responsibility for the different areas and stages of training, and must also agree on criteria of assessment which are clear and unambiguous.

The development of partnerships has major implications for a curriculum area such as information technology, which is taught mainly through other subjects. Practices concerning student teachers' use of information technology in school, which have developed informally and unsystematically, are likely to be more closely scrutinised by both students and staff across the team of schools in a partnership. As a result, comparisons may be made and norms of practice may develop across schools. Norms may primarily be in terms of the use of information technology by student teachers, but they may also reflect the role of IT in the teaching of the relevant subject or age phase in each school, and its wider role in management and administration. Partnership may thus offer the institutional mechanisms and impetus for greater coherence in the student's experience of using information technology in school.

Information technology's role in the curriculum is a diffused one and in important respects still unsettled. In this situation the activities of partnership, comprising discussion, planning and assessment across schools, could also become a powerful strategy for in-service teacher professional development in the use of information technology. A significant subtheme in what follows will, therefore, be the changing priorities of experienced teachers in the use of information technology.

TEACHER EDUCATION AT GOLDSMITHS' COLLEGE

The role of information technology in teacher education at Goldsmiths' College was strongly influenced by its participation from 1990 to 1992 in Project INTENT. The project worked within a philosophy that emphasised the close association of development with research (Somekh *et al.*, 1992). This was consistent with the emphasis upon reflective practice which is a distinctive feature of the partnership scheme to be described later in this chapter. The priority given to independent judgement and initiative was to prove highly significant when the partnership teams considered new arrangements for information technology.

Another feature of Project INTENT was the close involvement of management. At Goldsmiths' this meant that the project's three-member team included a newly appointed Professor of Education who was in line to become the next Dean. As a result, organisational impetus was given to developing an appropriate structure of working groups in relation to information technology, which cut across boundaries of subject and age-phase.

Prior to 1990, arrangements for IT in the courses for student teachers at Goldsmiths' included informal permeation of IT across all subjects (see Ruthven, 1984). This was described with approval by a member of Her Majesty's Inspectorate, in November 1991, as using information technology 'wherever and whenever it is appropriate'. However, despite its strengths, it had proved difficult to monitor and audit this arrangement. In 1990, the new working groups decided on arrangements for distributing responsibility for information technology across teacher training courses that would be easier to sustain and more effective than previous arrangements. Student teachers would continue to be provided with informal opportunities for the use of information technology in all their courses. But these would now, in almost all course elements, include occasions on which the whole of a class would have opportunity for 'hands-on' experience within a context that was appropriate to that course element. Such occasions, clearly identifiable to staff and students, would be timetabled to ensure that enough computers were to hand for use by all students. This form of permeation would occur, for example, in each of the primary curriculum areas. It was designed to meet national criteria for the accreditation of teacher education, which at the time specified that courses should contain 'compulsory and clearly identifiable elements' of IT (DES, 1989a).

By 1993, new government directives prompted a radical review of the arrangements for monitoring students' use of information technology with children (DfE, 1992, 1993). There was a move away from the specification of course content for the purposes of course evaluation to the use of exit criteria in the form of profiles of student competences. At Goldsmiths' there was general agreement for using competences to monitor students' experience with information technology. This was premised on the term competence being understood in a formative and imaginative way. The language of competences did not require a narrow, reductionist interpretation (Murphy *et al.*, 1993). More general misgivings about the concept of competences (Smith and Alred, 1993) were to be treated as warnings rather than as barriers against its use.

THE DEVELOPMENT OF THE NEW SCHOOL–COLLEGE PARTNERSHIPS

The next priority was to improve the student teachers' use of IT with children. This student experience occurred in college as well as in schools. New informal bilateral arrangements between the college and individual schools were led by the college, mainly at first within the undergraduate BA (Ed.) course for primary teachers; they included regular visits by children from a neighbouring primary school to work with students in college and using IT as a resource. A full account is given in Byrne Hill (1992).

Goldsmiths' had already developed partnership arrangements with a small group of secondary schools in its postgraduate programme. The initiative for this small-scale scheme within one subject had come from teachers in the schools and the subject tutor in College (Goldsmiths' College, 1992). After 1993 the government required that all secondary courses should increase the element of training based on the school site. This model of decentralised partnership was therefore extended, with modifications, to all secondary subjects and subsequently to the postgraduate primary course and the undergraduate courses. For most purposes the partnerships were initiated and run by teams of college- and school-based tutors. Each team in the secondary programme represented a subject and comprised from ten to twenty-eight teachers. It was co-ordinated by a college tutor and each of the school-based tutors was normally responsible for two student teachers.

Some significance attaches to the terms used. 'School-based tutor' was preferred to 'mentor', because the term implied that the role included responsibility for assessment and joint planning as well as for advice and counselling. Tutoring was understood as significantly more than a 'taking care of' role. The term 'mentor' was occasionally used informally, but was not considered to be sufficiently clear or rigorous for formal arrangements in teacher education, with its pressing needs for accountability and quality assurance. It should be noted that these teachers were not a cross-section of the teaching profession. They were selected or came forward because of their experience in teaching their subject and their interest in professional development. They may therefore be considered to have reflected more deeply than the average teacher, especially in relation to the importance of the school as a context for teacher education.

NEW PARTNERSHIP TEAMS

The new partnership teams were immediately presented with the question of how to provide all students with appropriate opportunities for the 'planning and management of lessons in which children learn with information technology alongside other resources' (HMI, 1992). In early meetings of the new partnership teams the discussion focused on IT provision in terms of access to equipment. Discussion then moved on to the identification of essential uses of IT in each of the subject areas. The enhanced responsibility for the training of teachers prompted unusually forthcoming responses from school-based tutors about what each of them believed and practised.

The postgraduate programme for secondary school teachers took the lead in the development because it was able to build on the existing small-scale scheme. Partnership arrangements with the schools for the ten secondary subjects were adopted in two stages and came into effect in autumn 1992 and autumn 1993. The arrangements are currently managed by partnership teams which meet termly. An individual or small committee within each school co-ordinates arrangements across all the subject departments that are working with the College. Not once, however, at any partnership team meeting was any significant reference made to a wider school structure or authority in relation to the curriculum role of information technology.

During 1993–4 the partnership teams were presented with a series of initiatives prepared by the Goldsmiths' College IT in Teacher Education Committee. This innovative committee, chaired now by the head of the department of teacher education, was part of the legacy of Project INTENT. It proposed that all students should give a fully planned and evaluated lesson involving IT during their first teaching practice in the spring term. The writing up and evaluation of this lesson would count as one of the pieces of assessed work. The committee agreed that an early priority for the partnership teams was that students should have adequate, school-based opportunities for the use of information technology.

The main obstacles were believed, at the beginning, to be the wide diversity of, and limited access to, IT equipment in schools. Therefore school-based tutors were surveyed to obtain a description of the IT facilities available in each teaching subject. The feedback from this survey significantly altered the terms of the inquiry, because it emerged that in most subjects in most secondary schools the extent and quality of the IT resources were not the major constraints. School-based tutors widely recognised that the equipment did not have to be state of the art. On the contrary, the planning of an adequate student teacher's experience with IT could be based on minimum resources, for example a word processor, a database and a spreadsheet. IT literacy for the student teacher was not primarily concerned with knowing more about computers, but knowing how to make an IT application work as an integral part of an activity. More fundamentally, therefore, the survey of facilities prompted discussion of the nature of the competences in IT that school-based tutors expected of beginning teachers. Henceforward, efforts to foster students' competence in the use of information technology were subsumed within the wider responsibilities of the new partnership teams.

The College's IT in Teacher Education Committee responded to this feedback from the partnership teams in early 1994. It proposed, first, that the partnership teams should discuss the feasibility of a student teacher's entitlement to use information technology in work with children that was *specific to each school.* This statement of entitlement would take appropriate account not only of differences in equipment, but also of differences in subject philosophy and in understanding the role of information technology within a subject. Second, the committee inquired whether it might be possible in the longer term for teams to agree a minimum student entitlement *across the schools* for each subject, and to describe the form that it might take. Discussion within the teams subsequently explored further questions relating to the competences that school-based tutors expected of beginning teachers, both in terms of expertise with IT and its relationship with curriculum and classroom management. Spelling out responses to these questions would achieve a number of purposes. Students would know what opportunities to prepare for, and what competences they were expected to achieve. Both schools and College would be clearer about what new teachers needed from them and what each partner was providing.

The following section summarises the response of the partnership teams according to subject. It is based on the opinions of 147 school-based tutors in a cross-section of 74 schools in south-east London and north Kent. These are drawn partly from the questionnaires which team members completed in May 1993 and partly from the discussions which occurred at subsequent partnership team meetings during 1994 as the teams responded to the College's IT in Teacher Education Committee's request for their views on the feasibility of a student entitlement to the use of IT in school. In the commentary that follows the presentation of the responses from each subject, a comparison is made between what school-based tutors believed to be important and the recommendations of government guidelines both at the time and more recently. This is useful as a test of the feasibility of government policy for IT.

THE FEASIBILITY OF A STUDENT ENTITLEMENT TO THE USE OF INFORMATION TECHNOLOGY IN SCHOOL

Science (twenty schools)

The school-based tutors in science distinguished between how they expected students to use information technology as a general professional tool and what they expected of students in the classroom. As general preparation they expected students to have already learned before going into school how to use information technology for:

- lesson planning;
- the production of classroom materials;
- organising information about pupils on a database or a spreadsheet.

Students were reported often to lack these general skills; a few were even physically apprehensive of computers.

On the students' use of information technology in the classroom, however, school-based tutors believed that they should be less specific. Any tight statement of entitlement concerning the curriculum uses of information technology was liable to run into serious timetable problems. One example illustrated this point: the use of a database for the study of patterns of illness by a Year 8 class could not be rescheduled to match the timetable of a student teacher. Tutors preferred to put the onus for the classroom use of information technology on student teachers, to offer them a 'menu of suggestions', and at the end of a teaching practice to require student teachers to provide an adequate answer to the question of what they had managed to do. A menu might comprise, for example, use of three of the following: a database, the graphical facilities of a spreadsheet, a hyperstudy, secondary sources on a CD-ROM, word processing with less able pupils, and data logging. All schools possessed appropriate data logging equipment, but the tutors did not consider that they should require students to be able to use it. They argued this on grounds of what they believed to be the equipment's complexity. It would be more appropriate, in their view, for students to choose from a menu.

Summary and comments

- *Student teacher entitlement*: student to choose from a menu.
- *Cross-school entitlement*: feasible on the basis of a menu which allows choice to schools as well as to students.
- *Essential competences of new science teachers*: (a) general: word processing, desktop publishing, data handling and use of a spreadsheet; (b) in the classroom: a range of flexible competences which were not specified in detail.

School-based tutors would not expect students to develop competences either in data logging or in modelling (for the formulation and testing of hypotheses, using spreadsheets or simulations). These are areas in the teaching of science, however, where the appropriateness of using information technology is much emphasised in the guidelines published by the National Council for Educational Technology (NCET, 1993, 1995g) and by the School Curriculum and Assessment Authority (SCAA, 1995). There were no suggestions that the use of information technology was limited significantly by problems of access to equipment.

Mathematics (twelve schools)

School-based tutors agreed, with one dissenting voice, that new teachers of mathematics should be familiar with the following: LOGO, a graphics calculator, data handling and use of a spreadsheet (particularly for statistical analysis). Students' knowledge of curriculum software was reported as varying widely, a few being unfamiliar even with spreadsheets. In general, use of mathematics-specific software, such as mathematical games, did not present students with problems.

A major difficulty in school-based tutors' arrangements for student teachers was that of providing them with access to computing facilities. They found it demanding enough to book computer rooms in order to meet the regular needs of pupils. It could be next to impossible to match students' requirements as well. Some students were found to be markedly ill at ease in a computer room and needed the support of an experienced teacher. The availability of technical support in computer rooms varied widely.

The mathematics tutors had recently decided that all students should be required to 'use information technology in some aspect of their work in school' during the summer term practice, and that from 1995 this should become a compulsory element of the course. School-based tutors offered no comment on students' general information technology skills. In mathematics students are required and strongly supported, from the beginning of their college course, to word process all course work and to produce worksheets using a desktop publishing package.

Summary and comments

- *Student teacher entitlement*: student to choose an area of work.
- *Cross-school entitlement*: feasible; it has been agreed and incorporated into the course from 1994–5 on the basis of student choice, monitored by tutors.
- *Essential competences of new mathematics teachers*: use of LOGO, data handling and a spreadsheet. Competence in word processing and desktop publishing were also assumed.

Consideration of any more ambitious entitlement to the use of information technology in mathematics was prevented by the reported difficulties of access to, and of support for students within, central computing rooms. The competences expected of new teachers matched broadly the guidelines of NCET (1993, 1995d) and of SCAA (1995) for the use of information technology in mathematics. There was some disparity, however, between the competences in new technology sought by school-based tutors and the opportunities that they could reliably offer.

Music (twelve schools)

The school-based tutors in music were emphatic that a student's most important quality is the ability to learn quickly within a given environment. No particular competences in information technology were expected of student teachers on their arrival in a school. Music equipment in schools varied widely, including different kinds of keyboard, amplifier, synthesiser, sound processor, stereo, video- and tape-recorder. Almost all departments had computers but 'not as many as we want'. The school-based tutors expected schools to assume responsibility for supporting students in using the particular equipment in a school. The school would 'teach [students] the basics'. School-based music tutors did not expect the College to do this. The same applied to the use of computers for composition. Schools would teach this to student teachers, with students being expected to work a good deal in their own time.

Summary and comments

- *Student teacher entitlement*: support in using appropriate but school-specific equipment.
- *Cross-school entitlement*: feasible only in general terms. Each school has specific expectations that are framed by the nature of its equipment.
- *Essential competences of new music teachers*: general IT skills and a readiness to try out new kinds of equipment.

As yet the likely elements of a minimum entitlement have not emerged. The wide range of possible expectations of a music teacher in relation to information technology, combined with the variety of equipment, have contributed to a distinctive consensus among school-based music tutors. This is that the major responsibility for ensuring the competence in information technology of new music teachers should, and could safely, be entrusted to schools. The guidelines of NCET (1993, 1995f) and of SCAA (1995) on the use of information technology in music are particularly open-ended and suggestive, rather than prescriptive. The strategy developed by the music team is consistent with them.

Art (twenty-eight schools)

School-based tutors in art agreed on the basic competences that they were looking for. Student teachers should have familiarity and some facility with:

- word processing for the creation of worksheets;
- painting software;
- a graphics package that could be used for design and lettering, and for repeat patterns in textiles.

A further suggestion was that student teachers should be able to use CD-ROM to access secondary sources in the teaching of critical and contextual studies (this was part of AT2 in National Curriculum art until 1994).

At first school-based tutors were worried about the particular equipment in College and elsewhere that students might have learned to use. The tutors in the art team are from local authorities which support a variety of different equipment. They were readily persuaded, however, that experience in College of an application on any make of equipment would be adequate preparation for using that kind of application in school.

School-based tutors stressed that the most helpful approach to information technology in art was that it should be 'use-led'. In art a computer should be one among a range of tools, with pupils using it normally for part of a task. It is not inappropriate, therefore, to have just one or two computers in a well-equipped art room. Beginning teachers need a 'have a go' attitude in such a situation, where there is rarely a technician. Student teachers are likely to have to trouble-shoot for themselves, for example when a printer driver is needed. The danger here is the kind of situation in which three pupils on one computer absorb most of a teacher's attention. The response of many of the school-based tutors has been to develop a cascade tradition of pupils helping one another.

Summary and comments

- *Student teacher entitlement*: ready access in the art room to a computer with appropriate graphics software.
- *Cross-school entitlement*: feasible in terms of classroom access to suitable equipment.
- *Essential competences of new art teachers*: word processing, desktop publishing and the use of graphics software.

No school-based tutor suggested a competence relating to the manipulation of digitised images. This contrasts with the central place of image manipulation in the guidelines for the teaching of art suggested by NCET (1993, 1995a) and by SCAA (1995).

Drama (eleven schools)

Most school-based tutors in drama were tempted, at first, to answer the question of what competences in information technology they expected in new teachers by replying: none at all. There were 'plenty of opportunities' in drama for using information technology, but the tutors held no expectations. After discussion, they recognised that, in reality, they did expect student teachers to be computer literate, but that they could not themselves give any help towards achieving this. Student teachers should not be frightened of computers, even if current staff were. New teachers should be at ease with and supportive of the 'climatic change' in the use of information technology that is occurring in schools.

Some school-based tutors expected to 'learn from students'. Several were 'impressed' or 'stunned' by the quality of the worksheets and lesson plans that had been desktop published by students. The most obvious other uses of information technology in drama teaching were believed to be in the preparation of resources and in administration, with some reference being made to the use of CD-ROM.

Summary and comments

- *Student teacher entitlement*: none suggested.
- *Cross-school entitlement*: not feasible.

- *Essential competences of new drama teachers*: computer literacy, including basic competence in desktop publishing and data handling.

The college-based tutor suggested some possible reasons for the distinctive approach of the school-based drama tutors to information technology. She believed that their views were often influenced by the fact that drama teaching is located, typically in schools, in a room that is cut off from other facilities. Their distinctive views were also shaped, she believed, by the difficult political relationships that often divide drama from English. These difficulties inhibit the sharing of ideas and practices, including experience in the use of information technology.

The teaching of drama is not covered in the recommendations of either NCET (1993) or SCAA (1995).

English (twelve schools)

School-based tutors in English, like tutors in other subjects, held general professional expectations of student teachers in relation to their use of information technology, as well as views of what was essential to the teaching of their subject. All English students should be able to produce worksheets, including graphics, through the use of a desktop publisher. In the classroom they should be capable of organising small tasks which include use of a computer. Commonly this would involve use of either a text disclosure programme or a word processor.

For these classroom purposes all student teachers must, in the view of the school-based tutor, be competent in word processing and desktop publishing. A more general requirement was for students to be versatile in working with different sorts of equipment. It has been increasingly common in the schools with which members of the team are familiar for the more recently acquired, stand-alone computers in English departments to have a graphical interface, and the networked machines available to whole classes to be IBM-compatible.

Only in the longer term might school-based tutors expect new teachers to be able to run the kind of special event involving information technology where a class makes an excursion to a pre-booked computer room. On these occasions colleagues might be corridors away, and there might be no help available in the use of software. There were enough horror stories still in circulation among English teachers at the time for school-based tutors to be cautious in their expectations of student teachers in this direction. They were agreed, however, that students should be provided with opportunities to familiarise themselves with the school network.

The school-based tutors said that computer versatility of student teachers in English should also include readiness to use library packages such as CD-ROM, and to use databases for holding reading records and information about popular literature.

Summary and comments

- *Student teacher entitlement*: use of a word processor and text disclosure software with small groups of pupils, together with an introduction to the school network.
- *Cross-school entitlement*: feasible; already agreed and incorporated in the English course from 1992–3 (details are given below).
- *Essential competences of new English teachers*: word processing, desktop publishing, data handling, together with flexibility across equipment.

The partnership agreement between English tutors included from the beginning, in 1992–3, a cross-school student entitlement to the use of information technology. Students were to go into schools in pairs during the spring term. During this practice each pair of students would teach one class collaboratively. In particular, all students would be given the opportunity to run a unit of work for their shared class in which the use of information technology would be prominent. In the summer term students would be asked, again working in pairs, 'to develop some clearly identifiable IT-related resources for each English department, in line with the department's perceived needs in this area, and to present those resources formally at department meetings' (Moore, 1992; see also 'University A' in NCET, 1991).

The guidelines of NCET (1993, 1995c) and of SCAA (1995) offer a range of related uses of information technology in English. These provide for choice. They support the partnership tutors' strategy of integrating the use of technology when it is relevant, and where it will be part of the learning process rather than its focus (NCET, 1991).

Modern languages (twelve schools)

School-based tutors agreed that a student entitlement to classroom use of information technology should comprise opportunities to use word processing and a selection of modern languages-specific programs. The latter included language games and text manipulation software. Beginning teachers were expected to be able to use a word processor to prepare teaching materials and to be familiar with well-known modern languages packages.

At the beginning of the partnership, the feasibility of an entitlement appeared to depend on resolving a problem of poor fit between the availability of equipment and the organisation of the typical modern languages classroom. School- and college-based tutors had worked on this problem in the National Council for Educational Technology's Flexible Learning Project (Harris, 1992). This project aimed to encourage the use of information technology in the learning of foreign languages through changes in classroom organisation; in particular, through developing group work in the place of whole class teaching. The modern language tutors had rare access to computer rooms. Therefore, if they were to incorporate the use of information technology into their teaching, they needed to be able to organise work around a stand-alone computer for groups of pupils. Small group use of a stand-alone machine would not fit easily, however, into classrooms that were teacher-dominated.

In 1991 partnership tutors reported considerable difficulties over access to equipment, with often acute need for overhead projectors, tape-recording equipment with headphones, television or video, as well as problems of access to appropriate computer facilities. Half the project schools did not have a stand-alone computer that was readily available for use by modern languages staff. By 1995 these difficulties had eased and all tutors were able to make a commitment to providing students with classroom opportunities to use word processing and popular modern languages packages, with a few offering further facilities such as data handling and CD-ROM. The teaching situations available might be either small group or whole class. Most of the modern languages departments had an agreed IT policy.

Summary and comments

- *Student entitlement*: use of a word processor and of a selection of modern languages packages, with use of further facilities as departments gain access to them.
- *Cross-school entitlement*: feasible in terms of the use of a word processor and of a selection of modern languages packages.
- *Essential competences of new teachers of modern languages*: word processing and familiarity with a selection of modern languages-specific programs.

The scope of students' use of information technology in the teaching of modern languages has developed significantly during the period of partnership. The guidelines from NCET (1993, 1995e) and from SCAA (1995) suggest numerous related ways of using information technology in the teaching of modern languages, from which teachers are expected to make choices appropriate to their circumstances. This is broadly in line with the provision that is being offered to students by the school-based tutors.

Design and technology (fourteen schools)

School-based tutors expected all student teachers to use word processing and desktop publishing for hand-outs and worksheets. On the whole schools possessed adequate computer-aided design (CAD) equipment, but students' knowledge of how to use it varied widely. Most students needed time with this equipment in school in order to develop their own understanding and skills. Many experienced teachers, however, were not able to use it. It would be too much, in the school-based tutors' view, to expect all student teachers to use CAD in a teaching context with children. A few schools could offer support to students in using CAD with small groups of pupils.

Summary and comments

- *Student entitlement*: this could vary from schools in which students used CAD with a small group of pupils, to schools which assured students of opportunities to familiarise themselves with equipment.
- *Cross-school entitlement*: feasible only in terms of student access to computer-aided design equipment in order to develop personal competence in using it.
- *Essential competences of new teachers*: word processing and desktop publishing, together with a readiness to work with different kinds of equipment.

Thus school-based tutors in design and technology varied widely in what they could offer as a student entitlement. They reported the main constraint as limitations in the expertise of experienced teachers. The guidelines of NCET (1993, 1995b) and of SCAA (1995) for the role of information technology in the teaching of design and technology give prominence to drawing packages, computer-aided manufacture (CAM), control systems, databases and spreadsheets. A minority of school-based tutors could commit themselves to supporting students in work with a group of pupils in one of these areas. The others could not make such a commitment.

Social studies (ten schools)

School-based tutors in social studies expected student teachers to be able to use information technology both in administration and in the classroom. Administrative uses included using a word processor to write profiles and pupil assessments, and the use of a spreadsheet to organise marks. The competences in the classroom that school-based tutors expected of student teachers were:

- use of desktop publishing to create a newspaper;
- use of a spreadsheet or of survey software that produces graphs;
- use of CD-ROM, with A level pupils, to access original sources such as newspapers for evidence-based work.

Student teachers were also expected to be able to supervise pupils in word processing their course work for GCSE.

Summary and comments

- *Student teacher entitlement*: use of an appropriate desktop publisher and either spreadsheet or survey software, and in some schools CD-ROM.
- *Cross-school entitlement*: feasible on the basis of opportunities to use a desktop publisher and either a spreadsheet or survey software.
- *Essential competences of new teachers*: word processing, desktop publishing, and use of a spreadsheet and CD-ROM.

Neither NCET (1993) nor SCAA (1995) offered guidelines for the use of information technology in the teaching of social studies. There is a slight paradox here: social studies is one of those subjects in which school-based tutors expressed greater confidence about being able to provide students with opportunities to use information technology which matched the agreed requirements of the subject. They felt less constrained by the difficulties that were mentioned in the responses of other teams.

CONCLUSION

In their earlier discussions, college tutors had assumed that diversity of, and uneven access to, equipment in schools would require most statements of student entitlement to be school-specific. Any cross-school entitlement would be in the most general terms. The discussions in the partnership teams that were formed as a response to government policy in 1992 (DfE, 1992) showed that, on the contrary, school-based tutors in a number of subjects were able to agree without difficulty to a significant cross-school student entitlement to the use of information technology in work with children. In a middle group of subjects, where the cross-school entitlement would involve a large element of choice by students from a menu of options, there was scope for partnership teams to firm up the range of choice when this became more appropriate to the subject and other circumstances supported the change.

There was little support for an entitlement that was specific to each school. The only basis that school-based tutors found for such an entitlement was one that reflected recognition of the difficulties, in some schools and subjects, which prevented them from offering students proper opportunities to develop the competences that were agreed to be appropriate to the subject. Overall, there was a significant degree of consensus within partnership teams on which uses of information technology were central to a subject.

The readiness of most teams to accept the feasibility of a cross-school entitlement was facilitated by the school-based tutors' views of the kind of uses of information technology that was central to their subjects. In all subjects school-based tutors predominantly expected new teachers to possess generic skills in information technology, rather than knowledge of software that was subject- or even equipment-specific. This was consistent with the emphasis in the National Curriculum on capability, as in the original title of the subject, Information Technology Capability (DES, 1990). Capability may be taken to imply a content-free set of skills and understandings. School-based tutors' understanding of required competences in terms of content-free skills and understandings thus enabled them to accept more readily the feasibility of a cross-school entitlement to the use of information technology.

The decision to broaden the scope of the inquiry from the feasibility of a student entitlement to include the competences expected of beginning teachers reflected a sense of the growing importance of the school-based tutors' role in decisions about how new teachers should be trained. Their view that the competences required of new teachers are generic, rather than application-specific, was immediately recognised as an important factor in the planning of courses. It added further weight to the view of HMI, as reported by Hodgkinson and Wild (1994), that, on grounds of what was achievable in the time available, one-year courses of training should 'focus on improving student competence in basic or generic skills . . . while aiming always to improve levels of student confidence'.

The inquiry showed less disparity than might have been expected between the competences in information technology that school-based tutors sought in new teachers, and the kinds of expertise that they were able to give student teachers the opportunities to develop. The much greater disparity that appeared in some subjects was between what school-based tutors expected new teachers to possess in expertise and what the guidelines of NCET (1993, 1995a–g) and SCAA (1995) suggested are appropriate areas of teacher expertise. A striking instance of this disparity appeared in design and technology, but it also occurred in science and in art. In these cases school-based tutors and NCET and SCAA held significantly different views about which major generic skills in information technology were central to the teaching of their subject. Most disparities involved both the use of more complex kinds of equipment and the development of generic skills that were unique to a subject.

It is difficult to comment on how representative were the views of the partnership tutors of other teachers. As mentioned earlier, all tutors identified strongly with their subject, to which information technology was a more or less helpful contributor rather than a partner with its own curriculum responsibilities. Each of the teams had developed through personal contacts between school-based tutors and the college-based tutor. An example of the influence of college-based tutors on the views of school-based tutors may be seen in the latter's attitudes to word processing and desktop publishing. In all subjects at College, students were required to word process at least one of their pieces of coursework and were introduced to the facilities to do so. In some subjects at College, however, there was a strong emphasis also on desktop publishing. It was in these same subjects (particularly mathematics, English, art and drama) that the school-based tutors showed most awareness of the extent of what student teachers could achieve in the desktop publishing of classroom materials.

Another feature of the responses to the inquiry was the contrasting predicaments of subjects which required use of bookable computer rooms for whole class use, and subjects in which a prevailing pedagogy permitted regular use of a stand-alone machine by small groups of pupils. The subjects which relied largely on use of bookable facilities had greater difficulty in making a commitment to provide student teachers with opportunities to use information technology in ways which were designed to contribute to their professional development. The uses of information technology tended to be constrained by what the timetabling of the room allowed.

The size of the samples inhibited the drawing of conclusions, or even the floating of hypotheses, about individual subjects. The subject and other factors that were identified, however, were valid for the schools concerned. The opportunities and difficulties that were reported might have been more or less significant in a larger sample of schools. The predicaments, nevertheless, presented a distinctive and significant challenge to the subjects whose school-based tutors reported them.

Partnership implies local, grass-roots knowledge and initiative in the training of teachers. The early experience of partnership that has been reported here shows both the importance of the local initiatives that partnership encourages, and the parallel need for careful sharing, discussion and criticism of the results of this experience.

REFERENCES

Byrne Hill, G. (1992) 'Work with children in the use of information technology', in *Developing Information Technology in Teacher Education* (DITTE 6). Coventry: NCET.

DfE (Department for Education) (1992) *Initial Teacher Training (Secondary Phase)*, Circular 9/92. London: Department for Education.

—— (1993) *The Initial Training of Primary School Teachers: New Criteria for Course Approval*, Circular 14/93. London: Department for Education.

DES (Department of Education and Science) (1989a) *Revised Criteria for Approving Courses*, Circular 24/89. London: HMSO.

—— (1989b) *Information Technology in Initial Teacher Training: A Report of the Expert Group* (the Trotter Report). London: HMSO.

—— (1990) *Technology in the National Curriculum*. London: HMSO.

Goldsmiths' College (1992) *PGCE (Secondary) Course: A Partnership Approach*. London: Faculty of Education, Goldsmiths' College.

Harris, V. (1992) 'How do student teachers respond to using IT in language teaching and what support do they need?', in *Developing Information Technology in Teacher Education* (DITTE 4). Coventry: National Council for Educational Technology.

HMI (Her Majesty's Inspectorate) (1992) *Information Technology in Initial Teacher Training: Two Years after Trotter*. London: Department of Education and Science.

Higham, J. and Macaro, E. (1993) *Information Technology in Initial Teacher Education: The Modern Languages Perspective*. York: University of York.

Hodgkinson, K. and Wild, P. (1994) 'Tracking the development of student information technology capability', *Journal of Information Technology for Teacher Education*, 3(1): 101–14.

Moore, A. (1992) 'The incorporation of information technology elements in a PGCE English course', in *Developing Information Technology in Teacher Education* (DITTE 6). Coventry: National Council for Education Technology.

Murphy, R., Mahony, P., Jones, J. and Calderhead, J. (1993) 'Profiling in initial teacher training', *Journal of Teacher Development*, 2(3): 141–6.

NCET (National Council for Educational Technology) (1991) *Information Technology in English in Initial Teacher Training: A Survey of Practice*. Coventry: NCET.

—— (1993) *Getting IT Across: Developing IT Capability at Key Stages 3 and 4*. Coventry: NCET.

—— (1995a) *Art: Approaches to IT Capability, Key Stage 3*. Coventry: NCET.

—— (1995b) *Design and Technology: Approaches to IT Capability, Key Stage 3*. Coventry: NCET.

—— (1995c) *English: Approaches to IT Capability, Key Stage 3*. Coventry: NCET.

—— (1995d) *Mathematics: Approaches to IT Capability, Key Stage 3*. Coventry: NCET.

—— (1995e) *Modern Languages: Approaches to IT Capability, Key Stage 3*. Coventry: NCET.

—— (1995f) *Music: Approaches to IT Capability, Key Stage 3*. Coventry: NCET.

—— (1995g) *Science: Approaches to IT Capability, Key Stage 3*. Coventry: NCET.

Ruthven, K. (1984) 'Computer literacy and the curriculum', *British Journal of Educational Studies*, 32(2): 134–47.

SCAA (Schools Curriculum and Assessment Authority) (1995) *Information Technology and the National Curriculum: Key Stage 3*. London: SCAA.

Smith, R. and Alred, G. (1993) 'The impersonation of wisdom', in D. McIntyre, H. Hagger and M. Wilkin (eds), *Mentoring: Perspectives on School-based Teacher Education*. London: Kogan Page.

Somekh, B., Blackmore, M., Blythe, K., Byrne Hill, G., Clemson, D., Coveney, R., Davis, N., Jessel, J., Taylor, C. and Vaughan, G. (1992) 'A research approach to information technology development in initial teacher education', *Journal of Information Technology for Teacher Education*, 1(1): 83–100.

Chapter 13

Do electronic communications offer a new learning opportunity in education?

Niki Davis

Electronic communication has become one of the newest strategies to support learning. The most important aspect of this is the ability for learners and teachers to communicate and to collaborate regardless of time and distance. Of course, the printed word has permitted this for many years, but books and other writings are usually 'finished' static communication. In contrast computer-mediated communication can permit learners in many locations and time zones to collaborate and support each other in their learning. This chapter provides an overview of recent applications and reports on the ways in which electronic mail and other applications have been used in the classroom. However, most of the chapter is devoted to an illustrated discussion of applications to support student teachers and the continuing professional development of teachers.

BACKGROUND

Over the last fifteen years or so communication mediated by computers has grown in volume and variety. Many of these computer systems have been connected with one another and those networks have linked to form a vast global network, often called the Internet. The original Internet served the needs of researchers. Today there is wider participation. The process is continuing to expand rapidly and to merge with many aspects of cable, telephone and satellite networks, resulting in the concept of Information Superhighways around the world (DfEE, 1995). This futuristic communications channel is frequently perceived as containing valuable information on just about any topic, within and outside the curriculum. It also provides flexible messaging system between millions of people, including researchers and other experts. Additional services such as video conferencing, leisure and commercial activities are also developing rapidly. The aim is lifelong learning, hopefully including the professional development of teachers.

By 1996 electronic communications had proved their value to enhance learning, but most activities have been outside the normal curriculum. In future, the structure of teaching and learning may change to permit communications technologies to play as important a role in education as they do in commerce. This chapter reviews evidence of progress towards achieving such potential, and the knowledge and understanding that teachers and their managers will require to permit such an achievement. Teaching and learning opportunities which become available through electronic communications are described, including a brief outline of the services and a range of case studies of their application to education for the purposes of enhancing the curriculum and professional development of teachers.

APPLICATIONS OF ELECTRONIC COMMUNICATIONS

There is a wide range of applications of electronic communications to teaching and learning, as shown in the box. They range from information banks to individual communication as a conduit for information. At one end of the range, banks of information are available from which teachers and learners can retrieve information much as they do from libraries. The difference is that access and volume are virtually unlimited. Many of the world's university library catalogues are available to search. Although it isn't possible to pick a book off a shelf, the full text of other files is available, including abstracts of published work, data from space missions and regional information from many parts of the world. Some information can be up-to-the-minute, for example news services or weather map 'movies' of the previous twenty-four hours. In August each year in the UK a timely service called ECCTIS provides up-to-date information enabling students to match their exam results with the remaining places available in higher and further education.

Electronic communications can be used in a 'store and forward' mode, rather like a mixture between a library catalogue and an answering machine. Participants connect to their host computer to collect and send information at a time that suits them. The host computer can also be considered as a link to remote equipment. This has frequently been a large computer; for example, NASA make a supercomputer in the USA available to schools, and access to surveillance cameras, telescopes and microscopes is also possible.

Electronic communications can also be used in real-time mode, with both participants on-line at the same time; it feels more like a telephone call. This point-to-point communication permits a range of applications including video conferencing and collaborative work using personal computers running the same programs. For example, video conferencing has also been used to link classes for discussions and to provide a 'remote' guest speaker, possibly through a satellite link. Further information on the technical aspects of electronic communications is provided by the National Council of Educational Technology (NCET, 1994), and a range of services and facilities in relation to open and distance learning is described in Mason (1994).

Learners in all phases of education may also publish their work in such systems. Over 10 megabytes per day of discussion messages were flying between universities in May 1994 and since then the growth has been exponential. These messages are between groups as well as individuals. Classes can be linked to work

Telecommunication activities in education: from information retrieval to information provision

Banks of information

- many of the world's library catalogues are available to search on the Internet;
- files on current issues produced for research or 'political' purposes;
- government and regional information.

Real artefacts to use

- full texts of newspapers or Reuters' pre-published material;
- full texts of classical books;
- weather and acid rain data in the form of Quicktime movies.

Resources to use from a distance

- super-computing;
- simulations;
- scientific, geographic and mathematical data.

Project work

- newspaper days with news collection and publication;
- projects on current or historical issues;
- science or mathematics projects promoting learner participation.

Discussions to monitor and/or join in (or advise, manage, etc.)

- computer education issues;
- teacher education, e.g. science;
- getting to know learners in different places, e.g. Kidsnet.

Teaching of a topic

- presentation of a paper or an argument, possibly by video conference;
- collaborative teaching/learning of a set of related topics;
- demonstration and/or workshop using IT tools at a distance.

Individual communication

- feedback on assessment, teaching, etc.;
- collaborative writing of papers, grants, etc.;
- asking for a specific piece of information, appointment or help.

collaboratively. Others comprise less formal interest groups; they post messages on a particular theme on a communal electronic notice board. Individuals using the Internet include electronic pen pals and those negotiating their collaborative work. That is the other end of the continuum of electronic communications: the ability to send messages to individuals or groups around the world for immediate reception or collection at the convenience of the reader.

Electronic communications are also used for management purposes. Many universities describe their courses on the World Wide Web, which is a colourful part of the Internet. Within universities, campus-wide information services permit the electronic publication of directories, calendars, minutes and discussions. Schools are also developing similar provision of information. In addition, a national service provided by British Telecommunications (BT) called Campus Connect provides management services, including the ability to transmit exam entries directly to examination boards. These management applications are not the focus of this chapter and so will not be discussed further. However, it should be noted that curriculum applications may enhance management applications and vice versa. This is because the information and equipment can be used for dual purposes. For example, students can design – and update – information to publicise their school.

Unfortunately, it seems that every time a new opportunity is created it is accompanied by a threat. In this case increased access is accompanied by unauthorised and possibly malicious use. Access without authorisation is called hacking and is a criminal offence. Students need to become educated in their responsibilities with electronic communications just as they are in other aspects of personal social and moral education, and educational institutions need to take security precautions in the use of electronic information, just as they do with other valuable items on the school premises.

THE POTENTIAL FOR TEACHING AND LEARNING

There is a wide range of applications that support teaching and learning. I will take one in detail to illustrate the ways in which teachers and their institutions have developed good practice with electronic communications.

One American service, AT&T Learning Network, which became available in the UK during 1994, provides a managed facility. Dial-up access to the Internet is complemented by technical support and curriculum guidance, including project management and student materials. Classes which enrol are placed in a Learning Circle with about six others (at least one of which is overseas) and they all work on the same theme. Co-ordination, provided by AT&T, identifies clear stages, including guidelines for good social behaviour and deadlines within project work to ensure a positive learning experience which is celebrated with a joint publication by all involved. The stages acknowledge that it takes time to get ready, to open a collaborative enterprise, and to permit everyone to plan their own part of the project before exchanging work. The final publication is a collaborative venture arising from this work. Margaret Riel (1994) has researched the value of this activity in relation to the skills that employers find valuable. Her findings show that these activities foster the knowledge and skills that employers say they want, such as good communication skills and the ability to work in teams.

There are several general themes for Learning Circles which capitalise on the different perspectives and resources available to share across the locations. For example, 'Places and perspectives' encourages students to explore the history, culture, government and geography of their region and to compare it with their distant peers. In introducing students to Learning Circles the curriculum guide provides sound advice for all those who use electronic communications in education:

> Tell your students that they will be working co-operatively with student teams in distant locations to carry out the Learning Circle projects. Encourage them to take their roles seriously as the information they will provide will represent themselves, their school and their community to others. Everyone is both teacher and learner in Learning Circles.
>
> (Riel, 1990, p. 14)

Teachers and students are encouraged to exchange information about themselves by electronic message and ordinary post. The addition of a small amount of personal information, or 'colour', at the end of messages brings the communications alive, adding both context and culture. This view of other people is one of the most powerful aspects of using electronic communications, but is difficult to measure. Each group of students (or an individual) sponsors a project, such as 'Regional legends and local history'. According to Margaret Riel, all teachers and students find this collaborative work exciting. The quality of learning and the final joint publication benefit from comparative data from other locations and this raises self-esteem. The quality of peer learning during the six-week projects can be seen from this interchange between students and their teacher:

> 'Hey, Nainoa, Kawehi, Nohea! Look what we got from Texas. They are studying anthropology and want us to write about marriage and families in native Hawaiians.'
>
> 'Look did you see the answers to the questions that kids in Utah asked about Alaska? They describe what it is like to live without sunlight. I just can't imagine that.'
>
> 'This one says "a question for Hawaii". What is it?'
>
> 'They want to know if, by early settlers, we mean the Native Americans or the Puritans. I guess we would want to know about both. What do you think?' . . .
>
> 'Mrs Tanaka, can Albert and I write back about life comparisons in the 60s and 90s for Canada's project? We already interviewed my uncles and aunts.'
>
> 'I think that would be great. I am impressed to hear that you already did the interviews.'
>
> (Riel, 1990, p. 47)

In the UK we have similar services and BT's CampusWorld service is the parallel to AT&T's service. Like AT&T, CampusWorld has a national flavour. The cultural aspect can be used to good effect, helping students to learn to take an external view of their writing. Let me illustrate this with an account provided by one of CampusWorld's consultants. In this case the curriculum activity was the collaborative writing of a story in chapters. The editorial role was taken by one primary class who had generated the project and written the first chapter. They received a later chapter from one of their partner schools and the editorial team were discussing the dialogue provided for a Native American. It was an old-fashioned stereotypical view of a Red Indian as told to children a generation or two ago. One child in the group said that children in America might read their story: she would be unhappy with this view, if she were them. She brought the editorial group round to her view and they replied with a tactful message asking for changes in the chapter. They were dismayed to hear nothing for two weeks and feared that the writers had been offended. They need not have feared. The chapter was returned with a different ending which involved an alien. The apology explained that the delay was caused by a break in project work to take examinations.

This story also highlights a difficulty for schools. Synchronisation of project work across term times, which vary between region and country, required careful management. The Australian long 'winter' vacation is an extreme example. There are more local-organisational issues too.

Institutional management decisions strongly affect use of electronic communications. Teachers will be influenced in the ways in which they can connect to the Internet by the location of the computer system, the telephone line and the modem which connects the two. Part of the solution has been to place such resources in a central area such as the library with appropriate support staff to oversee individual student use as well as occasional use by larger groups. Another aspect of the solution is to empower students to send and receive messages on behalf of the group. As this requires senior management support many teachers have had to work more independently, with the result that the use of communications is restricted to their classroom. In Davis (1994), I describe three further case studies which took place in UK schools with the help of the teachers who applied them: European studies in secondary education, e-mail days for small primary schools, and a foreign languages 'newspaper day' in a secondary school.

Schools have traditionally received only one 'identity' for e-mail. Rarely have teachers had their own, unless as a result of their personal initiative. This has had an effect on the way in which individual and group work can develop. E-mail, like the personal computer, was designed for individual use. Artificial constraints arise when this one identity is shared. This is similar to the contrast between a school telephone line and the personal telephone on a manager's desk.

In many universities the converse applies and staff and students can have their own personal 'identity' and mail box. The computer system is able to support individuals, for example through facilities that enable them to mark messages that have been read and highlight items of personal interest. Where this occurs it is possible to develop lively discussions between individuals and groups.

POTENTIAL FOR PROFESSIONAL DEVELOPMENT

Professional development can be improved through the application of IT, especially communications. The best case is when IT enhances a teacher's learning. Most of the applications in the box on page 169 can be used for professional development. I have been involved in this area of research and development for over ten years. Perhaps the style could be described as development with research because, with my colleagues, we have tried to fit our perceptions of the potential of electronic communications to the needs of teachers and learners. This 'technical action research' is informed, at one end, by an exploration of the strengths and weaknesses of the communications channel, for example e-mail. At the other end, it is informed by observation and action of ourselves, our students and practising teachers. In this way we have developed a range of case studies which employ electronic communications in a way which demonstrates their educational value and identifies the new issues that they raise. Several case studies will now be described briefly, first within initial teacher education and then for the purposes of continuing professional development.

Initial teacher education

Collaborative approaches have proved worthwhile in initial teacher education. I have designed the application of electronic mail in several ways to stimulate student teachers to consider multicultural themes and to take a comparative view of education. The activities are cross-curricular in many ways: they develop IT and communication skills as well as collaborative work and a consideration of approaches to flexible learning. I will take two examples to illustrate this. The first originated in the USA in the form of a competition for teams of student teachers. The second was designed from a similar curriculum activity in the school classroom. (The e-mail day for small schools described in Davis, 1994, is the primary school version.) Both case studies were applied simultaneously to primary and secondary teacher education and thus also increased awareness across the phases of education.

The case competition

The University of Virginia has developed the use of case competitions to help teachers to learn how to behave according to a set of professional procedures. This has been adapted from professional training strategies for lawyers and doctors. In a case competition teams of teachers must work as a team to: identify issues in the case; consider the values and reasons underlying the actions of people; seek knowledge, and use it to develop a rationale for action with an accompanying forecast of courses of action and speculations of the consequences. Case competitions have taken place locally in the USA and there is an annual national competition in the University of Virginia. I observed a case competition in April 1994 and afterwards worked with colleagues to plan an electronic, or virtual, version.

The first international 'virtual case conference', held in May 1994, increased access to this mode of problem-solving teacher education by eliminating the need for teams to be on the same campus. Instead, the time scale of the competition was lengthened from a weekend to a month and communication took place electronically. Five teams of student teachers in three different countries took part. The student teachers considered the case of a newly qualified middle school science teacher in a school with a possible theft problem, when a group of 'playful' boys breaks a mercury thermometer. As is often the case, science was not her main teaching subject: 'She was worried about letting students conduct experiments, because so much could go wrong, and she wasn't comfortable with the subject matter' (Kent *et al.*, 1995, p. 142).

Teams in the USA, Canada and the UK considered the case, supported by on-line discussion with experts and each other. Each put together a reflective report analysing the situation and providing advice. As one of the tutors, I can confirm that the development of reflective practice and the students' growing understanding of comparisons between educational systems was a delight to observe. The project and its context are described in detail in Kent *et al.* (1995).

E-mail days

Projects for student teachers to encourage collaboration across courses, institutions and cultures have taken simpler thematic forms too. The first e-mail day for student teachers took place in November 1990 with a multicultural theme. This is a theme within all initial teacher education courses. The introductory briefing material was provided by Professor Tony Adams of the Department of Education, University of Cambridge. I was the overall project co-ordinator and taught several primary and secondary classes in Exeter. The third partner institution was the University of Linkoping in Sweden. The groups were introduced to the tasks and each other at the start. Thereafter, they worked in small groups, writing and using e-mail to:

- outline a plan for a lesson in their main subject which included the multicultural theme (week 1);
- provide constructive feedback to other students' plans (week 2);
- consider appropriate classroom management of an outburst of cultural tension (week 3).

There was a wide range of creative ideas across many subjects and age-groups. For example:

- Compare creation stories which explain the natural environment and surroundings in different cultures for 11–13 year olds (Cambridge).
- Class to make a collection of regional recipes possibly within a historical context and add some recipes from other cultures. Compare nutritional value (Exeter).
- Train pupils to inform themselves on subjects not available in texts for language training in English, French, German or Spanish. Train pupils to use e-mail as a means of getting really interesting information not imposed by the teacher (Linkoping, Sweden).

Recent applications

Cross-curricular activities such as these are now very difficult to arrange because of the time pressures imposed by increased school-based training. For this reason electronic communications are starting to take a different role: to link student teachers based in schools back to the university tutors and resources. In Exeter dial-up electronic communication via modems is being developed for three main purposes:

1. library access, including reservation of books;
2. support from the personal tutor and other students;
3. curriculum activities, through documents and messages for discussion groups.

Other university departments of education are also developing the use of electronic communications for similar activities (Attwood, 1994). In common with Exeter, they find that there are major organisational and access issues. In Exeter we have loaned a modem to partner schools to facilitate communication. However, shared access to a computer, modem and telephone line within a school can cause problems, and communication during the school day can be difficult for a student on teaching practice. The Open University has been able to overcome many of these issues in their part-time PGCE because they are using a distance learning mode of study. Student teachers are given a personal computer and a modem as part of the course and have sole use of it from home while studying. It is given to the host school on completion of the course. Many of these students make excellent use of discussion groups which are set up for them by the Open University (Sellinger, 1996). In addition to general topics each subject discipline has its own section. For example, science student teachers have been swapping lesson plans, worksheets and teaching strategies with occasional supportive, provoking or reflective messages from their tutors.

CONTINUING PROFESSIONAL DEVELOPMENT

One of the main benefits of electronic communications listed by US teachers has been the development of their teaching and reflection on the process of learning, even where the school curriculum is the main focus (Honey and

Henriquez, 1993). Therefore activities described in the previous section have an effect on teachers' professional development. Electronic communications can also be applied more directly. Several years ago I created what I called the UK national electronic network for pre-vocational education and training, called ResCue. It was created in association with all the further education Regional Curriculum Bases (RCB) across the UK. The aim of the network was to develop new practices in teaching and learning with an emphasis on basic skills in the context of vocational activities. This required teachers to change their practice and to develop resource-based learning with relatively few resources. ResCue was therefore designed to hold a catalogue of published resources which had been especially keyworded for basic skills and vocational topics. Each RCB held a collection of these resources for inspection and loan. A second catalogue held a collection of donated assignments in full text. Teachers were encouraged to collect this text and edit it to suit their students. Notice boards advertising in-service training events in each region were also available on-line. (More detail of ResCue can be found in Davis, 1988.)

ResCue's success on the Campus 2000 network service (now CampusWorld) was limited because relatively few teachers had the IT skills and confidence to make use of such a service. Many staff felt that the IT area of their college was 'out of bounds' to them. Somekh (1989) discusses these social and cultural contexts of schools that can hinder access to IT. However, access to IT is improving both in terms of skill and access. The political potential of the Information Superhighway appears to be giving rise to many new projects. Several in the USA are taking the approach of building a community of practice among teachers in the hope that it can become self-sustaining.

The first project which recognised the importance of building a community was probably LabNet. Ruopp *et al.* (1993) developed an approach which used electronic communications as a focus for the collaborative development of project-based active science and mathematics teaching. The LabNet community comprised over 1,200 science and mathematics teachers from the USA and Canada. Introductory face-to-face in-service workshops for teachers covered both science and telecommunications. The teachers then went back to their classrooms to change their approach to science teaching to one which set problems for their students and encouraged the students' active exploration of science concepts to solve them. This was such a major change of practice that the teachers needed support from others and wanted, like the student teachers in the UK Open University, to share ideas and resources. They also shared discussions of scientific concepts, complementing each other's knowledge of both science and pedagogy. Electronic links aim to support the development of a community of practice: the teachers shared their experiences and supported each other during the process of professional development. The central research and development team consider that electronic networks appear to offer the following vehicles for professional development (Muscella and DiMauro, 1995, p. 167):

- support for substantive reflective conversations;
- a particular focus (i.e. writing, science, school change, reflection on practice);
- creation of an environment that fosters colleagueship; and
- putting teachers at the helm of their own professional development.

The central LabNet team has been researching the aspect of collaboration with particular zeal because of its importance to the community. Muscella and DiMauro (1995) report a two-month-long conversation on scientific method, called 'Against method', in which science teachers hundreds of miles apart in Minnesota, California and Massachusetts 'delved into the nature of science, exploring how scientists develop and test their theories'. I agree with their opinion that it is hard to imagine this conversation taking place in any other but an electronic forum, except perhaps a university seminar. Science teachers are simply too isolated. However, such revitalising conversations must be worth striving for. Other forms of networked discussion for teachers are popping up all over the world. One example is the CONNECT network for Scottish teachers created by the Scottish Council of Educational Technology.

Potential of multimedia communications

Today new services are becoming available which provide intensive professional development 'on the job' using multimedia telecommunications. In Exeter we are developing case studies using telecommunication lines which can carry a range of media simultaneously, including telephone, multimedia and video. In this way the screens and video can be shared between a learner and a teacher or consultant. Together they can develop knowledge and skills in an intensive collaborative partnership. The Multimedia Communication Centre at Exeter has created a range of applications which can be seen in practice or on video (Wright, 1995). The range includes:

- cell biology;
- IT in education, e.g. CD-ROMs;
- psychometric testing and guidance;
- artist in virtual residence.

For example, Linda Baggott shared her electron micrographs which she had captured for fundamental research in reproductive biology. She used them to communicate new scientific concepts and practices to A level students and their teachers. Other services enhance school practice by developing an overview of the educational applications of complex software, CD-ROMs and the Internet itself. The session is accompanied by hands-on trial, with the consultant standing by to respond to the learner's needs. Occasionally the consultant or on-line teacher is a professional in a field other than education. For example, we have linked an artist to teachers and students in a school so that he could talk about his paintings, which were displayed on the computer screen from a PhotoCD. The artist is able to magnify a section of the painting and to use other software, an electronic whiteboard and video to illustrate techniques and concepts to the distant audience. The artist can also respond to the work done in schools because images, captured using a video camera, can be displayed on both screens. Again, the video can be enhanced using the software tools. This work is now being extended to enable viewing without the artist present. It is planned to hold high-definition pictures of artistic works and video interviews on a video server for dial-up access at any time. An appointment can also be made with the artist for a tutorial or seminar in 'real time'. I expect that many services will be created as the world Information Superhighways develop. Some may seem similar to a cable TV service, some will have a closer association with the familiar telephone, while others will be more closely derived from computer software and networks. In the future the medium carrying the signal will be of no consequence to the user and services will be run over a range of telecommunication channels. This is similar to today's telephone networks: the route and the bandwidth are immaterial as long as the signal is adequate.

Multimedia communications also appear to be valuable in the supervision of student teachers. Exeter has developed a model for the development of teaching which categorises into themes the complex process of becoming a teacher. This permits student teachers, the associated school staff and university staff to communicate more effectively. A focus for this communication is the 'conference' in which a student teacher articulates a chosen teaching episode. The student teacher designs the themes for this episode and the plan is produced in the form of an agenda for teaching. A teacher in the school annotates this agenda while observing the student teaching it. The annotated agenda forms the basis of the supervisory conference with the university tutor. The student may also gather pictures and student work to illustrate the episode. Early work using multimedia telecommunications for the supervisory conference with the university tutor suggests that the telecommunication enhances the student's reflection. We think this may be because the student teacher recognises that he or she must take the lead in preparing for the supervisory conference, and because of this, and the individual focus of the telecommunications link, the student gains more insight into the process of teaching and learning. There are also efficiency gains for the university staff involved as they do not have to undertake long journeys to supervise students. This can be a considerable gain of time and energy for staff in a rural environment who often have to travel for hours for a supervisory conference of half an hour.

USING ELECTRONIC COMMUNICATIONS EFFECTIVELY

In summary, electronic communications can open up the classroom, or a whole school, to the world. It can be a means to enhance and extend curriculum and professional development on-site and over time.

However, its use must be accompanied by increased responsibility of the learner and a consequent restructuring of the teaching process towards facilitation. The increased flexibility of learning will draw support staff into the process and they too require development and support. It is possible for there to be only one teacher using electronic communications in a school, but if the institution as a whole adopts the practice the potential is multiplied. Institutions with a shared resource collection/library should consider locating a set of the equipment and telephone line there, while remembering that sharing resources is never easy. Communications skills will be at least as important as technical IT skills in our future lives. Staff will need to know about relevant applications for electronic communications and best practice in their use. Given the wide range of applications, the best place to start will be to address a need or enthusiasm. In the longer term, electronic communications must address institutional needs because, in common with the telephone line, they are not a 'one-off' cost.

Institutions which balk at budgeting implications should note how vital electronic communications have become in commerce and leisure and realise that their potential in education has hardly been touched. The effect of information technology on organisations may be seen as similar to that of a catalyst promoting an evolutionary and then a revolutionary change (NCET, 1995). This is true of most IT applications and electronic communications are probably the most extreme example. Communication is a fundamental process of education. When the mode of communication changes, the organisation must change also. I have illustrated ways in which electronic communications can support both personal and group communication in many ways. Yet the potential has hardly been tapped. Once educational organisations have undergone a revolutionary change many more opportunities will open up for learners throughout their lives.

Electronic communications do offer new learning opportunities in education. In order to realise these opportunities the organisation of learning will change, hopefully developing learner autonomy and continuing professional development for all, including teachers. This is the goal: to develop today's Information Society into tomorrow's Learning Society; a society that will communicate through global Information Superhighways using electronic communications.

ACKNOWLEDGEMENTS

This chapter has been informed by research funded by International Computers Ltd (ICL), British Telecommunications plc, the Joint Information Systems Committee (JISC) of the UK Higher Education Funding Council, the Department for Education and Employment Learning Methods Branch, and the University of Exeter.

REFERENCES

Attwood, G. (1994) *Partnerships in Initial Teacher Education: An Overview of Recent Research Projects.* Coventry: National Council of Educational Technology.

Davis, N.E. (1988) 'Supporting professional development with IT networks', *Programmed Learning and Educational Technology*, 25(4): 344–7.

—— (1994) 'Electronic communication', in J. Underwood, *Computer-based Learning: Potential into Practice.* London: David Fulton, pp. 41–58.

DfEE (Department for Education and Employment) (1995) *Superhighways for Learning: A Consultation Document.* London: DfEE.

Honey, M. and Henriquez, A. (1993) *Telecommunications and K-12 Educators: Findings from a National Survey.* New York: Center for Technology and Education, Bank Street College of Education.

Kent, T.W., Herbert, J.M. and McNergeny, R.F. (1995) 'Telecommunications in teacher education: reflections on the first virtual team case competition', *Journal of Information Technology in Teacher Education*, 4(2): 137–48.

Mason, R. (1994) *Using Communications Media in Open and Flexible Learning.* London: Kogan Page, in association with the Institute of Educational Technology, Open University.

Muscella, D. and DiMauro, V. (1995) 'Talking about science: the case of an electronic conversation', *Journal of Information Technology in Teacher Education*, 4(2): 165–81.

NCET (National Council for Educational Technology) (1994) *Networks for Learning.* Coventry: NCET.

—— (1995) *Managing IT: A Planning Tool for Senior Managers.* Coventry: NCET.

Riel, M. (1990) *Learning Circle Curriculum Guide: Places and Perspectives. High School Level.* Newark, NJ: AT&T Learning Network.

—— (1994) 'The SCANS report and the AT&T Learning Network: preparing students for their future', *Telecommunications in Education News*, 5(1): 10–13.

Ruopp, R., Gal, S., Drayton, B. and Pfeister, M. (eds) (1993) *LabNet: Toward a Community of Practice.* London and Hillsdale, N.J.: Lawrence Erlbaum Associates.

Sellinger, M. (1996) 'Beginning teachers using IT: the Open University model', *Journal of Information Technology for Teacher Education*, 5(1).

Somekh, B. (1989) 'The human interface: hidden issues in computer mediated communication affecting use in schools', in R. Mason and A. R. Kaye (eds), *Mindweave.* Oxford: Pergamon.

Wright, B. (ed.) (1995) *Multimedia Communications Brokerage*, Report OL 229. Sheffield: Education and Training Technologies, Department of Education and Employment.

Part Three

The management of IT development in educational institutions

Introduction to Part Three

Parts One and Two of this book focus upon the importance of curriculum development and teacher professional development in using IT effectively in teaching and learning. The third vital ingredient is the development of the organisation to provide a *compatible* climate. The organisation will need to support and adopt changes taking place in the learning process. The three dimensions of innovation – curriculum, professional development and management of the organisation – can either support each other or cripple effective development. Innovation is unlikely to flourish in a restrictive environment. Project INTENT and the PALM project are among the few innovative projects with IT which have attempted to work with all three dimensions simultaneously. It seems that a failure to attempt this integrated approach is one reason for the patchy nature of IT in education today.

Part Three of our book is written for teachers as well as managers, because we maintain that the best team for the effective management of IT is one whose members span different roles and responsibilities in the organisation. The reflective approach taken by managers in these final chapters is similar to that advocated for teachers and teacher educators in the first two parts of the book. This is not surprising, since development is about learning and change and requires the same kind of support for participants whatever its setting. One head teacher described his use of action research to develop a collegiate management style in school as follows:

> At the start of the project my role as researcher/head was fully involved in the cycle as I outlined the research and put some of my plans into action. In the second stage I was able to withdraw a little as staff took on activities related to the research. In the final stages my role becomes fully absorbed as I become a participant in the action research rather than a leader of it.
>
> (Bone, 1993, p. 76; quoted in Lomax and Parker, 1995)

The development of IT in educational institutions is rarely a one-step transformation. The National Council for Educational Technology's Educational Technology Project developed a model of change through IT that can be used to support schools and possibly university departments of education (NCET, 1995). The model describes five stages of IT deployment:

1 localised;
2 co-ordinated;
3 transformative;
4 embedded;
5 innovative.

The model moves from an evolutionary stage in levels 1 and 2 through a transitional stage into a revolutionary change in levels 4 and 5. The revolution is of school organisation, and the range of potential benefits accruing from IT increase with the level. This model is based on a business model developed during the 1980s by MIT's 90s Research Group (ICL, 1992) with support from NCET's project. The NCET document also offers guidance to managers. This starts with a recommendation to map their organisation on to the five levels of the model. They are then encouraged to initiate a variety of actions with the aim of harmonising the school's profile and moving it forward (NCET, 1995, p. 8, Figure 2).

Our approach in this part of the book also focuses on strategies for managers and those managed, but the style is different. The authors of each chapter describe and analyse their experience, providing a picture of the complex process of management, together with the strategies that proved useful and the issues that arose in particular contexts. This approach recognises that the context of each organisation is unique and that management builds upon this. Therefore, the specific examples provided here are intended to give readers ideas which can be adapted to their own context – the more easily because they are rich in detail rather than being broad, generalised recipes of the kind often found in books on management.

The first chapter, by Bridget Somekh, Geoff Whitty and Rod Coveney, outlines the two-level partnership between a senior manager and those who led the development of IT in the five institutions involved in Project INTENT. It provides a fascinating look behind the scenes – one which only became visible to the actors after the first year or two. The contrast in management styles constructs and sharpens the issues. The importance of micropolitical factors is explored to achieve a better understanding of the management of change. Key concepts and strategies are derived empirically, and then compared and contrasted with some well-known theories of innovation.

In Chapter 15 Rod Coveney, one of the Project INTENT managers, compares and contrasts two major innovation processes which were implemented in Worcester College of Higher Education at the same time – a higher education quality audit and a development project (Project INTENT). Most educational organisations have had increasing audit pressures from bodies interested in quality such as the Office for Standards in Education (OFSTED). In these days of financial and other pressures, it is interesting that Rod notes the similarity between the two approaches in terms of cost and staff time, and that both caused 'latent hernias' which had to be managed. Project INTENT, however, had an action research approach which proved to be important to the continuing development of teaching and learning in the College. From Rod's personal standpoint the value of the staff development, for him as a manager, arising from Project INTENT was considerable.

IT resources require management across a department and an institution. Chris Taylor provides an overview of the issues facing senior managers and IT co-ordinators in deciding what to buy, how to deploy it and what kind of support to provide for users. The focus is on the provision of IT resources for curriculum purposes, but many of the issues discussed are also relevant to the use of IT in administration. The conflicting demands of accommodation, security, safety, staff and curriculum development must all be managed within the financial constraints of education. The process is ongoing and cannot be left to the 'techie' as it is so closely related to teaching and learning itself.

In Chapter 17, Jon Pratt describes an approach to teacher appraisal which maximises opportunities for staff development and organisational change. He begins by analysing the changing role of head teachers as a result of increased pressures upon schools and greater internal control over budgets. Many schools are required to collect and confront significant amounts of evidence about their practices for the first time. He draws upon his extensive experience of appraisal training and consultancy with schools, showing in particular how the methods and techniques associated and pioneered through action research are being brought into the mainstream of management practice – especially in relation to IT.

The final chapter of the book focuses on an integrated approach to staff and institutional development. Niki Davis describes strategies which were used successfully within Project INTENT, and complements these with examples taken from partner schools. The strategies involve work with three interrelated sets of stakeholders:

- committees and managers to promote the development of IT policy and resources;
- teachers and tutors to encourage adoption of IT and development of its use;
- support staff (and contexts) to enhance teaching and learning.

The process of professional development is three-fold: it involves the initiators of change (sometimes called the 'change agents'), the stakeholders and the institution. The latter only exists in terms of the interrelating roles and relationships of the first two. As they learn more about each other's aims and contexts, they gain the information and understanding which enable them to adapt their practice and begin to change the organisation(s) within which they work. We hope that this book will encourage you, the reader, to engage in these processes and to become a learner constructing new practice in both personal and social contexts.

REFERENCES

Bone, D. (1993) *How Can I Develop a Collegiate Management Style in School and Encourage the Senior Management Team to Fully Involve Staff?* MEd dissertation, Kingston University, Kingston-upon-Thames, Surrey.

ICL (International Computers Ltd) (1992) *A Window on the Future*. ICL Briefing for Management on the Findings of the Management in the 1990s Research Programme. London: ICL.

Lomax, P. and Parker, Z. (1995) 'Accounting for ourselves: the problematics of representing action research', *Cambridge Journal of Education*, 25(3): 301–14.

NCET (National Council of Educational Technology) (1995) *Managing IT: A Planning Tool for Senior Managers*. Coventry: NCET.

Chapter 14

IT and the politics of institutional change

Bridget Somekh, Geoff Whitty and Rod Coveney

The management of change across a whole institution is never easy. Managers often have an important role in facilitating change, but theirs is by no means the only one. They certainly cannot bring about effective change without the involvement of others, nor are they necessarily the key people in initiating it. Ironically, change is often made more difficult because managers concentrate on trying to get other people to change, not realising that they may need to begin by changing their own management strategies – and probably also some aspects of organisational structure. In the light of this, we hope that the experiences described in this chapter will be of interest not only to managers – whether they be in schools or university departments – but also to those lower down in the organisational hierarchy who can carry change forward much more easily if they develop skills in 'managing their managers' (sometimes known as 'upward management'). Our particular concern here is the introduction of information technology across a whole institution, but the approach to managing change that we describe is also applicable to other innovations, including the difficult, but all too familiar, situation when many innovations are being introduced at the same time.

Popular books on management tend to present a mixture of wise precepts and prescriptions for action. Our own experience of management has led us to believe that these are often too general to be of much use, so in this chapter we want to do something rather different. The aim of the chapter is to describe an approach to managing change that may be of practical value, while stressing that, since no two institutions are the same, the approach will always need to be adapted to fit the context in which it is being applied. To enable readers to do this, we think it is important to present a detailed analysis of the impact of this approach in an actual case where it has been tried out. This will entail consideration of some of those less tangible features, such as institutional culture, management style and micropolitics, that are often neglected but in reality play a crucial role in either supporting or blocking the change process. Although the example we use is drawn from higher education (HE) institutions, much of the research that went into developing our ideas was carried out in secondary schools. (See, in particular the Support for Innovation Project funded by the Employment Department and Suffolk and Norfolk LEAs between 1986 and 1988: Somekh, 1988; SIP, 1989.)

COMMON PROBLEMS IN INTRODUCING INFORMATION TECHNOLOGY ACROSS AN INSTITUTION

Very few educational institutions have so far managed the introduction of information technology across the whole institution effectively. 'Patchy' was the word Her Majesty's Inspectorate (HMI) used to describe the use of IT in initial teacher training institutions (ITTEs) in its 1988 report, and at various times over the last five years it has proved notoriously difficult to find examples of whole schools using IT effectively when there has been a specific need (e.g. for purposes of evaluating the effectiveness of government initiatives, or to develop tests for the IT attainment targets in the National Curriculum). Although many institutions have made some progress, effective change in IT across the whole institution appears to be inherently difficult. There seem to be four main reasons for this, which are outlined below.

Cultural alienation and stereotyping

Most people who have never used a computer make assumptions about its purposes and use. These are culturally constructed. Computers emanated originally from the world of engineering, and their appearance – and in some cases their mode of operation and language on the screen – still belongs to the engineering culture. Those who develop expertise in computer use acquire a technical language and in-front-of-screen behaviours which serve to set them apart from novices, and give them a sense of power that they frequently learn to turn to advantage. (Often there may be very tangible pay-offs in terms of career opportunities.) Specialists in disciplines such as literature, history or art cannot feel at home in this environment until they bring their own uses to it and 'make it their own'. It is not far-fetched to say that frequently the computer conjures up for them, subliminally, the ubiquitous machines of science fiction and the implied threat of a future depersonalised, or even dehumanised. Gender further complicates the issue since many men and women have a tendency to see computers as the province of the male. The vehemence with which some people reject computer use, and the real difficulties and therefore high costs of giving them 'training', are indicators of the extent to which the computer is perceived to threaten their culture and values.

Compartmentalisation

In the early days, computers typically came into secondary and HE educational institutions through the mathematics department or, more rarely, the science department. However, because of the departmental divisions in the institutional structure and hierarchy, the normal progress was towards establishing separate departments of computer studies. Individuals were duly appointed to be heads of these new departments and given charge of the computers and the keys which locked the computer room (often called a laboratory, which served to underline the computer's cultural origins). The expectation was firmly established that computers were a specialist discipline rather than a general tool, and it has proved very difficult to change this perception. All cross-curricular initiatives are hard to establish in institutions with a departmental structure (e.g. 'language across the curriculum' following the Bullock Report: DES, 1975) and information technology is probably no worse in this respect than others (Whitty *et al.*, 1994). Nevertheless, in the late 1980s the very people who might have led whole school development were often reluctant to do so, sensing that it would undermine their own power base by effectively taking away their rooms, machines, subject discipline and specialist examination teaching.

Equitable allocation of resources

Computers, of course, are expensive. In any institution the allocation of money is part of a political process, contested by different interest groups. It highlights issues of power and serves to delineate management style. This means that even if senior managers retain the power to allocate sizeable sums of money (which they often do not, depending instead on a committee-based decision-making structure), they make decisions about its allocation on the basis of a large number of stated and unstated considerations. These are likely to include established budgeting traditions, perceived fairness, the informal standing of the individuals concerned (are they liked by colleagues?), 'trade-offs' for services rendered, bargaining for services required, and so on. This creates a 'catch 22' situation for IT: it is only when all colleagues across the institution have adequate access to computers that they will perceive money allocated to purchase computers to be well spent, but without considerable resources being allocated this precondition can never be met. The exception, of course, is the maverick principal who has decided to make IT the central plank of the school's development and a marketing strategy in its own right. There are one or two well-known examples of this among secondary schools, such as Stanley Goodchild's Garth Hill during the 1980s which capitalised on its location in the Berkshire 'silicon belt'. However, even City Technology Colleges, with generous funding and new forms of school organisation, have not always used their lavish IT resources to best effect in the classroom (Whitty *et al.*,1993, p. 119).

Responsibility without power

It is common practice in most institutions to give special responsibilities to individuals for some aspects of the corporate endeavour. In institutions with a line management structure there is usually a group of people who share this responsibility, working to the head of department or sector leader. A problem commonly arises when responsible individuals do not have control of adequate resources or decision-making powers to put in train the necessary action to fulfil their responsibility. This problem, summed up by the phrase 'responsibility without power', is much more common in relation to IT for two reasons: first, the amount of money needed to establish, and thereafter to maintain, IT equipment is much larger than that needed for most other aspects of institutional work; second, the cross-curricular nature of IT means that, in order to be effective, the IT co-ordinator in secondary schools and initial teacher education establishments needs to be able to influence not only members of the IT department but all colleagues across all departments.

Even in primary schools where there is no departmental structure, the wide-ranging responsibility to work with *all* colleagues is difficult to fulfil. For both these reasons, effective management of change in IT may only be possible with the active involvement of at least one member of the senior management team who has some capacity to work across departmental boundaries. But that is not to say that change has to be an entirely management-led undertaking. Rather, those initiating change from below need to be able to draw upon the resources of management at key points if their efforts are not to be continually frustrated by the very features of organisational structure and culture that need to be changed.

PARTNERSHIP IN THE MANAGEMENT OF CHANGE: A TWO-LEVEL APPROACH TO WHOLE INSTITUTIONAL DEVELOPMENT

To address these problems and thereby manage the development of IT effectively within the participating institutions, the Initial Teacher Education and New Technology Project (INTENT) adopted an approach to IT development based upon Fullan's model of educational change (see below). An action research methodology provided the opportunity to research the effectiveness of the resulting change process within participating initial teacher education establishments.

INTENT's aims were to enable all tutors – regardless of their subject specialism and of whether their focus was on primary or secondary teaching – to prepare student teachers to use computers in their teaching of children. They went well beyond developing improved specialist courses in computer use or computer awareness. The implication was that all tutors should use computers in their own teaching of student teachers as well as in the preparation of teaching materials, and should be ready to supervise student teachers using computers either on teaching practice in schools or on occasions when children and their teachers came into the higher education institution (see Somekh, 1993). These aims were ambitious, given the state of IT development in ITTEs in 1990. However, the project was timely since the criteria for accreditation of initial teacher education courses required all students to acquire IT competences (DES, 1989); in that sense the project's aims fitted an urgent need of the participating ITTEs.

In developing strategies for putting these aims into practice, the project co-ordinator was strongly influenced by the ideas of Fullan, although this was often not a conscious influence and was never made explicit to other members of the team. In his book *The Meaning of Educational Change* (1982), Fullan emphasises the complexity of the social processes of change. Individuals at all levels – teachers, students, heads, inspectors, local and national policy-makers – have significant roles to play if change in practice is actually to occur. In particular, those responsible for implementing change need to 'make sense' of what it is about and why it is being suggested. This 'personal meaning' is essential because of the strong link between the commitment to change of teachers (and other professionals) and their professional values. Fullan also stresses the importance of 'integrating general knowledge of change with detailed knowledge of the politics, personalities and history peculiar to the setting in question' (Fullan, 1982, p. x). He draws upon a considerable body of research to illustrate the 'multivariate nature of change', that is, its dependence for successful implementation upon people at different levels in an institution and the large number of expected and unexpected ramifications that it gives rise to. He points out the importance of an educational innovation being seen by those concerned as 'authentic' in the sense that its main purpose is to improve educational practice. There may be many reasons for an educational innovation being suggested (to cut costs, promote good public relations, further the career of one or more individuals) and it may be reasonable for teachers to resist an innovation if they do not consider it to be educationally worthwhile.

Fullan sets out the classic stages of an innovation:

- its source (where did the idea come from and why?);
- its adoption (the decision of an institution to initiate the work);
- its implementation (teachers and students putting the new ideas into practice);
- its institutionalisation (changes in practice established as the norm so that they will continue without any special support).

He describes each of these stages in detail, exploring likely problems and giving practical advice drawn from research evidence on how to tackle them and on the importance of the roles of all the different players. He stresses the importance of staff development and participation, good relationships between teachers, support from the head, a clear time-line, good communications and an internal (or local) consultant to support teachers. Among several examples of successful change, he describes the action research approach of John Elliott (1976, 1979) and says that this 'indicates that collaborative research between an outsider and teachers on practical and theoretical aspects of instruction can constitute a fundamental staff development experience' (Fullan, 1982, p. 270).

In the light of Fullan's model, there were several features of Project INTENT which served to develop the team's commitment to the aims of the project and the outcomes of its action research, including writing for publication. First, the project had high-level endorsement. The funding from the National Council for Educational Technology (NCET), and the interest of HMI in its progress, acted as instrumental imperatives for senior managers 'who had taken the money and felt an obligation to deliver'. Second, it was perceived by participants to be 'authentic' in Fullan's sense. An intrinsic commitment to the project's aims developed which, as one team member put it, 'shone through and carried us along when times got "sticky"'. Third, while the institutional goals were diverse, there was a strong sense of corporate vision and corporate responsibility. In part this was because the co-ordinator offered direction and leadership to the team, but also because she 'used' the strengths of different team members – and the respect in which they were held by others – to develop commitment and vision. Fourth, the project in many ways modelled its own message, in the sense of valuing the contributions of all equally, adapting its management strategies according to need, changing its organisational structures as necessary, and encouraging upward management within the institutional teams. These same strategies were then applied in the individual institutions to a greater or lesser extent.

The significant elements of the INTENT approach to IT development, based upon Fullan's analysis of the innovation process, and also upon the work of Elliott (1976, 1979, 1980, 1991, 1993a, 1993b) consisted of:

- individual decision-making within each institution about the exact focus of development work and strategies to put it into action (*to ensure a fit with local needs and institutional culture*);
- a senior manager in each institution working in close collaboration with a staff development tutor (or two half-timers) (*to ensure high-level support and good communications*);
- the staff development tutor relieved of course teaching responsibilities for a year in order to support colleagues in using IT (*to provide internal consultancy*);
- a second project year during which work continued without external funding for the staff development tutor (*to encourage the shift from implementation to institutionalisation*);
- action research (of a kind) carried out by both the 'senior manager' and the staff development tutor into the effectiveness of their own roles in promoting IT development (*to ensure staff development and the development of 'personal meaning'*);
- tutors who were encouraged to carry out action research into their use of IT (*to support staff development and the development of 'personal meaning'*);
- residential meetings of the inter-institutional team of senior managers and staff development tutors (*support and co-ordination in the widest possible sense*);
- external support from a full-time national co-ordinator (*support and co-ordination*).

In the remainder of the chapter we will examine the impact of this approach to change upon practice. By focusing on what actually happened in five initial teacher training establishments we hope to indicate the complexity of the power play between factors such as declared purposes and local cultures; organisational policies and individual needs; organisational structures and personal power; and the project's vision and the institutional vision. We hope these accounts will enable readers to draw preliminary conclusions about which aspects of the approach could be applied in their own contexts.

We will then use these accounts to draw some conclusions of our own and suggest some key factors about the process of change which we learnt from carrying out this work. In the final section these ideas will be discussed briefly in the light of the changes in Fullan's theory of innovation set out in the revised edition of his book (Fullan, 1991).

THE FIVE ITTES

In order to provide an insight into the various contexts in which Project INTENT was carried out, we provide some brief sketches of the participating institutions. These concern the styles of management employed in each institution and the strategies adopted by some of the key individuals and groups involved. For purposes of anonymity, the term ITTE (initial teacher training establishment) is used throughout, and the title 'principal' for the most senior manager with responsibility for teacher education.

ITTE A

ITTE A was led by a strong principal of great personal charm, a skilful negotiator on the national scene who had impressed the sponsors with her commitment to IT development even before the project was announced and bids to participate were invited. The ITTE, which was part of the then polytechnics and colleges sector of HE, was organised hierarchically with some power devolved to committees, the most significant of which for the project was the Learning Resources Committee whose Chair was appointed to the role of INTENT staff development tutor. During the time of the project the larger institution of which the ITTE was part was re-restructured (in a two-stage exercise over several months) from eleven 'schools' into four divisions and in the process the post of deputy principal of the ITTE was removed. There was considerable uncertainty at this time for a number of individuals about the security of their posts. The ITTE, however, achieved the status of a division, which we speculate might have been less likely if the principal had been less politically astute. The principal's management style *vis-à-vis* the project could be described as 'benign, hands-off interest'.

ITTE B

ITTE B was led by a strong principal with a clear vision for institutional development. The ITTE was an institution in its own right (with affiliations to a university) and management was hierarchically organised in a line management structure with some powers vested in powerful committees. The principal could wield exceptional powers on occasions but normally worked through the formal decision-making channels (e.g. in the case of one difficult issue he said, 'Fortunately, I didn't have to make that decision alone'). During a time of economic recession this ITTE was undertaking considerable building works as a result of the entrepreneurial talents of the principal. There was also a great deal of curriculum innovation, of which the development of IT and the work of the project were a part. The principal's management style could be summed up as opportunistic, entrepreneurial and politically astute leadership. He had a concept of the management of change as a two-stage process in which he himself played two distinct roles: first came the pioneering stage during which he led from the front, mapped out the vision, nurtured individuals and exercised exceptional powers as needed; then came the stage when the innovation had become part of the formal policy and structures of the institution when he retreated to 'the crow's nest' and offered perhaps 'counselling' but no further special treatment ('The principal is making me fight for every member of staff – so nobody can turn round and say, "It was handed to you on a plate"'). He saw himself as having particular skills 'in getting things moving', but described his role in day-to-day management as that of the non-expert (neither an academic nor a conventionally trained manager), 'able to listen and see where things can be encouraged and facilitated . . . but bowing to others' greater experience or more specialised knowledge'.

ITTE C

ITTE C which had originated from the amalgamation of a university and a teacher training college in the 1970s did not have a formal line management structure. Instead, power was formally vested in committees of academics in which all had an equal voice; and informally vested in the three 'active' members of the five-person professorial team who could, if necessary, take decisions without recourse to the formal structures, although they used these powers only with caution. This ITTE was led by a powerful professor with a national reputation as a media commentator. He placed a high priority on research and defended the right of individuals to pursue their own 'enthusiasms'. His approach to institutional development was one of 'establishing through strengths', one of which happened to be IT (he named three colleagues as having 'international reputations' in the field). He was not prepared to coerce individuals to put time into initiatives which did not interest them, although he emphasised individuals' obligation to self-management of their own professional development and was prepared to use strategies such as generating pressure from students in order to create professional guilt and thereby 'lean on' people. His management style could be described as benign autocracy heavily disguised by strategic and political acumen. He had a strong sense of loyalty to the 'ethos' of the ITTE and the importance of guarding it as 'a place where people want to be'.

ITTE D

In ITTE D there were two management styles operating side by side. The principal headed up the old-style institutional structure of five relatively autonomous departments, with differential status in terms of teaching responsibilities and resources. Individualism was encouraged, and those who were active and favoured stood out from those who were inactive and largely unseen by management. Something of a 'club' culture had built up around the principal who had presided over what was seen as a 'golden age' of the institution. This existing organisational structure and culture had, however, been radically destabilised by the recent incorporation of the ITTE within a prestigious university, bringing major changes in staffing and resources. A requirement to develop research had become paramount and, alongside funding cutbacks and changes in government policy for initial teacher training, this was seen by many as posing a threat to the institution's reputation for teaching excellence. The appointment of a new professor – and principal-in-waiting – with an established reputation and considerable practical experience as former manager of another ITTE, was seen as presaging changes in both the structure and culture of this ITTE. INTENT provided this new professor, who was the INTENT manager, with a mechanism for promoting change. An interdepartmental committee was established to develop an agreed IT policy and promote IT development, together with departmental subcommittees involving (and thereby, in the view of one colleague, giving 'ownership' to) a large number of colleagues. To some people, this appeared to signal a shift towards a new coherence and more open management practices, while others viewed the development as rampant managerialism.

ITTE E

In ITTE E there was strongly devolved management. The principal of the ITTE remained remote from the project and effective management was in the hands of the INTENT manager, who held a senior position in the line management structure. Although decisions were normally taken according to due processes at committees, power was vested in post holders and 'fast track' action could be taken when needed. Great care was taken to embed the work of the project in the formal policies and structures of the ITTE, by ensuring that its arrival and progress were noted in the minutes of key meetings and by integrating its work with the work of particular course teams. The ITTE had an elaborate administrative structure, involving detailed paperwork in line with the expectations of the Council for National Academic Awards. However, paperwork did not appear to be produced cynically, but was used to develop policy and evaluate practice. The INTENT manager was, in the words of one colleague, 'trusted by everyone'. He had an unusual capacity to live with ambiguity rather than foreclose on decisions for the sake of convenience. He was always clear that the ITTE's central purpose was to provide high-quality learning experiences for its students, no matter what the difficulties. His management style can be summed up as reflexive, procedural but personalised, and imbued with a strong sense of morality and fairness. In the face of continuous pressure to change imposed from outside (revised criteria for accreditation of courses, new contracts for staff, shrinking resources, increasing student numbers, revisions of the national curriculum) he saw himself as playing the parts of 'plate-spinner in the circus act' and 'personal coach' (i.e. provider of individual support, coupled with uncompromising demands for the necessary action within the rules of the game).

INSTITUTIONAL ETHOS

The nature of Project INTENT was therefore different in each of the institutions, which had very distinctive histories, management styles and forms of organisation. Hoyle (1976) has identified some of the differences between bureaucratic and non-bureaucratic patterns of organisation in schools, which can be characterised as follows:

> *Bureaucratic (hierarchical)*
> Fixed and rigid roles for teaching staff
> Clear and definite rules for almost every eventuality
> Rigid timetabling, pupil grouping and curriculum division
> Head holds a lot of power
>
> *Non-bureaucratic (collegial)*
> Very few rules; those that do exist are general, allowing individual interpretation
> Flexible timetabling, pupil grouping and curriculum
> School policy decided by all teachers.
>
> (Cited in Halpin and Whitty, 1992)

No particular school is likely to be a pure example of either type of organisation, but there are many schools that tend in one direction rather than the other.

Much the same is true of higher education institutions. Traditionally, in 'old' university departments of education, professional autonomy and academic freedom have meant that line management is weak. Formally, decisions are usually made by elected committees or by vote of the entire faculty (e.g. at a meeting of the school board), but informally the professors have a great deal of power. In the former polytechnics and colleges, there has typically been a line management structure with a principal, senior management team and departments. A senior appointment (e.g. of a principal lecturer) has nearly always entailed taking on responsibility for leading a department or section (Somekh *et al.*, 1992).

While oversimplified, these descriptions are broadly recognisable in terms of the experience of Project INTENT which worked across the (then) polytechnic/ college and university sectors. Not only did the broad distinction made here between the traditions of the two sectors ring true, so also did the characterisation of the tension between the ideology and reality of the collegial model in some institutions. In particular, those institutions espousing a 'collegial' model were often perceived by more junior colleagues as examples of 'restricted' collegiality, in which the leader shared power with a limited number of colleagues, rather than 'pure' collegiality, in which all members had an equal voice in determining policy (Bush, 1995). Where collegiality is mediated through a committee structure, it may be the case that unless junior colleagues adopt the proactive role of 'extended professionals' (Hoyle, 1969) their potential for collegiality will remain latent. Effective collegiality, therefore, may be a function of extended professionalism, which of course needs to be nurtured by the institution.

These different traditions had an impact on how Project INTENT was conducted in different institutions. So too did the micropolitics of the various institutions. The study of 'micropolitics' concerns 'the overt and covert processes through which individuals and groups in an organisation's immediate environment acquire and exercise power to promote and protect their own interests' (Malen, 1994). No one contemplating change can ignore the micropolitical dimension in developing a strategy, and national projects like INTENT are only likely to be successful if they are sensitive to the micropolitics of the institutional settings in which they operate.

PROJECT INTENT IN ACTION

The project co-ordinator began with a commitment to something like 'pure' collegiality within the project team, while accepting that change within institutions would require institutional teams which recognised (but did not entirely succumb to) existing patterns of power and authority. It will be clear from the institutional sketches that some of the institutions involved in the project approximated to the collegial model and others to the bureaucratic one, even if, as indicated above, most of the 'collegial' institutions displayed 'restricted' rather than 'pure' collegiality (Bush, 1995). In most cases, the selection of the INTENT team reflected these characteristics. In the 'collegial' institutions, it was important to recruit as 'manager' someone of professorial status. In the more 'bureaucratic' institutions, the involvement of a senior line manager was required. Where the team that was selected to promote the innovation was too far out of line with these requirements problems were encountered.

The difficulties of adopting a 'collegial' approach within an institution with a line management structure were evident in the case of ITTE A. Here, the principal had the ultimate power over all major decisions (e.g. whether to buy PCs or Apple Macs for lecturers' personal use), which placed her in the position of receiving lobbyists and reaching considered decisions on the basis of the information given to her. As a result she was kept well-informed about INTENT's work because, as she put it, 'I think that [the INTENT staff development tutor and manager] have seen the political advantage of carrying your Principal along with you.' It is not clear whether she understood the project's developmental purpose and the need for all the research carried out under its auspices to be oriented towards promoting colleagues' professional development. Arguably she did not, as she selected for the role of staff development tutor a trusted and committed colleague with good organisational abilities who might have made an excellent 'INTENT manager' but who found it difficult to give colleagues 'tutorial' support since she had never been a school teacher and had – at the start of the project – only minimal IT skills. Inevitably, this led to disagreements between the staff development tutor and 'manager', who at the start of the project was not in a position of sufficient seniority to be able to unlock resources or steer the project through the formal committee structures of the ITTE; six months into the project, he was still negotiating with the principal for 'a slot at a management team meeting'.

During the first three months of the project it had been decided that the staff development tutor and the manager would reorganise the division of labour between them, and work more as a partnership of equals. Predictably, this led to a certain amount of tension between them. The principal clearly did not see any role for herself in acting as a broker between them in order to secure the project's purposes, but instead played the part of a detached observer, saying in March 1992 that she had noted disagreements between them, 'but I predicted that'.

By the end of the two years of the project the staff development tutor had made a considerable contribution to the project's research output by carrying out a series of surveys of student and staff attitudes towards IT and competences in using it, and the manager had contributed to a joint paper presented at a conference. However, in terms of the development of colleagues' confidence and competence with IT, there was arguably little result over and above what would have been achieved anyway (as the principal said, 'It's perhaps fortuitous that what we've been trying to promote internally has chimed with the external culture, although we wouldn't have tried if it hadn't looked likely to start with').

In terms of the development of the individuals who took the roles of staff development tutor and INTENT manager there appear to have been some positive pay-offs as, by the end of the project, both had been promoted to more responsible posts. But this suggests that the project had come to serve the needs of the pre-existing structure. What it did not appear to have done was to change the culture in any way that would have enabled the INTENT staff development tutor and manager to become an effective team, partly because it did not pay sufficient attention to the impact of that culture in the first place.

In an institution used to clear line management, the approach adopted produced continual irritation for both the staff development tutor and the INTENT manager over their roles. For example: who was 'managing' the project internally? should all communications to colleagues come from both individuals jointly? It is likely that the ambiguity could have been better tolerated within an institution with more collegial traditions.

ITTE C appeared superficially to be much more of a collegial institution. By and large, there was space in it for the two INTENT staff development tutors (one of whom was a new appointment and new to the processes by which the institution was managed) to be able to work with staff who wanted this, while not posing a major threat to two powerful individuals with international reputations for specialist research in the IT field who worked completely independently of them. Approximately 70 per cent of staff had been newly appointed in the past three years and almost all had some IT experience/skills. This meant that their professional development needs, although real, were not as acute as at other institutions. Partly because of this, ITTE C was the most advanced institution in the project in terms of IT use, sometimes wanting to engage in issues relating to more 'cutting-edge' technology than the others.

ITTE C had developed, however, a characteristically academic form of collegiality. There was a strong tradition of the rights and responsibilities of the individual. This meant that there was, almost universally, a pride in the traditions and national standing of the institution, but there was also a very strongly defined sense of 'the way things are done here' and it was easy for individuals to invoke this as justification for resistance to new ideas. The institution was very much a product of the people who worked there. This was a collection of creative, independent, clever people, many of whom could be abrasive and were, to varying degrees, inherently competitive. For a new member of staff coming from a much more bureaucratic institution, this was not always an easy place to work: suggestions made in open meetings were easily discounted – change could only be brought about by knowledge of the committee structures and astute lobbying: it helped to have personal charisma or a strong ally in high places. Hence, this was a place where it was difficult to restructure a course which involved a number of departments, because there was little tradition of interdepartmental planning. The focus for development provided by a national project could be useful in this context as a means of driving collaborative endeavour, and it was the opinion of one member of staff that 'the PGCE course would not have been restructured if it had not been for INTENT and the IT development work'.

Within this curious mixture of collegiality and rampant individualism, considerable power was vested in three powerful professors who had international reputations for research excellence and considerable status in the university as a whole. The active involvement of one of these three as INTENT 'manager' in the institution usually served to help INTENT and IT development more generally. However, a rhetorical commitment to 'pure' collegiality meant that the INTENT terminology of 'manager' was inappropriate in this context. Paradoxically, though, when this terminology was used, it led to frustration because it implied that staff development tutors were not managers. In reality, of course, collegiality was somewhat more restricted than the rhetoric suggested and occasionally the project became involved in a 'power play' between the professors. One of the three, the principal, provided strong leadership and a clear vision of the institution's commitment to excellence. He saw IT as having important educational potential, provided it was in the hands of good teachers who used it creatively to support students' learning. The twin goals of the institution were to achieve high standards in teacher training and excellence in research. Although the action research approach of the project was not the methodology commonly used by many of the lecturers for their own research, the emphasis the project placed upon research *per se* proved an effective incentive for colleagues to participate. The contribution of this institution to the INTENT publications was considerable, as were its achievements in terms of changes in teacher training practice. This breadth of achievement was a tribute to the flexibility and energy of the lead staff development tutor – who began work with serious doubts as to the value of action research. On the other hand, there was an energy and opportunism about the institution as a whole and Project INTENT fitted well with its twin goals.

In ITTE D there was also latent conflict between professors, but the institution was already sufficiently destabilised by other developments for INTENT to be able to take active advantage of the ensuing ambiguity. At the time of the project, both the staff development tutors were outsiders in terms of what Handy and Aitken (1986) might term the 'club culture' – 'rich in personality, mythical stories and folklore from the past' – that surrounded the current principal. In this respect they had little influence. However, one saw himself as having been part of the 'club' twenty years previously and had recently commented that he enjoyed his twenty-five years in the institution 'partly because I know everyone and can approach them directly'. The principal himself was known for an early book on IT in which he warned readers to guard against the potential evil of the computer-as-a-teaching-machine, while there were other staff with a strong interest in the social and political implications of IT. Although there were those with an interest in the applications of IT in design and technology, there was little encouragement to the staff as a whole to give it any priority. At the time when INTENT began, the two people who acted as joint staff development tutors were not part of any IT department and their obvious enthusiasm for IT was perceived by colleagues to arise from personal interest but not from any ambition for personal gain in terms of status or career.

The involvement of the new professor in INTENT meant that there was an opportunity for the enthusiasms of the staff development tutors to receive sponsorship at a senior level. Great emphasis was now being put on research as a result of the move into the university sector and the forthcoming 'research selectivity' exercise. In the absence of much funded research in the institution, it proved possible to characterise INTENT as a research – albeit an action research – project, which would generate publications as well as institutional change. The attempt to involve more staff in decision-making about IT than had usually been the case in the past could also be seen as a move towards a less-restricted form of collegiality. Initially, though, it was seen by many as a form of what Hargreaves (1994) has termed 'contrived collegiality' and was thus treated with suspicion not only by those with an investment in existing ways of doing things but also by those who were calling for the development of a more genuinely 'collaborative culture'.

One department appeared highly resistant to involvement in INTENT, partly as a defence of departmental autonomy and partly on the basis of prior negative experiences with IT. However, a cycle of implementation was agreed which allowed individual departments to develop their own action plans, with the help of the staff development tutors, and these were to feed into the development of an institution-wide action plan. This gave departments a greater sense of ownership and involvement in institutional change than they had experienced in the past.

It has to be recognised that the 'space' for this to happen resulted from the micropolitics of the relationship between the principal and his expected successor. The latter used INTENT as a sort of 'dummy run' for more far-reaching proposals for change. In the event, he left the institution before these could be implemented, but as far as IT was concerned, considerable progress (from a low-level start) appeared to have been made across a number of teaching areas by the time the project came to an end. A very different kind of 'space' for INTENT's development work was created by the unique partnership between the two staff development tutors and the fact that they made no claim to any particular power base. Their working relationship was one of trust and mutual support, in which they sometimes spent considerable periods of time together discussing ideas and planning joint initiatives, but also tolerated each other's idiosyncrasies. Since neither of them sought power within the institution, they were able to use the structure created by the principal-in-waiting to co-ordinate the efforts of colleagues without arousing serious animosity.

Most of the structural and micropolitical factors we have considered so far would apply to the reception given to any major innovation in the institutions concerned. However, as indicated earlier, there are some aspects of IT that give rise to more specific micropolitical considerations. One of these is the tendency for there to be IT specialists who have developed the field in isolation from the rest of the institution. Such people may control substantial resources but be reluctant to see them diffused throughout the whole institution. The rationale for Project INTENT, however, was that IT should be permeated throughout an institution's initial teacher training. Decisions had to be taken about how far this was best achieved by enlisting the support of IT specialists or by by-passing them. A factor in the progress made at ITTE D was that there had never been an IT department, only ad hoc arrangements for giving students classes in using IT. This was not the case at any other INTENT institution.

ITTE B was an institution with two strongly developed, quite separate cultures located respectively in 'the academic departments' and 'professional studies'. Although it is an oversimplification, in general members of the academic departments were steeped in the culture of their subject disciplines and took pride in passing on the knowledge and traditions of that discipline to the future teachers who were their students. Within the institution, their closer affiliations with the university and the status of subject knowledge over practical skills and competence had traditionally given them higher status than their colleagues in professional studies who dealt with the practicalities of teaching and classroom management. Project INTENT, through force of circumstances, became a strongly disruptive force that intervened in the balance of power between these two cultural groups. This was because the project provided the principal with an opportunity to provide support for the development of a new technology department. The start date for the new department was brought forward a year, thus enabling the resource of a full-time staff development tutor to be channelled into staff training and development work for the new courses. Moreover, the presence of the project within professional studies appears to have been a factor in the appointment of the staff development tutor (who was a member of the professional studies department) to the new post of head of technology. In a complete break with tradition, professional studies would be closely aligned with an academic department – one which, although new, was clearly seen by the principal as something of a flagship in the institution's development. The new head of technology had a national reputation in IT, in particular in leading development work in the use of LOGO in mathematics teaching in the primary school. However, her background was in primary teaching and her colleagues in the IT department had academic credentials in technology which made them well qualified for the new post. Two very different kinds of technology department were possible, and Project INTENT played some part in tipping the balance towards one grounded in the professional culture of teaching rather than the culture of technology.

This decision was clearly contentious in terms of the micropolitics of the institution. Nevertheless, the existing culture had already been destabilised by entrepreneurialism and expansion. Slow-moving, bureaucratic structures were already giving way to 'fast-track' decision-making under the guidance of a principal who saw himself on a voyage of discovery in which he sometimes led from the bridge and sometimes retreated to 'the crow's nest' to look out for what lay ahead.

A key factor in the success of INTENT's work in ITTE B was the personality of the staff development tutor. She played two different key roles, moving in the second year to become the INTENT 'manager' and working with two colleagues who took on the role of staff development tutor as a partnership. Her quiet persistence and strongly consultative style enabled her to gain colleagues' confidence. She was also politically astute and able to forge alliances and avoid confrontation, which proved to be essential qualities, given the highly politicised position that the project found itself in within the institution.

ITTE E was probably the institution which most nearly matched the project's aspirations for a collegial working style. Action research had, for many years, been an important feature of the institution's work and the INTENT 'manager' had considerable understanding of how this methodology could be used to combine the process of staff development with the development of IT in teacher education. Within the school of education the culture was one of benevolent bureaucracy with a strong overlay of consultative collegiality. The formal line management structure of the institution provided an overarching framework within which some subject groups took the opportunity to carve out a more isolated position. There remained an ambivalence about the extent to which line managers had authority to make demands of colleagues and the extent to which they could only make requests and negotiate. This was particularly true in the case of the relationship between the professional studies department and subject departments. The latter retained operational responsibility for the development of professional applications with their subject specialist students. The fact that the staff development tutor was drawn from a subject department and, therefore, had 'subject-cred' helped to reduce the potentially negative effects of this tension.

A strength of the project in ITTE E was that it was fully embedded in the institutional structures and caused the minimum of unhelpful disruption. The INTENT 'manager' had responsibility for managing development within initial teacher education and INTENT easily became an extension of his role. The staff development tutor (a new member of the mathematics department) was asked to work closely with course teams in the core subject areas of English, maths and science so that from the start of the project she had an official role in course development. The head of IT was given a formal role as INTENT evaluator, so that he remained very much in touch with the project's work although not a member of the project team. This inclusion of the project within existing structures necessarily created some tensions, but these were dealt with by all concerned with considerable sensitivity. For example, INTENT did not fit with the expectations of the head of IT. The project's approach appears to have been focused more upon teaching and learning processes and less upon the acquisition of IT skills than he had expected. He remained supportive of the project's work, but there were times when its direction and style were almost certainly not as he would have chosen: as he said at the end, 'It has certainly not turned out as I had expected.' Nevertheless, he provided technology support and built upon the project's work in planning for IT development, as well as contributing to the project's publications. Similarly, where the leadership of some course teams was not fully committed, members were unsure about their involvement in IT development, and the staff development tutor found it stressful to be in a position of working with colleagues who had not volunteered. Nevertheless, in two departments IT development over the two years was impressive and it was possible to address central issues of students' IT competences because all students had had the same IT experiences. This was considerably assisted by the staff development tutor's work in developing a system for profiling competences which was adopted universally (Vaughan, 1992b).

The 'manager' and staff development tutor worked well as a partnership, using action research extensively to develop their own roles in managing change and ensure that as much as possible was achieved (see Vaughan, 1992a, and Coveney, 1992a, 1992b). By planning carefully, by setting ambitious aims coupled with support, and by continuously evaluating and revising the approach through action research, they were able to achieve a great deal. However, ultimately the project's achievements in ITTE E depended upon the commitment of these two individuals and their capacity to overcome problems and make things work.

USEFUL IDEAS FOR THE MANAGEMENT OF CHANGE ACROSS A WHOLE INSTITUTION

Project INTENT demonstrated the power of a special initiative to provide support for change. It provided clear goals, but also sufficient flexibility within which individuals were able to interpret them to enable the whole team to develop commitment to these goals. To take advantage of the lessons from INTENT, readers will need to think of ways of creating a special initiative or 'project' in their own institution. Project INTENT institutions were certainly fortunate in having funding from the National Council for Educational Technology to cover half the salary of a member of staff for one year, as well as a national co-ordinator and funding for inter-institutional meetings. But all the rest of the resources for a two-year project came from the participating institutions themselves.

'Projects' are often seen as one-off, expensive experiments that make little impact upon the system as a whole. But there are many ways of setting up a change initiative or 'project' on a smaller scale, using the existing resources of the institution, or tapping into an available local resource. This kind of small-scale project has many of the same advantages even without the same level of funding or external support. Small-scale projects can often have an impact on the system as a whole.

While the following ideas about the management of change should not be seen as a set of solutions, some or all can be adapted and used to devise strategies to support change in all kinds of educational institutions:

- Setting up a 'project', especially if it has links with other institutions, enables special priority to be given to an initiative so that management can provide it with extra resources in the short term without being perceived to be unfair.
- Nevertheless, the 'project' needs to be sufficiently integrated with existing institutional management structures to ensure that its work continues after the special funding comes to an end.

- A change initiative or 'project' needs to strike a balance between fitting the existing culture of an institution ('the way things are done around here') and challenging that culture.
- A change initiative or 'project' needs to identify and build upon the key factors which motivate individuals at *this* time, in *this* institution.
- A change initiative or 'project' needs to identify and make use of existing 'spaces' or ambiguities in the institutional structure, or in the informal power structures.
- The key to the process of change is the hearts and minds of the individuals who have the power to make it happen. One good way of engaging their hearts and minds is by involving them in some way – however small – in researching the effectiveness of the innovation with the aim of improving its implementation.
- The two-pronged strategy of a staff development tutor working closely with a senior manager is very effective. This is because it provides support for colleagues on a one-to-one basis as needed, while simultaneously making it possible to put into place supportive structures, to allocate essential resources, and to highlight the importance of the initiative to the institution as a whole.
- This partnership between 'coal face' and senior management (assuming it involves regular discussions) always uncovers surprising misconceptions on both sides. This new mutual understanding of the perspectives of 'them and us' can reduce tensions and enable a genuine cross-fertilisation of ideas.

In 1991, Fullan published a new edition of his book, entitled *The New Meaning of Educational Change*. It contains substantial revisions to his original theory of innovation, although these are integrated within the text without any special indication and they need to be teased out by a comparative reading. Fullan's changes are interesting in the light of what we learnt about the management of change from Project INTENT. First, it is clear that the INTENT approach was informed as much by Elliott's theory of change as by Fullan's original model, and hence the work of INTENT provides useful confirmation for Fullan's new ideas which tend to be much more in line with those of Elliott (1991).

By comparing Fullan's revised model – and the ideas of one or two other theorists – with the knowledge of managing change gained in Project INTENT, we have developed five interrelated key concepts for understanding the management of change.

The first key concept is 'messiness'. Fullan (1991) emphasises that change is a messy mixture of problems and excitements (ibid., p. 345). The accounts we have given of the work in the five INTENT institutions confirm that each individual setting is unique and change is strongly shaped by context – therefore there is no neat set of procedures that a manager can adopt and apply in an unproblematic way. It is not even possible to plan change within a given context and pursue its development step-by-step in a logical way, since 'the what and how constantly interact and re-shape each other' (ibid., p. 47). Morgan, in the introduction to his book *Images of Organization* (1986), stresses the importance of managers having the ability to 'read the situation', which he explains as 'the ability to develop deep appreciations of the situations being addressed'. This ability was often exemplified by both staff development tutors and 'managers' in Project INTENT in their ability to act strategically and with sensitivity in working with colleagues. In part it depends upon knowing the context really well and being able to anticipate what alternatives may happen. Dreyfus (1981) refers to this ability as 'situational understanding' and Elliott (1993b) calls it 'practical wisdom'. In his revised theory Fullan moves away from his earlier step-by-step, rational approach and puts forward the same idea, suggesting that in addition to drawing on knowledge about change we need to 'employ this knowledge in a nonmechanical manner along with intuition, experience and assessment of the particular situation, each time adding to our store of common knowledge' (Fullan, 1991, p. 348).

Our second key concept is the power of individuals to make a positive contribution to bringing about change. In Hoyle's terms they embody an 'extended' rather than a 'restricted' notion of professionalism (Hoyle, 1969). Instead of assuming that they can only be reactive, individuals – including those with very little formal power in the institution – use their understanding of the structures and micropolitics of the institution to adopt a proactive stance. This idea, central to Elliott's vision of the teacher's ability to bring about change through action research, is described by Fullan in the somewhat defensive metaphor of 'facing change head-on' which he further describes as 'exploiting change before it victimises us' (Fullan, 1991, p. 345).

Our third key concept is partnership. In Project INTENT we saw that change could be effected by bringing people together to work collaboratively: staff development tutor with colleague, 'manager' with staff development tutor, and other variations on this theme of partnership. At a time when the politicisation of education nationally had induced a sense in all the ITTEs of 'change fatigue', INTENT provided an opportunity to examine a change initiative critically and in some depth. Fullan, moving away from his original emphasis on personal meaning now emphasises the importance of making 'shared meaning'. He says, further: 'The interface between individual and collective meaning and action in everyday situations is where change stands or falls' (Fullan, 1991, p. 5). His analysis of power has shifted away from the notion of top-down managers supporting and facilitating change at grass-roots level, to a more complex analysis of power residing at all levels. He sees this power of individuals being 'most often used not to do things', but more positively he suggests that 'Like-minded individuals and small groups of individuals can create their own critical masses' (ibid., p. 348).

Our fourth key concept is to make teacher professional development central to the process of planning and implementing change. In INTENT, support for staff development was the central strategy for managing change. Building on

Elliott's ideas, ITTE tutors were encouraged to carry out action research on their own teaching, implementing changes to improve their practice and writing up reports of their work for publication. As Fullan puts it (ibid., p. 289): 'teacher development and school development must go hand in hand. You cannot have one without the other.' The only problem was the extreme pressure under which all involved were working. A little more 'space' at all levels would have given professional development and partnership a better chance.

Our fifth key concept is the integration of theory and practice, what Fullan calls 'the desirable, if elusive, goal'. So much change fails at the implementation stage because its purposes are subverted by people who do not understand its fundamental aims. The theory of IT use in education emphasises its power to transform the learning process; yet in practice, the use of IT, more than any other innovation, can become little more than a technical procedure which has little or no impact upon the process of teaching and learning. Building on the work of Elliott, the action research approach to managing change adopted by INTENT focused upon integrating IT use in teaching training with growth in tutors' understanding of the educational purposes of its use.

CONCLUSION

Overall, Project INTENT was most successful where it was sensitive to, but not hidebound by, the structure and culture of the organisation and the micropolitics of the institutional life. Attempts at shared decision-making within a traditional line management structure created confusion unless they were handled with sensitivity, while it was difficult to accommodate the bureaucratic structures needed by some institutions with the collegial cultures – even of the 'restricted' variety – of others. However, sensitivity to a context within which innovation is to take place does not necessarily involve uncritical acceptance of the status quo. Sometimes, INTENT was able to take advantage of ambiguities and partially implemented changes. In a few cases, it was able to bring about change not only in relation to IT but also in the ways in which institutions tackled policy development in cross-institutional fields more generally. Nevertheless, it was clear that, whatever the enthusiasms of the staff development tutor, involvement of a manager was often crucial to making progress. This involvement, in turn, was easier to sustain in the context of an externally driven project where there was a high level of visibility as well as clear accountability for funding. Thus, although many of the specific achievements of INTENT were genuinely 'bottom-up' initiatives, their likelihood of success was considerably enhanced by being part of a larger endeavour. Managers and staff development tutors could, for example, use their recognised responsibility for the project's aims to bring about change within the institution. It was important for the project to engage with the political realities of institutional life; at the same time the project provided opportunities for 'managers' and staff development tutors to acquire new leverage on institutional power structures.

ACKNOWLEDGEMENTS

We would like to thank our colleagues in Project INTENT who made a substantial contribution to our thinking: Maureen Blackmore, Katrina Blythe, Graham Byrne Hill, David Clemson, Charles Desforges, Malcolm Glover, Andrew Hamill, John Jessel, Wendy Nuttall, Chris Taylor and Gay Vaughan.

REFERENCES

Bush, Tony (1995) *Theories of Educational Management*, 2nd edn. London: Paul Chapman.

Coveney, Rod (1992a) 'Managing staff development within initial teacher education courses: reflections on conflicting priorities', *Developing Information Technology in Teacher Education*, no. 3. Coventry: National Council for Educational Technology.

—— (1992b) 'Ways into staff development', *Developing Information Technology in Teacher Education*, no. 5. Coventry: National Council for Educational Technology.

DES (Department of Education and Science) (1975) *A Language for Life* (The Bullock Report). London: Department of Education and Science.

—— (1988) *A Survey of Information Technology within Initial Teacher Training*, A Report of Her Majesty's Inspectorate. London: HMSO.

—— (1989) *Initial Teacher Training: Approval of Courses*, Circular 24/89. London: DES.

Dreyfus, S.E. (1981) 'Formal models vs. human situational understanding: inherent limitations on the modelling of business enterprise', Schloss Laxenburg, Austria: International Institute for Applied Systems Analysis, mimeo.

Elliott, John (1976) 'Developing hypotheses about classrooms from teachers' practical constructs: an account of the work of the Ford teaching project', *Interchange*, 7(2): 2–22.

—— (1979) 'How do teachers learn?', unpublished paper, Cambridge Institute of Education.

—— (1980) 'Implications of classroom research for professional development', in Eric Hoyle and Jacquetta Megarry (eds), *Professional Development of Teachers: World Year Book of Education*. London: Kogan Page, pp. 308–24.

—— (1991) *Action Research for Educational Change*. Buckingham, Bucks., and Bristol, Pa: Open University Press.

—— (1993a) 'What have we learned from action research in school-based evaluation?', *Educational Action Research*, 1(1): 175–86.

—— (1993b) *Reconstructing Teacher Education*, ed. John Elliott. London and Washington, D.C.: Falmer Press.

Fullan, Michael G. (1982) *The Meaning of Educational Change*. New York: Teachers College Press.

—— with Suzanne Stiegelbauer (1991) *The New Meaning of Educational Change*. London: Cassell.

Halpin, David and Whitty, Geoff (1992) *Secondary Education After the Reform Act*, Units S1/2 of Open University Course EP228, 'Frameworks for Teaching'. Milton Keynes, Bucks.: Open University.

Handy, Charles and Aitken, Roy (1986) *Understanding Schools as Organisations*. Harmondsworth, Middx: Penguin.

Hargreaves, Andy (1994) *Changing Teachers, Changing Times*. London: Cassell.

Hoyle, Eric (1969a) 'How does the curriculum change? 1. A proposal for inquiries', *Journal of Curriculum Studies*, 1(2): 132–41; 1(3): 230–9. Reprinted in R. Hooper (ed.) *The Curriculum: Context, Design and Development*, Edinburgh: Oliver & Boyd.

—— (1969b) 'How does the curriculum change? 2. Systems and strategies', *Journal of Curriculum Studies*, 1(3): 230–9.

—— (1974) 'Professionality, professionalism and control in teaching', *London Education Review*, 3(2).

—— (1976) 'Barr Greenfield and organisation theory: a comment', *Educational Administration*, 5(1).

Malen, Betty (1994) 'The micropolitics of education: mapping the multiple dimensions of power relations in school polities', *Journal of Education Policy*, 9(5/6): 147–67.

Morgan, Gareth (1986) *Images of Organization*. Beverly Hills, Cal., and London: Sage.

SIP (Support for Innovation Project) (1989) *Thinking Schools*. Cambridge: Cambridge Institute of Education.

Somekh, Bridget (1988) 'Support or interference: observations on working with school-based in-service education of teachers', *Cambridge Journal of Education*, 18(2): 191–208.

—— (1993) *Project INTENT, 1990–92: Final Report*. Coventry: National Council for Educational Technology.

—— with M. Blackmore *et al.* (1992) 'A research approach to IT development in initial teacher education', *Journal of Information Technology in Teacher Education*, 1(1).

Vaughan, Gay (1992a) 'Staff development strategies: a staff development tutor's perspective', in *Developing Information Technology in Teacher Education*, no. 4. Coventry: National Council for Educational Technology.

—— (1992b) 'Profiling: a mechanism for professional development of students?', *Cambridge Journal of Education*, 22(1).

Whitty, Geoff, Edwards, Tony and Gewirtz, Sharon (1993) *Specialisation and Choice in Urban Education: The City Technology College Experiment*. London: Routledge.

Whitty, Geoff, Rowe, Gabrielle and Aggleton, Peter (1994) 'Subjects and themes in the secondary school curriculum', *Research Papers in Education*, 9(2).

Chapter 15

Managing change in educational institutions

Reflections on the effects of quality audit and a staff development project

Rod Coveney

INTRODUCTION

This chapter is based on the results of experience in a variety of management contexts so I hope that a brief personal history will assist the reader to relate to the origins of the views expressed. As the Registrar at Worcester College of Higher Education I, together with a Registry staff of sixteen, have responsibility for student admissions, progress and completions as well as the operation and development of the quality assurance systems of the College.

Originally I joined the staff of the then College of Education in 1967 as lecturer in physical education, became Head of Physical Education in 1979, Director of Studies for BEd in 1983 and Assistant Dean in the School of Education in 1990. My role as Registrar is, therefore, a relatively new one for me and it combines the 'prickles and challenges' of all its predecessors. Imagine the Registrar as a gymnast (as, in a former life, he was) maintaining a one-arm handstand (the support arm on a moving base) while spinning three hoops, one on his free arm and one on each of his legs. The moving base is representative of the national context of higher education – a source of policy, funding and students but unpredictable, even capricious in its influence. The spinning hoops represent the proper expectations and needs of students on the one hand, of the staff who teach and research on one of the legs and of the College's quality assurance system and management structure on the other leg. A major responsibility of the Registrar is to help maintain the system in dynamic equilibrium. As long as the behaviour of the base is not too unpredictable the challenge is within the scope of a well-practised, skilful gymnast. The real skill, however, lies in creating a sufficient reserve to manage and survive caprice, which is the responsibility of the Principal assisted by the College's strategic management team.

But how does all this contribute relevantly to a book entitled, *Using Information Technology Effectively in Teaching and Learning*? My background as a gymnastics coach and in teacher education includes a particular interest in learning generally and the acquisition and analysis of perceptual-motor skill. Use of the Open University mainframe via its telephone link to study centres in 1973 and the statistical package for the social sciences in my research activity on the

Birmingham University mainframe later in the decade served to make an initial connection between my academic and professional interests and new technology. Matters developed apace so that by the mid-1980s I was the proud owner of a BBC Model B and skilled at a level equivalent to first class honours in the use of *Wordwise*. In the College, by the end of the decade initial teacher education courses had access to a dedicated teaching room with twenty-four BBC Masters and had incorporated a twenty-hour introduction to IT in both the BEd and PGCE programmes.

In parallel with these latter developments my own role changed from half teaching, half management to full-time management. By management I mean, at least for the purposes of this discussion, striving to create the optimum conditions in which colleagues can operate effectively in the pursuit of institutional and personal goals. (It is the conflict between these that makes life both interesting and frustrating.) During the last five years I have managed three staff development projects, one of which involved IT – Project INTENT (Initial Teacher Education and New Technology). I was also responsible for the preparation and management of the College's Quality Audit by the Higher Education Quality Council (HEQC). While at first sight these were quite different initiatives, each was concerned with factors which affect the quality of students' learning experience. The former example (micro: teacher education) was specific to IT in teacher education; the latter example (macro: College-wide) was general, involving all the activities of the College which support teaching and learning. I think that some of the processes involved in the audit could be applied to a staff development project and, in an informal, small-scale but unsystematic manner, they were used from time to time during the course of Project INTENT. Conversely, IT processes, in the form of the College management information system, assisted in preparations for the audit with regard to both the assembly and analysis of data and the preparation and presentation of the documentation. My initial message, then, is that lessons from both these experiences can, if learned, be applied. So read on.

The following narrative is set in Worcester College of Higher Education, a medium-sized college of some 4,000 students (2,700 full-time undergraduate students, 33 per cent of whom are in initial teacher education; 1,200 part-time undergraduates; and 300 part-time graduate students of whom 70 are registered for research degrees). A former Council for National Academic Awards (CNAA) validated institution, whose courses are currently validated by Coventry University, the College is preparing to apply for its own taught degree-awarding powers during the 1994–5 session and is working towards the achievement of university status at the turn of the millennium. The College's mission is to:

> play its full part nationally in providing high quality, accessible learning opportunities to a wide range of students and other clients. It also serves the needs of its regional community, local industry and commerce, in partnership with other local providers of education and training.
>
> (Worcester College of Higher Education, 1994)

So much for background. My purpose in this chapter is to compare the effects of Quality Audit and those of the staff development Project INTENT on the management of change in the College. In order to do this, the first section will describe Quality Audit and how it sets out to investigate institutional quality assurance (QA) procedures and structures. This account will provide the context for a case study, based on the experience of the College, which will analyse the preparation for, conduct of and actions taken following a Quality Audit. A second case study will analyse how Project INTENT, an externally funded staff development project, was managed and how it affected (i.e. led to changes in) the College. The conclusion of the chapter will consider the lessons to be learned by managers from both these experiences – lessons which can be applied to IT both within and outside higher education.

CASE STUDY 1: QUALITY AUDIT

Background and purpose

Quality Audit has two principal aims: to provide higher education institutions (HEIs) 'with an opportunity to render themselves accountable for the quality of their educational provision to all those who have a legitimate interest in what is being offered in Higher Education' (Williams, 1994, p. vi); and secondly, as a result of the first, to provide the HE sector with detailed information about itself and its practices and hence aid its improvement and development. In the drive for accountability, therefore, the taxpayer as provider of funds has been assured that there are QA procedures in place which have a developmental function and which, through a formal evaluation process, have revealed aspects of work in the higher education system which require development. The issue here concerning managing change in institutions, which will be followed up later, is not whether the discoveries made prior to audits were unknown but whether any remedial actions would have been taken had the discoveries not been made public. This move towards public accountability was anticipated by the contractual terms of the staff development project described later in the chapter.

The notion of quality applied to education has sometimes been described as either *fitness for purpose* – the extent to which an institution enables its students to achieve appropriate learning outcomes and academic standards – or *customer satisfaction* – the extent to which the institution meets the requirements of its students. In fact most HEIs have sought to address both these approaches to quality in their QA procedures. In each of the two case studies here both these concepts and the interplay between them feature in the background to the narrative and provide a link between the various parts of the chapter.

The role of the Division of Quality Audit (DQA), a division of the Higher Education Quality Council, is 'to undertake audits of institutions of HE with a view to ensuring public accountability for the maintenance and enhancement of academic quality and standards' (HEQC, 1994a). The HEQC 'invites' an institution to be audited and, once the invitation has been accepted, provides it with an outline timetable for the submission of documentation, which must be based upon criteria provided by HEQC, and an approximate date for the visit. The compulsory criteria require an account of the systems for the management of the institution with particular regard to its quality assurance arrangements, for example the academic board and its associated committee structure; the validation and review of programmes; teaching, learning and the student experience; student classification and assessment; feedback and enhancement processes; staff employment and development and the accuracy of promotional material. A broad range of other criteria provides an institution with some scope to match its documentation to its mission. A team of auditors (three plus an audit secretary) is appointed; they read the initial documentation, request further information and, with the DQA officer responsible for the audit (who also reads the documentation), decide a timetable for the visit which identifies the personnel they wish to interview and at what time during their visit. Teams typically spend three days at the institution and meet between 100 and 150 people in order to follow lines of inquiry derived from their scrutiny of the documentation. They then prepare a draft report which, some three months after the visit, is sent to the institution to correct for factual accuracy, after which it is published to the institution and one month later nationally.

Institutional preparation: what had to be managed?

Preparing the documentation

The timescale for this varied from four to six months, although recently some institutions have had as much as a year's notice. To manage this process, and given the diversity of the sector, an institution typically decides whether to vest responsibility for the preparation in an individual or a committee. Much depends upon the size and complexity of the HEI. In the case of Worcester, the operational responsibility was mine, guided, in the case of strategic and tactical decisions, by the strategic management team (SMT). An example of the former type of decision concerned the extent to which the College's transitional status (in terms of growth in numbers and the extent of curriculum development and change) should be stressed as a context. A further issue concerned the development of a critical appraisal of the College's quality assurance procedures, their effectiveness and proposals for their development (which also forms a compulsory criterion). An example of the latter tactical decision concerned the emphasis given to particular sections of the criteria with regard to how best to communicate with a team of auditors, at that time unknown to the College, none of whom might be drawn from the former CNAA sector.

The documents required were collected and organised into a coherent selection which was intended to convey to its audience a clear picture of the College, its mission and strategic plan, and its QA procedures and mechanisms.

As a former CNAA institution, once the broad framework of contents was decided this was not a difficult task – but it was time consuming. I was assisted by two temporary clerks (recent young graduates, relatively inexperienced in the world of work but relatively skilled in searching and selecting documentation). They were involved full time for six weeks in the preparation of the initial documents and for a further month in the preparation of follow-up documentation and the programme for the visit. No account was kept of the cost of reprographic services but the staffing cost to the College in terms of time spent was around £15,000 and the estimated total cost was not far short of £20,000. Seven sets of documentation must be prepared for the HEQC and even this medium-sized, single-site College required at least three other sets for its own use. The grand total of documentation assembled measured half a cubic metre.

What was learned in the preparatory phase?

The preparation of documentation and associated management activity provided the following benefits. Although the College was well versed in annual monitoring activity, had recently reviewed its combined studies degree and undergone HMI inspections in both humanities (including ITE) and science, this was a first opportunity since its 1987 CNAA Institutional Review to look at the institution as a whole. Although during the previous year the strategic plan had been fully revised, which had involved all committees and given all individual staff the opportunity to contribute to it (both ideas and editorial advice), the preparation of the documentation did provide a stimulus not unlike an annual spring clean. Like the results of an annual spring clean it was discovered that the contents of some of the shelves had been mislaid. One clear value concerned the confirmation of institutional self-knowledge. By the time the documentation had been sent to the HEQC I had shared my preliminary thoughts on the anticipated findings of the audit report with the SMT. The result of this process was used in several ways. It led, for example, to immediate operational developments intended to shorten the timescale involved in committee work on the annual monitoring process. It also helped in deciding on the level of detail needed to respond to the auditors' request for further documentation, as, for example, the extent of the changes which the College was undergoing and their effects on the complexity of committee structures became more apparent.

It was also necessary to decide how best to prepare the whole College for the visit. As a small institution it was anticipated that the proportion of staff interviewed would be relatively large compared, for example, with a multisite university in excess of 10,000 students. The College's staff development programme for the previous year had included sessions on both the quality audit and the Quality Assessment[1] exercises which had been well attended by managers, teaching and support staff. This was augmented, at the start of the academic year, half way between news of the visit and the submission of the documentation, by a revision paper which described the audit process and the anticipated contents of the documentation. I also attended a meeting of each School's teaching and support staff to explain the action plan and timetable for the visit. Having spent my formative years in physical education I described this process privately to friends as a sort of pre-match briefing, to which their response was to express the hope that I did not suffer the same fate then threatening the England soccer manager of the day, Graham Taylor. (He was sacked.) This was followed up by monthly news sheets on progress, including the contents sheet of the documentation, and briefings for the members of key committees thought likely to be involved in the visit.

The institutional visit

An audit team comprises four members, three auditors and an audit secretary, who receive the documentation soon after it is submitted. The team normally meets once before the visit, the result of which is a request to the institution for further documentation and decisions about the programme for the visit. Typically the secretary arrives at the institution on the Tuesday afternoon prior to the three days of the visit to check administrative and domestic arrangements. The visit proper lasts from Wednesday to Friday, during which time the team see some twenty-five different groups of staff and students totalling between 100 and 150 persons. There is no doubt that an audit team works very hard. From 9 am to 4.30 pm is spent in almost continuous meetings with groups of staff and students and the evenings in the writing and discussion associated with formative evaluation. Meetings with students typically feature in the team's working lunches. The programme is designed to allow the team, when following a particular line of inquiry, to triangulate between managers, staff and students using the documentation as a reference point. In order to maintain consistency of approach amongst the many different audit teams working nationally, the protocols for an audit visit are followed precisely. Auditors do not tour the campus, or visit the senior common room. They spend their time in one or two rooms and are visited by the different groups which make up their programme.

A policy decision was taken by the strategic management team (SMT) as soon as an invitation to be audited was received that the College wished to obtain maximum benefit from the audit. 'Going over the top' was to be avoided but a helpful, professional and courteous stance was to be adopted for all parts of the process. This resulted, as already stated, in particular attention being given to the requirements of audience when preparing the documentation. Care was also taken with the domestic arrangements provided for the team during their stay. They were given reasonable and convenient accommodation in which to work, with adjacent parking, and were kept supplied with the necessary coffee, tea and buffet lunches to enable them to 'keep going'. As a result the audit team provided the College with good value for money for the time they spent at Worcester.

Once the participant groups in the programme had been agreed upon, they were briefed during the ten days prior to the visit. The auditors had decided, for example, to meet members of a validation panel and the subject team whose proposal had been scrutinised. The briefing for this consisted of reminding colleagues of the documentation which had been provided for the auditors: the validation programme for the previous academic year as well as case study materials of the particular validation event, including the validation report, procedures for validation including the guidelines for the responsibilities of panels and for the preparation of proposals. Colleagues were reminded of what they already knew and had routinely experienced.

What was learned during the visit?

The meetings held on the first day of the visit were purposeful but tense. The auditors had met only once previously and did not know each other. Each chaired one-third of the first day's meetings, which tended to create some tension within the team while each was 'tested' in front of the others. Day two was much less tense and colleagues who were involved on both days believed that this was because the auditors had established a good professional working relationship and had begun to enjoy the experience. The dynamics of audit are, therefore, important and luck must play some part in this. The twenty-minute pre- and post-meeting briefings held for the College groups were valuable in confirming that the auditors' lines of inquiry were broadly as anticipated. This reassured colleagues who, without exception, rose to the occasion. The decision not to hold formal rehearsals based upon our anticipations also proved effective as colleagues responded to the auditors' questions, as opposed to giving answers practised in rehearsal.

The institutional report

> Audit reports describe the QA systems and procedures in institutions and comment upon practice. As such they have a significant developmental function for both the institution concerned and for other audiences.
>
> (Gordon and Partington, 1993, p. 3)

The report describes what the audit team learned during the visit and concludes with a section, to which readers typically refer on its receipt as a matter of priority, entitled 'Conclusions and points for further consideration'. This section of the report draws attention to *points worthy of particular commendation*, and those to which the institution *in developing its QA procedures may wish to give further consideration*. The language is restrained but the messages for managers are clear – particularly in so far as a response must be made to the HEQC not less than one year after the receipt of the report.

As a former CNAA institution whose courses are currently validated by Coventry University, also a former CNAA institution, one general area of concern noted by Roger Brown in *Learning from Audit* (1994, p. v) also featured in the College's report. This concern, stated in the context of a rapidly expanding institution, was directed at the relationship between the approval of programmes and resource allocation, in particular the improvement of links between learning resources and the academic development programme. (That said, in an HEI system where real funding is set to decline by 14 per cent in the next three years, resourcing is a matter which is seldom forgotten and will never be '*fully addressed*': Brown, in ibid.) There is also a sense that the evaluation of teaching and learning, staff development and student assessment (other factors noted as national issues by Brown) are all aspects which both relate to the issue of funding and are objects of universal HEI aspiration as worthy targets for development. For the HEI, deciding where to invest resources in these interrelated matters consumes a substantial proportion of management time.

But what of the other specific recommendations for further consideration in the Worcester report? In the context of '*a highly managed institution*' (HEQC, 1994b, p. 20) strongly committed to its clear mission and strategic plan and to the local community through its partnerships with local further education providers; with well-qualified staff and an evident concern for and commitment to the achievement of quality; with a supportive programme for staff development and the dissemination of good practice; with well-received teaching supported by a well-organised approach to research, the College was encouraged to continue to reduce the complexity of its QA procedures, to strengthen its procedures for their critical evaluation and to seek greater consistency in its approach to annual reporting. It was helpful to have the College's self-perceptions confirmed.

Actions resulting from the report

In order to address the better co-ordination of learning resources and academic development the College has revised the sequence of decision-making in order to ensure that resource issues are settled further in advance of the validation process. As stated previously, many of the findings of the report were anticipated. By the time of the audit visit the Academic Standards Committee had already strengthened its role as a critical evaluator of the College's quality assurance procedures. This process continues. New procedures have now been codified in a revised quality assurance document which will comprise part of the documentary evidence for the bid for degree-awarding powers. Given managers' awareness of the need to strengthen the ownership of these changes, they were implemented in an ongoing manner in association with a staff development programme. While this was a very sensible course of action, it was also costly in relation to all the other items on tutors' agendas, such as teaching in the context of a new undergraduate modular scheme with larger numbers of students to manage; Quality Assessment visits which were being undertaken in four subject areas; and coming to terms with changes in the quality assurance procedures.

From a management perspective the proposed bid for degree-awarding powers represents a clear imperative for these changes. As was the case during the Audit visit these challenges are being overcome, for tutors have created slack in the system to accommodate the range of this agenda. While the impetus for change is 'top down' (from the strategic plan), because the goals of the plan are shared throughout the College the motivation is also shared. The resulting pressures, however, are also typical of those encountered on a smaller scale in the second case study which is discussed next.

CASE STUDY 2: PROJECT INTENT

A staff development project

Staff development at Worcester has taken a variety of forms. In the relatively resource-rich 1970s, 5 per cent of the staff annually were able to benefit from a year's study leave which was used, in the main, to achieve a higher degree. By the mid-1980s, with more limited resources and with the requirement that all staff involved in ITE should formally maintain up-to-date teaching experience in schools, periods of study leave were reduced to one term. By the end of the decade, however, fresh opportunities for staff development emerged following a series of initiatives sponsored by agencies, some of which were not controlled by the Department for Education. These projects involved institutions making a formal competitive bid for inclusion by stating how it was intended to achieve the outcomes specified by the funders and how such outcomes were to be assured and evaluated. (As already noted, the terms of these staff development initiatives anticipated the principles of public accountability later applied to the procedures of QA.) So, for example, the College was involved in a major two-year project connected with the Technical and Vocational Education Initiative (TVEI) (1989–91) funded by the Training, Enterprise and Education Directorate (TEED) of the Department of Employment and in a series of projects connected with Enterprise Awareness in Teacher Education (1990–4), also funded by TEED. These projects were required to adopt formal management structures which related to institutional and course management procedures and to involve the participation of personnel from schools and, again typically, industry. The projects also involved a formal commitment from the staff participants who were to be 'developed', as the relationship with the funding body was contractual. All this was a relatively new experience for the College and, as a result, it became a more enterprising institution.

As outlined in the Introduction to this book, Project INTENT (Initial Teacher Education and New Technology) was a two-year project involving five HEIs (1990–2) funded by the National Council for Educational Technology (NCET), the purpose of which was to support the development work of IT in ITE. During the first year of the project a full-time staff development tutor (SDT) was appointed to each of the HEIs involved in order to initiate and support IT development. Each SDT collaborated with a senior member of staff (in the case of Worcester, me) who focused on issues relating to the management of innovation. The project had four main foci:

1 developing the quality of teaching and learning with information technology;
2 providing support for lecturers integrating information technology across the curriculum;
3 developing management strategies to enable 1 and 2 above; and
4 monitoring the process of institutional change.

Implementation: what had to be managed?

The preparation of the project

At the start of the year 1990–1 the management of initial teacher education courses at Worcester was vested in the Board of Studies for ITE which, as Director of Studies for BEd, I chaired. At its meeting in the summer of 1990 the Board heard that a bid had been made to participate in Project INTENT. The management of the project then fell to a small planning group which I led.

This group agreed the broad outline of the project, sought advice about the teams of tutors on which it should be focused and then delegated the detailed planning to the SDT and the personnel involved. All this was then reported back to the Board at its meeting in the autumn term. Of course neither planning nor actions were quite as neat as this. Much of the planning took place during the summer vacation after the details of autumn term courses had been decided. The national planning conference for the five institutions which participated in the project did not take place until the second week of September 1990. It was inevitable, therefore, that some colleagues returned in the autumn term to find that they had become involved in something for which they felt a less than complete sense of ownership. They soon grew tired of the typical manager's response that having accepted the money we were contractually involved and were expected to 'deliver the goods'.

Implementation

The plan adopted for the staff development work was for Gay Vaughan, the staff development tutor at Worcester, to attend planning meetings of the teaching teams involved in the project so that she could influence the discussion in relation to work on information technology. This also enabled her to assess the IT needs of each member of the team. Gay then liaised with each participating tutor in the detailed planning of the work. (It is important to remember in this context that the aims of the project were educational – as opposed to button pushing.) A typical schedule emerged in which Gay taught the first session with the tutor observing; she and the tutor then evaluated the experience and then jointly planned the next session. In practice this method was adapted so that Gay operated in a team teaching situation with tutors. Responsibility for leading the session passed between tutors as planned or as the situation demanded. Throughout the process Gay continued to attend team meetings so that she could acquire an overall picture of how the staff development was affecting teaching and learning in the curriculum.

What was learned in the preparatory and implementation phases?

The initial preparatory experience was not dissimilar to that associated with the period June–September 1993 with regard to the Quality Audit. Although the news about Quality Audit was public in June, the impact was not fully appreciated until September. The initial 'top-down' management process was also similar, as was the teaching staff dilemma of how to balance competing priorities of time with regard to planning the 'old year out' while also planning the 'new year in'. Where there is no additional time such conflicts do not have satisfactory answers. The challenge for managers is to try to create a climate in which tutors can be assisted to reconcile the conflicting priorities. (This is also a challenge for those with staff development responsibilities.)

Managing such situations in my experience, therefore, demands more than a routine structure can provide unless there is slack built into the system, or goodwill which can sustain it. The initial teacher education context at Worcester was one in which most tutors belonged to more than two teaching teams, and this often involved them in more than two different courses. This is a context which tends to spawn meetings for the purposes of planning and maintaining the coherence of teaching and learning, within the team and across each course. A staff development project had suddenly appeared and experience suggested that it would succeed only if it was integrated within the courses rather than being 'bolted on' to them.

If there was any slack in the system, it was soon used up. While the duties of course management can, with planning, absorb additional routine tasks, this makes it more difficult to cope with the unexpected. The issue of time, or lack of it, was also magnified by the cumulative effects of the contractual contributions 'in kind' which, in spite of attempts to spread them, fell differentially on the various teaching teams. (The project's funding provided for the HEIs to contribute half the cost of the SDT 'in kind'.) Preparation for the audit was a much less disruptive process. It involved fewer personnel and was more closely related to the routine life of the College.

Actions resulting from the project

Responsibility for the evaluation of the project at Worcester was undertaken by Andrew Rothery (for the details, see Rothery, 1992). His conclusions were that the aim should be to integrate IT for teaching and learning fully into the course process, and that this should be guided by a clear institutional policy. In order to ensure that staff development 'takes' and that new methods of teaching and learning are fully exploited, the role of the staff development tutor should be made permanent. He identified four main fronts on which further progress was crucial: co-ordination of the support to staff and students from the computing, media and library services, particularly with regard to the use of software and equipment; targeting staff development on teaching practice supervisors; promoting greater liaison between the College, LEAs and schools; and encouraging the development of profiling schemes to assist students' professional development and to provoke students' feedback on the quality of support being provided for the learning process.

Three years on, the College has established an institutional policy for IT (a process led by Andrew Rothery) and phase two of an action plan to establish a management information system will see the institution fully networked by September 1995 with a student–PC workstation ratio of 10:1 and facilities for JANET and Internet. Although Gay Vaughan remains a member of the Primary ITT teaching team in which she has a central, influential role, both in relation to IT and with regard to the development and use of profiling, it has not been possible to provide her with formal support as an ongoing staff development tutor. It is also a matter of concern that the pressure on HE resources, noted previously, has made the development of partnership arrangements with schools more difficult. Partnerships have strengthened liaison generally and also exposed the potential for raising standards both of students' performance and of IT teaching in schools. Provided that tutors' IT staff development can be sustained and the time found to work with school staff and students on using IT in teaching and learning more effectively in the classroom, the aspirations created by the project will eventually be realised.

While some of these developments cannot be claimed as solely the result of Project INTENT there is a sense that they might not have happened quite so readily had not some of the foundations – the perception of a need for an institutional policy and the heightened awareness of staff with regard to the use of IT in teaching and learning – been established and had the areas for development not been so clearly argued as a result of the evaluation. Actions required as a result of the audit report are similarly clear – associated as they are with changes to the QA systems and routines which govern College life. It is in this respect that the audit process has created demands of all College tutors which are similar to those experienced by the tutors who participated in Project INTENT.

MANAGEMENT ISSUES

According to Isenberg (1984):

> One distinctive characteristic of top managers is that their thinking deals not with isolated and discrete items but with portfolios of problems, issues and

> opportunities in which (1) many problems exist simultaneously, (2) these problems compete for some part of his or her immediate concern, and (3) the issues are interrelated.

I want to use this notion to develop a tentative analysis in relation to the objectives of the Project INTENT case study. It will also provide a framework for the comparison of the audit and the development project.

The first example concerns the decision to bid for Project INTENT. The project details were obtained by colleagues, with an interest in the particular area, who saw an opportunity for development. These were then discussed informally with course managers. Because of the limited timescale for assembling the bid the subsequent process was typically a spiral of action followed by analysis followed by further action. The rationale of the project, and how this would interact with the course process, was developed in less than a fortnight. The success of the enterprise was probably made possible because the academic structure and procedures for quality control proved a sufficiently robust but flexible framework to allow such a process to take place. (The Quality Audit report confirmed this.) The motivation for the activities, however, was as much derived from managers' perceptions of the importance of staff development as a means of keeping up with the demands being placed upon initial teacher education courses, as on colleagues' desire to develop the quality of their teaching. To satisfy these needs the institution had to acquire the necessary funding and with that imperative came a great deal of 'top-down' pressure. Similarly, the opportunity to be the first college of higher education to be audited and to capitalise on the benefits which could stem from a positive audit report also created 'top-down' pressures. The origin of each of these decisions could be classified under the umbrella term 'leadership'.

The importance of this management perspective is not always shared by colleagues whose main priority is teaching – even if the importance of staff and course development is readily acknowledged. (For an account of this alternative view with regard to Project INTENT, see Vaughan, 1992.) Since the time of the project a great deal of effort has been expended in the College to develop a shared understanding of and commitment to the goals of the strategic plan as well as a clearer connection between the contribution of all members of the staff to the goals of each annual plan of operation. This factor clearly impressed the quality auditors. That said, when a perceived lack of slack or space in the system causes colleagues to express doubt about the wisdom of undertaking so much development there is a risk that they may be perceived by managers as 'problems' which must be variously solved, manipulated or ignored. I think that the root of the issue of space in Project INTENT lay in the way in which ITE course content, design and staffing at the time were interrelated.

One interpretation of that situation is that in responding to the requirements of accreditation initiated by Circular 3/84 (DES, 1984) and developed by Circular 24/89 (DES, 1989a) both BEd and, more especially, PGCE primary courses became seriously overcrowded. This overcrowding was magnified by the attempt to deliver traditional course structures based upon the more generous 1:12 teaching ratios of the early 1980s which by that time had deteriorated to 1:18. This caused pressures which, to use a medical analogy, resulted in several hernias appearing at the weak points of the structures, some of which began to look quite serious. In this situation the aim of management should be to help colleagues keep the pressure down so that nothing bursts until new structures, based upon a better match between course context, staff and course development, and staffing can be designed and set in place. Nothing did burst and, in the period following quality audit when the intensity was more widespread throughout the institution than in Project INTENT, the systems and personnel also proved equal to the pressures.

Project INTENT was based upon an action research model which was chosen to match its educational, as opposed to button-pushing, emphasis which is exemplified in the work of Vaughan (1992) and the papers by Stratta (1992) Bullock (1992) and Ghaye (1992). What was unforeseen about this model at the time of the bidding process was its hidden cost implications, particularly in the second year of the project when there was no external funding except for meetings, travel and the support of the national co-ordinator. There was none to assist the completion of the writing necessary for disseminating its results. This was compounded by a complex set of motivational pressures, typical of each of the three projects in which I was involved but more intense in INTENT because it involved five institutions. These resulted from the motivation and commitment to the project of each of the institutional teams to undertake a careful evaluation of the first year which, as the project gathered momentum, resulted in the 'end loading' of the writing.

The situation following Quality Audit is not dissimilar with regard to hidden costs. The College's response to the audit report will be incorporated in the bid for degree-awarding powers and, although a senior member of staff has been seconded for a year to assist the project, and although this role includes a commitment to provide a staff development programme in order to reinforce the changes implemented as part of the response, and although there is a carefully constructed and detailed action plan, the latent hernias can sometimes be discerned swelling ominously in the background.

OVERVIEW: CHANGE IN AN EDUCATIONAL INSTITUTION – WHAT HAS TO BE MANAGED?

The pressures noted above exist more generally throughout the higher education system of the 1990s as a result of the externally generated forces created by the mechanisms which have been set in place to assure quality and which often provoke the grass-roots plea to 'leave us alone to get on with our teaching so we can actually succeed in improving its quality'.

The clarity of the College's strategic plan conceals a great deal of turbulence and unpredictability at all levels. This originates, for example, from the uncertainty caused by the present government policy of 'consolidation' with regard to numbers in HE. As a result the Higher Education Funding Council is involved in an annual process of setting maximum aggregate student numbers (MASN) which causes problems at all levels. In the first place it sets an uncertain context for the College's long-term goals. The effects of implementing (or stopping) a recruitment or curriculum policy in HE lasts at least three years and often longer. This affects the motivation of all members of the institution from policy-makers to cleaners. It also means that a disproportionate amount of resources is invested in trying to maintain student numbers within 1 per cent of the MASN and so avoid the financial penalties of under- or over-recruitment.

All this affects, and is affected by, the programmes for staff and curriculum development which are necessary in order to continue the process of changing from part of an elitist system of HE to part of a mass system; from an accountable system of HE to a system which is suffering from a surfeit of accountability; from a system based predominantly upon teaching to one based upon learning from a much greater variety of sources, some of which are unknown. It is also influenced by other changes which have been and are being implemented within the College. This has helped to create (or increase) tensions in the relationship between institutional structures and goals and individual tutors' operational structures and goals – the 'top-down, bottom-up' issue. This was the ITE context in which Project INTENT was conducted and it is the context in which the response to the quality audit report is being prepared.

LEADERSHIP: WILL IT BE UP TO THE TASK?

The major issue which affects my management role concerns the role conflict caused by a blend of externally imposed policy and the move, in HEIs, away from a collegiate to a managerial model of institutional responsibility and action. As Registrar at Worcester I am responsible for implementing and operationalising quality assurance policies, many of which result from the demands of centrally determined policy, and the resulting systems designed to render HEIs more accountable. A major problem at this time concerns the national context of 'consolidation'. Change is easier to manage in an expanding situation. The internal arena in which the game is played out is formed by the College's management and committee structures where external policy and the internal measures for translating that policy into practice are debated in a manner which resembles a type of democracy. At our present stage of development the boundaries between management responsibilities and quasi-democratic responsibilities are still evolving and are not fully understood. (The Quality Audit reported that some of our systems were '*complex*' and this was due, in part, to the unfinished agenda of boundary clarification.) As a result, in order to keep things running smoothly managers appear to participate in what sometimes understandably cynical colleagues see as a pseudo-democratic process, by mediating in political conflict and by exercising tactical, and it is hoped unobtrusive, control of the whole process.

If Bush (1986) is correct, in situations of ambiguity participants interact in an anarchic phase to identify problems and to propose solutions. This is followed by a political phase of bargaining and negotiation before a collegiate phase results in the acceptance of compromise policies and the working out of the detailed outcomes which result in commitment. This is all then enshrined in a bureaucratic phase which results in legitimacy and operational satisfaction. I have often wondered how long this cycle is supposed to last. Will the College's response to the Quality Audit report bring it to an end or shall I remain in the cycle for ever and derive my satisfaction from the effects of adrenalin which provides the motivational fuel for this 'management junky'?

But the context of the cycle is not quite as negative as this interpretation may imply. The changes which have stemmed from Quality Audit and Project INTENT have resulted in positive changes in students' experience. But because they have been connected with other changes it is difficult to be precise about their scale or extent. It is a fact that the goals of the College's 1993–4 annual operating statement were all achieved: recruitment targets were exceeded by 6 per cent; planned new programmes were validated and implemented; a positive Quality Audit report was received; IT, library and media services were unified into a single service; the tender to provide nursing and midwifery education in Hereford and Worcester was accepted by the West Midlands Regional Health Authority; extensions to the Students' Union facilities were completed; a new, international-standard, all-weather pitch was built; and the activities of the year kept within the overall planned budget. At the time of writing, the goals of the current year are all on target. The dynamic driving this process has been provided by clear institutional goals and a '*highly managed*' (HEQC, 1994b), well-led, well-motivated and committed staff.

SUMMARY

Project INTENT was planned just as the era of strategic plans in higher education institutions began. It resulted from concerns identified in the Trotter Report, *Information Technology in Initial Teacher Education* (DES, 1989b), to which the School of Education at Worcester needed to respond. The project was integrated (as far as possible) into BEd and PGCE teacher education courses. The invitation to undergo quality audit occurred at a time when the College's strategic plan was being revised. It was not envisaged as part of the plan but it was capitalised upon as a vehicle for examining and refining the design of institutional systems and, as a result, by improving their efficiency, providing further impetus to the achievement of institutional goals. The evaluation of Project INTENT provided an action list of priorities for development. The quality audit report had a similar result. The importance of the latter to the College's future, however, is considerably more important. Current developments in learning and teaching in the College closely follow the intentions of Project INTENT which are being universalised throughout the College. From a personal standpoint, the value of the staff development brought to me by contact with the other institutional teams involved in the project was immeasurable.

I did not begin this account with my usual disclaimer which colleagues have come to recognise: that I should not provide any answers to the problems discussed. Indeed, in the matters of pressure and balance to which I alluded at the start of this account, there is no one answer because the context is both fluid and dynamic. For me the acid test is whether the context can be influenced so that the optimum conditions are created in which staff development, course development and the development of more effective teaching and learning (i.e. the achievement of clear institutional goals) can take place. The management processes in which I have been involved have encouraged me to think and write about my responsibilities and have been instrumental in helping to create my better understanding of the 'portfolios of problems issues and opportunities' (Isenberg, 1984) which form their context. The following factors may contribute to the creation of optimum conditions for change in institutions: effective communications within and between all parts of an institution; building quality assurance strategies as far as possible into institutional structures and processes; and providing colleagues with the maximum freedom to realise their professionalism within institutional structures. I should make it clear that unobtrusive management should not be confused with a lack of leadership. It does not mean a neutral, 'hands-off' approach but one in which the manager remains as inconspicuous as possible whilst engaging in the process of 'releasing' the quality of colleagues' professional commitment to institutional goals which is fundamental to the whole process of improving the quality of teaching and learning.

ACKNOWLEDGEMENTS

I am grateful for the comments of colleagues at Worcester on initial drafts of this chapter. The responsibility for the views expressed, however, is my own.

NOTE

1 The Quality Assessment of Subjects is the responsibility of the Higher Education Funding Council for England. This process assesses how quality is delivered at subject level on a three-point scale: excellent, satisfactory and unsatisfactory.

REFERENCES

Brown, R. (1994) 'Foreword', in *Learning from Audit*. London: Higher Education Quality Council.

Bullock, E. (1992) 'Computers and the teaching of history in schools', in *Developing IT in Teacher Education*, DITTE no. 1. Coventry: National Council for Educational Technology.

Bush, T. (1986) *Theories of Institutional Management.* London: Paul Chapman.
Coveney, R.B. (1992a) 'Managing staff development within initial teacher education courses: reflections on conflicting priorities', in *Developing IT in Teacher Education,* DITTE no. 3. Coventry: National Council for Educational Technology.
—— (1992) 'Ways into staff development: exploring ambiguity in managing top-down–bottom-up tensions in initial teacher training institutions', in *Developing IT in Teacher Education,* DITTE no. 5. Coventry: National Council for Educational Technology.
DES (Department of Education and Science) (1984) *Initial Teacher Training: Approval of Courses,* Circular 3/84. London: DES.
—— (1989a) *Initial Teacher Training: Approval of Courses,* Circular 24/89. London: DES.
—— (1989b) *Information Technology in Teacher Training: Report of the IT in ITT Expert Group* (chair: Janet Trotter). London: HMSO.
Ghaye, A.L. (1992) 'Tales from the riverbankers: children and teachers becoming critical with the aid of computers', in *Developing IT in Teacher Education,* DITTE no. 4. Coventry: National Council for Educational Technology.
Gordon, G. and Partington, P. (1993) *Quality in Higher Education: Overview and Update,* Briefing Paper no. 3. Sheffield: Universities Staff Development Unit.
HEQC (Higher Education Quality Council) (1994a) *The Work of the Higher Education Quality Council,* Pub100 7/94. London: HEQC.
—— (1994b) *Worcester College of Higher Education: Quality Audit Report.* London: HEQC Quality Assurance Group.
Isenberg, D.J. (1984) 'How senior managers think', *Harvard Business Review,* Nov–Dec: 81–90. Reprinted in J. Henry (ed.), *Creative Management.* London: Sage Publications, 1991.
Rothery, A. (1992) 'IT in initial teacher education at Worcester: evaluation of a significant year', in *Developing IT in Teacher Education,* DITTE no. 4. Coventry: National Council for Educational Technology.
Stratta, E. (1992) 'Primary initial teacher education: computers and the teaching of history', in *Developing IT in Teacher Education,* DITTE no. 1. Coventry: National Council for Educational Technology.
Vaughan, G. (1992) 'Can professional development be achieved through course development?', in *Developing IT in Teacher Education,* DITTE no. 4. Coventry: National Council for Educational Technology.
Williams, P. (1994) 'Introduction', in *Learning from Audit.* London: Higher Education Quality Council.
Worcester College of Higher Education (1994) *Strategic Plan 1994–8.* Worcester: WCHE.

Chapter 16

Organising IT resources in educational institutions

Chris Taylor

CONTEXT

The practice of organising IT facilities in an educational institution may seem at first a simple business. You just take some computers, put them on tables in a suitable room and connect them to an electricity supply. Unfortunately, that is not the case. There are now directives from the European Union regarding the installation and use of such equipment in the workplace. There are also curriculum, management, personnel and social factors which are affected by the kinds of decisions that are made about the technology. Behind these decisions there are educational decisions which underpin the way in which the technology is to be used.

In this chapter I set out to provide practical information and suggestions for IT co-ordinators and senior management in both primary and secondary schools. Responsibility for organising IT facilities in educational institutions is usually vested mainly in one person who may have the title of IT co-ordinator. In practice, however, the development of IT always depends upon the support of senior management in order to secure finance for equipment, allocation of rooms, and technical support. Without this support the IT co-ordinator does not usually have sufficient power to promote effective development.

My experience of organising IT facilities is varied. Initially I was a primary school teacher living through the introduction of IT into my school; later I worked as part of the Computer Education Advisory Service of one of the country's largest LEAs; nowadays I am a lecturer in IT in teacher education. I have seen both the successes and difficulties institutions have experienced in introducing IT, in motivating and training staff and in ensuring resources are deployed effectively.

Historically, in British educational institutions the organisation of IT facilities has been managed in one of two ways. The computer room or laboratory is common in many secondary schools, and the single computer in a classroom is used in the majority of primary schools. Now that IT has to be taught across the curriculum to all pupils it is time to consider the effects of these arrangements and to look at other alternatives. It is also essential to consider those people involved in the use of IT and the decisions that affect them. These include, as well as IT co-ordinators and senior managers, students,[1] support staff, administrators and parents.

HOW SHOULD YOU MANAGE INFORMATION TECHNOLOGY IN YOUR CONTEXT?

There are two main approaches to the deployment of computers in schools and universities: either whole rooms are dedicated to IT or single computers are placed in each classroom. An intermediate approach is to provide clusters of computers in a variety of locations, each perhaps with a focus on one discipline or age-group. The advantages and disadvantages of each approach are listed below.

The computer laboratory

Advantages:

- ease of management and supervision of equipment;
- ease of use for whole class teaching;
- security simplified;
- peripherals and software can be shared.

Disadvantages:

- promotes a didactic approach;
- mixed ability teaching difficult;
- access can be restricted;
- health and safety difficulties multiplied.

A single computer in the classroom

Advantages:

- encourages a flexible approach to organisation;
- acts as a focus for group work;
- does not demand specialist support and facilities.

Disadvantages:

- time restrictions on students' access;
- may be of little use in a formal teaching situation;
- management is devolved to students;
- may increase security difficulties;
- increased costs if networked to the main computer room.

APPROACHES TO SHARING INFORMATION TECHNOLOGY RESOURCES

Networks

Computers can be used individually in a 'stand alone' mode or they can be linked together to form networks. In a network a group of computers are linked together, so that facilities such as hard disks, printers and software can be shared. Networks do require competent management but can be a cost-effective way of providing access to equipment. If set up securely they can be relatively free from virus infections or hacking, and software is relatively safe from interference. In a local area network (LAN), wires or fibre optic cables are used to link together all the computers in one room or throughout a building. Usually they are all connected to a network server which provides them with a shared source of software. It is useful to give those new to a computer network an analogy of the way it operates. This is particularly important if networks are slow or unreliable. (See, for example, my colleague Niki Davis's analogy between a network and Manuel, the waiter in the television comedy series *Fawlty Towers*, in Chapter 11 of this book.)

Wide area networks (WANs) enable communications between computer users at a distance, usually over telephone lines. They may be suitable for distance learning contexts, access to remote databases, electronic mail or conferencing. All this is covered in some detail in Chapter 13 of this book.

Single computers

The single computer in the classroom also requires managing and organising. Software needs to be available, either on a hard disk or in a disk box belonging to the class. A number of local primary schools in the Exeter area have decided to provide a work disk for each of their pupils, but some programs such as Front Page Extra are set up to save work to the program disk. Regular virus checking is recommended. A local secondary school had to shut down its IT rooms for two weeks while all disks were checked after a virus infection. A monitoring system will help you to ensure that all children have regular access to the IT facilities and also to record and assess their work. Some schools use a tick sheet by the computer and also collate an IT portfolio of children's work.

Clusters

Another possibility is to provide a cluster of computers in several different rooms. The purpose of this is to allow teachers scope to integrate IT use with other classroom activities while going beyond what can be achieved with a single computer. A cluster of four computers may be fitted into a room whilst still allowing space for other activities. At Exeter we use clusters in primary studies, technology, art, music, PE and modern languages teaching rooms. Clusters permit a diverse provision so that the resources are purchased to suit particular curriculum applications. The major difficulty with such an approach is that of management: security arrangements are more complex; a greater diversity of technical skill may be needed; software resources may have to be duplicated unless the computers are networked; and appropriate software licences will have to be purchased.

It is often a good idea to locate a cluster in the library or resource centre so that students have access to them together with books and learning resource packs, including software and support materials. The systems can act as a source of information, either by accessing on-line databases or from CD-ROM based reference material. At Exeter, in addition to a number of networked machines, we have an IT teaching room in our library which is available on open access.

Portable computers

The rapid development, decreasing size and cost of portable computers offer new possibilities and pose new challenges. Any classroom becomes a potential computer room with a set of portable computers. Recent projects funded by the National Council for Educational Technology (NCET, 1994) and the Scottish Council for Educational Technology (SCET, 1992) demonstrated the power of portables organised in a variety of ways. In some schools working with us at Exeter, all the children in a class were provided with a low-cost portable word processor. In two first schools, we provided smaller sets of machines which could be used by individuals or groups. These machines proved to be a valuable additional word-processing resource which complemented the classroom computers, and the young children found them easy to use. Once the teachers had overcome the difficulty of keeping the batteries charged, management was found to be simple. In a local secondary school 'pocket book' computers were found to be a valuable resource, even though the school had at first requested larger portables.

However, battery life is a problem in the more powerful machines: they may only offer a few hours use after each charge. Sharing machines may be difficult due to the size and position of their screens, and colour graphics are expensive. The less powerful, smaller machines offer better battery life but have limited screens and a smaller range of software and may cause difficulties in transferring files to desktop workstations. Portable computers are vulnerable to theft and damage and can be more expensive to repair if they use custom-made components. These problems should decrease with the rapid development of the technology.

WHAT ABOUT SUPPORTING THE STAFF INVOLVED?

All staff involved in using IT in their teaching will need access to staff development and training. It is valuable to set up a support system involving technicians and ancillary workers, to ensure that machines run reliably, that software is managed effectively, and that teaching is not unduly disrupted by technical hitches. At Exeter we have found that appropriate training is as important for support staff as for academics and administrative staff. Library staff who have complete familiarity with the computer and information systems available are able to advise staff and students on their use. In addition, it can be useful to give teachers access to the institution's computerised administration system if one exists. We have not yet managed to do this at Exeter due to complex issues of security, software compatibility and staff training. The cost of training and support for personnel in addition to that of hardware and software is often a hidden extra expense that requires careful planning and negotiation.

HOW SHOULD YOU ORGANISE TEACHING ROOMS?

It is important to provide a suitable environment for computer use. Costs will include such things as installation and security, as well as the provision of the correct furniture and lighting. The latter are becoming much more important now that students are likely to spend more time on machines as a result of better access. Ad hoc arrangements using existing furniture, 'daisy-chained' wiring and non-specialist lighting may no longer be acceptable. Computer systems require tables and chairs of the correct height for their users. Primary school furniture has been slow to adapt to this need. There are less obvious factors to consider too. Measures must be taken to prevent screen glare from sources such as the windows. Electrical wiring should be secured out of the way. Avoidance of magnetic emissions from VDUs is important, as is adequate ventilation to remove dust from laser printers. Where computers are likely to be used by a single individual for extended periods of time, Table 16.1 provides a list of requirements to comply with basic health and safety regulations.

Table 16.1 Requirements to comply with basic health and safety regulations for extended computer use

- Tables of sufficient height and depth to enable work at a suitable distance from the screen
- Tilt and swivel screen stands, adjustable keyboards
- Adjustable typists' chairs
- Flicker-free lighting and shades for outside windows
- Flicker-free screens
- Covered wiring, protected by a circuit breaker
- No undue noise (in particular no high-pitched, continuous hum)
- Adequate fresh air ventilation
- Positioning of machines so that no one is sitting near the sides or back of VDUs
- Regular breaks from VDU work at least every hour

WHO IS RESPONSIBLE FOR DRAWING UP A POLICY FOR IT?

Every educational institutions needs to draw up a policy governing how IT is to be used and what its role is to be. This policy should reflect both the educational philosophy of the institution and the pragmatic constraints under which it is to be implemented. A good policy is a forward-looking document, designed to give coherence and continuity to what might otherwise become a series of one-off arbitrary and fortuitous decisions, particularly where there are severe financial constraints. It will be about both the management and distribution of hardware, and factors affecting personnel. Decisions need to be made regarding the exact responsibilities of senior managers, whether there is to be an IT co-ordinator, how technical support is to be provided, and to what extent teachers, students, governors and parents are to be involved in the decisions regarding IT.

In a school, the preparation and implementation of such a policy is the responsibility of the head teacher, who may choose to delegate it to a senior member of staff. In a college, it will often be delegated to the IT staff by the senior management team. In every case it will need to be discussed and negotiated with all those whom it affects. Feedback from those who use the IT resources will be essential to enable their effective use.

Gavin Owen (1992) has researched the role of IT co-ordinator in secondary schools and the development of IT policies. He warns senior managers to be wary of delegating all the decisions on IT to any individual or group below the senior management team. Not only does this create difficult tensions in the management of an expensive and essential resource, it also suggests that IT policy should be led by developments in IT, rather than by the needs of teaching and learning across the whole curriculum. IT is too important to be left to the technophiles.

HOW WILL YOU KNOW IF IT IS HAVING AN IMPACT?

The best institutional policies will incorporate a system for monitoring the use of IT facilities. This will involve strategies to ensure that hardware and software are actually being used, evaluating the nature of their use and whether or not effective learning is taking place. What is important is not the monitoring technique used but the quality of the information gathered and how it is used. One method is to survey workstation use at random intervals over a period of time. If the systems are not being used effectively action can be taken to find out why. Student perceptions of the facilities can be very useful in identifying factors which otherwise might be overlooked. Effective monitoring is important to ensure good use of expensive and scarce resources, and it also helps to make a case for the maintenance and development of resources.

HOW CAN YOU PLAN FOR FLEXIBLE USE OF THE IT RESOURCES?

The use of IT resources for teaching is only part of the picture. If the use of IT resources is to be effective, students will require access to the facilities to undertake work in their own time. This is difficult in a computer room unless it is only timetabled part-time or sufficient stations are supplied to allow students free access to the spare ones. In my experience, the latter is not a totally successful solution. Students working on their own projects cause disruption to class lessons, no matter how quiet and considerate they try to be. The click of the keyboard can be distracting to a teacher trying to talk to a class. The reality is that there is a conflict between the needs of open access and the needs of teaching, and provision should be made to take this into account. An ideal situation is the provision of a dedicated open-access IT room close to the main computer area where a member of support staff is readily to hand. Alternatively, all students might have their own portable computers. If neither of these ideals is possible it may be worthwhile using portable dividing screens within a room to separate teaching and open-access areas.

Special facilities need to be provided if open-access areas are to be used by individuals outside normal hours. These include a toilet near by, an emergency telephone and adequate lighting outside the building to enable users to feel safe when arriving and departing. This is more fully described in Taylor (1992a). Although this applies mainly to higher education at present, future development in schools, such as more flexible working hours, may turn this into a priority.

HOW CAN YOU KEEP THE SYSTEMS SECURE?

The term 'virus' is a metaphor for computer programs written with malicious intent. They are often designed to be hidden from the user and they copy themselves from disk to disk. This can lead to major corruption of software and data. Viruses are often created by clever, innovative individuals who regard their production almost as a hobby. Fortunately, equally clever, innovative people spend their time creating virus protection software. To minimise problems, it is advisable to install and regularly update virus protection software on all machines. In addition, since viruses are very common, you may want to discourage both staff and students from bringing disks from machines used off the site. Some sort of record of the users of each machine is desirable in order to track down any infection if it should happen. To protect networks, only the system operator should be able to put files on to the file server hard disk.

Hacking is the process of trying to break through the security of a system (usually a network) either for curiosity or with malicious intent. Hackers can cause a great deal of damage by either the intentional or unintentional destruction of files. At Exeter we had one case of hacking which led to the loss of teaching files, programs and use of all the central computer services. Fortunately, it was possible to track down the culprit by careful observation and monitoring the use of the terminals. There is no absolute cure for hacking but regular maintenance should inform the system operator if it is happening. It is a criminal offence and deserves appropriate disciplinary measures. Schools can educate their students on the moral issues of these offences by considering extreme cases and their effects. For example, where computer networks hold medical and financial information the issue becomes clearer. Hacking for monetary gain is clearly a criminal activity, but 'hobby hacking' which inadvertently causes a patient to die is equally serious and likely to lead to a trial for manslaughter.

The problems of vandalism and theft are increased by out-of-hours use of IT facilities when there is no supervision. If the facilities are on open access, some means of recording the names of users and excluding unauthorised personnel is essential. Appropriate strategies include key code locks on access doors, closed circuit video, and securing items of equipment with locks. Computer equipment left unattended in cars is particularly vulnerable, as several of the contributors to this book know to their cost.

YOU HAVE THE MONEY: WHAT SHOULD YOU BUY?

Software

Curriculum applications are determined by software, which should be selected before choosing the hardware. Before deciding on software purchases you need to gather information on how individual staff intend to use the system. In a school it is likely that software will be needed to enable students to communicate and handle information, create or manipulate models and undertake measurement and control, in line with the National Curriculum. Some LEAs have developed a recommended toolbox of software for purchase or distribution to their schools.

Such a general-purpose toolbox of software might include: a word processor; a desktop publishing package; graphics packages for art work; another for graphing in maths; devices to experiment with computer control; music software; and data-handling programs. A number of these applications are available in integrated packages such as Microsoft Works which contains word processing, spreadsheet and database software. You may be offered computer systems with a bundle of software included in the price, but don't forget that this only adds value to your purchase if it is software you actually want to use! In addition to this, subject-specific software, such as science simulations or packages for use in the teaching of modern languages, may be appropriate, as may some CD-ROM reference collections.

Hardware

It is always difficult to make choices when it comes to purchasing hardware because technological development is so rapid that whatever is bought today will start to be out of date in six months time. To complicate this, advice from colleagues, advisers and manufacturers is likely to conflict. At present there are a number of standards, depending on the operating system software chosen for the computer system. Software is not always written for all these computer platforms, so the choice of a particular software package can determine the platform.

For further information on hardware and guidance in purchasing, the National Council for Educational Technology publishes an information pack called *Choosing and Using IT Equipment* (NCET, 1995).

WHAT NEXT?

There are many problematic issues regarding the provision and management of IT facilities, and you can expect to face up to some difficult decisions. For example, at Exeter we have recently had to decide how to go about upgrading an existing research machine (RM) network: do we buy the same make of computer to ensure software compatibility, or do we buy machines that are compatible with the university's central IT services? Should we attempt to put more of our computer rooms on to 24-hour access, which would meet student demand but use up funds on security which would otherwise be available to replace old equipment? To what extent should we continue to invest in Acorn-based equipment which is used in the local primary schools, but is increasingly being seen as non-standard? These are all complex problems to which there are no right answers. We all have to learn to make the best possible decisions with the incomplete information available to us at the time.

There are, however, some areas where decision-making may seem easier. For example, at Exeter we have decided that secretaries should be provided with new computers running Microsoft Word, enabling their former machines to be distributed to other members of staff. This has involved a considerable investment in training, and also in furniture to ensure compliance with European directives on health and safety. It has cost a considerable sum, but should lead to a direct improvement in administration. We have also invested in new equipment to meet the needs of students and lecturers, for example we have provided a range of facilities in the resource centre to enable both viewing and authoring of multimedia packages.

The future will bring additional challenges with increasing expectations of what IT can contribute to education. There is likely to be additional help as some companies are already developing services to relieve schools of the technical management of IT resources. However, the weight of responsibility for decision-making, policy development and practical IT development will continue to lie with the school's managers and teachers. The issues raised in this chapter will continue to need careful consideration and strategic planning, although their precise manifestations will continue to change as hardware and software develop and government policies shift to make new demands on schools and teachers.

NOTE

1 For simplification, the word 'student' is used throughout this chapter to refer to pupils in primary and secondary schools as well as students in initial teacher education.

REFERENCES

DES (Department of Education and Science) (1990) *Technology: National Curriculum Non-statutory Guidance*, March. London: HMSO.

EEC (European Economic Community) (1990) *Minimum Safety Requirements for Work with Display Screen Equipment*, Council Directive no. L156/14, *Official Journal of the European Communities*, 21 June.

Govier, H. (1996) *Draft IT Policy*. London: Micros and Primary Education (MAPE).

HSE (Health and Safety Executive) (1992) *Work with Display Screen Equipment*. London: HSE.

NCET (National Council for Education Technology) (1992) *Choosing and Using Portable Computers*. Coventry: NCET.

—— (1994) *Portable Computers in Action*. Coventry: NCET.

—— (1995) *Choosing and Using IT Equipment* (resource pack). Coventry: NCET.

Owen, G. (1992) 'Whole school management of technology', *School Organisation*, 12 (1).

Richardson, A. (1993) 'The implications of new educational technologies on educational accommodation and systems in the next 5–10 years', *Computer Education*, Feb.

Rowley, J.E. (1993) 'Managing, teaching and learning in an IT workshop', *Computer Education*, June.

SCET (Scottish Council for Educational Technology) (1992) *The Laptop Computer Project*. Glasgow: SCET.

Taylor, C.A. (1992a) 'Open access to IT facilities', *Developing IT in Teacher Education*, (DITTE no. 5). Coventry: National Council for Educational Technology.

—— (1992b) 'Creating an effective working environment', *Learning Resources Journal*, 8 (1).

—— (1993) 'Safety and your computer', *Microscope*, no. 38.

Chapter 17

Managing curriculum development

Using school teacher appraisal to find the means

Jon Pratt

APPRAISAL MAN

Figure 17.1 Appraisal Man
Source: *The Times Educational Supplement*, 25 December 1992

This character appeared as a 'subplot' of a cartoon in *The Times Educational Supplement* in 1992. It is, as far as I know, the first and probably only appearance of 'Appraisal Man' but the image and its metaphorical implications linger on in the hearts and minds of teachers currently wrestling, as they would see it, with compound innovations in their practice and demands upon their time and resources.

The cartoon character is worth examining as a metaphor, not only of school teacher appraisal to which it refers, but also of the perception many teachers have of the relationship between themselves as internal practitioners and those external agents who seek to make judgements about them.

Appraisal Man is mechanistic, yet clearly random and uncontrolled in his actions – once set going he will follow his own course blindly. The manager of Appraisal Man only has control in the sense that he can initiate his activity; henceforth control is arbitrary. Appraisal Man is intrusive, the magnifying glass indicating the purpose to 'detect', to uncover and reveal what has chosen to be hidden. The 'superman' persona suggests an innate and unquestionable superiority of judgement beyond the expertise of 'ordinary mortals'. Last, but not least, he is, inevitably, a man.

Now, this could be explained as typical of the paranoia of the teaching profession which has consistently resisted accountability – revealing the dichotomy between 'insiders' and 'outsiders' and the perceived quality of their judgements and perceptions. However, there has been and continues to be a change in the definition of the boundaries and borderlands between insiders and outsiders and this is particularly relevant to senior managers of schools in terms of professional development and change. There has been, during the early 1990s, an 'externalisation' of the management of schools in terms of the roles and relationships of head teachers and their deputies.

With the changing accountabilities of schools, Local Education Authorities (LEAs) and governing bodies, schools developed greater autonomy. This brought new and wider sets of responsibilities for school managers, during which they assumed roles and accountabilities which previously were rooted within the role of local authorities and local inspectorates.

A phrase which has become common describes the head teacher as the 'resident inspector' in a school, thus linking directly the insider and outsider roles that formerly were separated between school management and outside agencies like the LEA. In the same way, LEAs have tended to emphasise the concept of 'partnership' between their officers and head teachers with the message of equality of status replacing older hierarchies.

This idea of the 'resident inspector' is interesting because for many it contains an implicit contradiction; the evaluation and monitoring role of an 'inspector', in their view, can only be performed effectively by a person who is 'outside' the school as an institution, with the associated ideas of objectivity. Similarly, for many head teachers, particularly of small schools, the associations of the term 'inspector' would appear to be in direct conflict with the nature of the relationships they foster within their school and the management styles which emanate from those relationships.

Yet the demands of formal inspection (through the Office for Standards in Education's (OFSTED) cycle in England and Wales) have brought a sharper focus on the accountabilities of the management of schools to demonstrate both development and the maintenance of standards of quality across a wide range of activities. Heads have learned, soon enough, that this can not be sustained by a four-yearly burst of concentrated energy prior to an inspection but must be addressed through an on-going process of 'quality assurance' and school development.

So head teachers and members of schools' 'senior management' are placed in a role which bridges what may have been perceived as the domains of the 'insider' and the 'outsider'. How well equipped are they to achieve this difficult balance?

OFSTED inspectors, of course, have the support of training, an exhaustive prospectus and manuals of procedures and strategies. LEA inspectorates have developed ever more sophisticated techniques for monitoring and supporting school development, with particular attention being paid to the nature of an 'evidential base' upon which evaluative judgements can be made, and the techniques of analysis through which such evidence can be processed and used.

Although a number of schools will have developed quite sophisticated techniques themselves to guide their development, many head teachers will either have had little access to and awareness of these 'tools' or processes, or they may find it difficult to apply these, or similar, techniques within the framework of relationships and ways of working which they find in their schools. The net effect of this situation may be that development in schools, curriculum and professional development in particular, and the decisions that inform that development are based upon very little systematic collection and analysis of evidence. Rather, intuition and hunch inform change – often effective but not always reliable.

This chapter seeks to explore the difficulties school management may have in creating genuine whole school development in the use of information technology in teaching and learning, because of the lack of, or difficulty in, introducing systematic techniques of information gathering and analysis, for the reasons outlined above.

I wish to suggest that innovations and, specifically, school teacher appraisal, which may have not been universally welcomed by schools, their managers and staff, have the potential to deliver to schools precisely the tools and techniques, embedded in positive relationships, which schools need to make real progress.

To do this I would like to look first at experiences of working with head teachers and their colleagues during the training for appraisal; and second, at a case study of one school which sought to link appraisal to the development of IT within the school.

'ONE BLUE, TWO YELLOWS, A RED AND A GREEN'

'Do you know: we've got one blue, two yellows, a red and a green!' This was exclaimed with some excitement by the head teacher of a small, five-teacher primary school at the end of a session during the appraisal training day shared with two other schools in Cambridgeshire.

She was referring to the outcome of an exercise, variants of which are commonly used in management training, in which each teacher was issued with about sixty coloured cards in one of four colours. Each card contained some skill or aptitude such as 'Performing on stage or in public' and 'Analysing and summarising information'. The four colours represented skills in each of four domains:

- information processing and ordering skills;
- physical and manual dexterity skills;
- creative and expressive skills;
- interpersonal and management skills;

although participants were not informed of the significance of the colours at the outset.

In addition, each person had four 'header cards' which were used to head columns entitled: 'Very competent', 'Competent', 'Adequate at present', 'Needs development'. The instructions given to participants (the detail is important here) were:

1 Arrange each card under the appropriate heading according to your own personal assessment of your stage of development.
2 Invite a colleague to look at your card layout. They may:
  - challenge any placement you have made but only positively (i.e. where they think it belongs in a higher category of competence);
  - ask you to explain and explore the reasons for particular placements.

  They may not:
  - move any cards themselves;
  - force you to change any cards against your will.
3 Repeat the above for your colleague.
4 Reflect on and make final changes to your layout. Consider any 'colour bias' – what does this suggest to you?
5 Request that you can look at the layout of colleagues who work in the same team/year group/department. What differences/similarities are there? What implications are there for the way you work together?
6 From your own layout select just two cards, one from the Undeveloped column and one from the Competent column, both of which conform to the following criteria:
  (a) it is something which would actually improve your life/work by developing it further;
  (b) it is something that it is possible for you to develop further.

The head teacher was responding to stage 5 above and was excited about the way they could use the information to ensure that they shared skills and supported each other.

I asked her: 'Surely you know about the respective skills and enthusiasms of your staff?'

'Yes, informally, I do. But this is the first time we have been able to share this sort of view of ourselves, in a way which is neither threatening to individuals nor appears to be critical of areas of weakness.'

Knowing the school, I was aware that there was a very positive and supportive framework of communication and mutual support, based largely upon relatively informal frameworks of consultation, discussion and decision-making. What was clear, however, was that such a social context, while necessary and supportive of teacher morale, was essentially non-analytical in structure and ethos. The head teacher admitted that she found it difficult to address issues of concern while being an intimate partner in the relationships of the school.

A common assumption may be that managers – and this could apply as much to a head of department in a large secondary school as to the head teacher of a small primary school – have to change the nature of the relationships with their colleagues, in order to achieve what they would perceive as an objective and analytical frame of reference. More often than not this would be assumed to be a more hierarchical or authoritarian position.

The error is to confuse analysis of situations with the judgement of situations and to assume that close professional relationships automatically preclude rigorous and effective judgement.

The head teacher in this situation was not changing her relationship with her colleagues – indeed, as a 'trainee' with her colleagues she was in a 'more equal' position. The difference was that these structures and techniques allowed and encouraged rigorous analysis and judgemental processes to take place, which exploited professional intimacy rather than conflicting with it.

REFLECTING ON THE PROCESS

Teachers universally found this exercise a fascinating and rewarding process and were keen to discuss its implications. A consensus of ideas and views, drawn from work with over forty schools, is reflected below. Quotations are taken from the observation of teachers working on the exercise.

Clarity of structure

Despite the dangers of engaging in a prescriptive and mechanistic process, the highly structured approach allowed teachers to engage with the analysis of a complex range of skills and perceptions with ease and confidence. Unlike traditional checksheet-based systems the potential for reflection, review and change offered by the cards was a major factor. This, in turn, led to a surprisingly intensive focus on the precise meaning of language in its application to self-evaluation and analysis. Words like 'performance', 'planning' and 'constructing', for example, challenged participants to apply alternative meaning to context and to consider both literal and figurative meanings: 'If you mean building literally in "Building and Constructing", I am hopeless; I can't put two bricks together!

But I do think I can "build" understanding and agreement in meetings and situations like that.'

A key factor was the sense that the structure allowed a progressive narrowing of focus that moved from a wide perception of a comprehensive range of skills to choices based upon clear criteria. This was clearly different to a process of arbitrary selection, which many teachers felt had been the basis of any professional reflection and development they had experienced before. The sense of a shared basis for reflection which may lead to quite different outcomes for individuals was an important feature which is explored in the case study which follows.

The role of the partner

The vital importance of the role played by the partner in the process of examination was clear. The constraints placed upon the partner emphasised the role as one of questioner and 'reconstructer' of information and perceptions, rather than that of judge based upon superior perception and understanding.

Participants observed that their partners called upon 'evidence' to support their challenge of individual card placings. Sometimes this evidence was of the sort that was not normally available to the teacher: 'You say that your teaching is rather routine or dull, but children who have joined my class from yours are always talking about particular projects they did.'

On other occasions the evidence was offered for reinterpretation and recontextualisation by the partner: 'You have put "Performing on stage" as "Undeveloped" but I have seen you really holding the attention of children and adults alike during your assemblies – you are about the only who can!'

'Yes, I suppose that is "performing" if you look at it like that.'

Requiring their partners to 'look at it like that' was seen by all as being of great value, bringing a rigour and intensity to the process that was surprising given the artificiality of the exercise in its context and timing.

Even where, for logistic reasons, teachers from different schools were paired together, they were surprised at how important the partner role was. Indeed, there was often interesting discussion about the actual advantages of a 'naive partner', which was followed up in subsequent developments in schools.

The rules suppressed any tendency to 'bully' or, alternatively, gave individuals the tools with which they could resist such tactics.

Yet, critically, there were concerns and challenges here. Wasn't this a 'soft process'? Look, this is all very well but isn't it the appraiser's job to judge, to be critical, to tell the appraisee what is good and bad?'

My response was to offer the view of the appraiser role as: 'The responsibility to ensure that critical judgements *are made*, not to *make* them.'

Development or improvement

The final stage of selection focused on the importance of making actual development practical and realistic according to clear criteria.

Teachers found it unusual and difficult to be asked to choose from the 'Competent' column, reflecting a strong view that professional development largely, and appraisal definitely, are concerned with weakness and failure: 'Surely the purpose of appraisal is to discover your weaknesses so that you can put them right?'

The 'you don't have to be sick to get better' adage is disturbingly difficult for teachers to accept. The question: 'What are you doing quite well but would like to do even better?' needs powerful reinforcement.

In many cases a more sophisticated and collaborative view of appropriate individual development became apparent. This was represented by remarks like: 'My IT skills aren't particularly developed but we work so closely together that I know there is support there if I need it.'

What teachers found reassuring was the clarity with which 'routing' could be established from their specific development choices through to something that represented a much more holistic view of their capabilities and skills. Over this a comprehensive 'template' of individual choices could be placed which was consistent, even in its variety, with a collective view of the teacher's role.

In this sense individual choices were convergent with an agreed specification despite the apparent diversity of development choices. This was an important feature of the case study which follows.

Action or reflection – a necessary luxury?

The final task given to the 'pair' of teachers was to take one development area defined by a chosen 'card' and, through discussion, analyse the key issues involved for that teacher. These then had to be expressed as specific written questions, which invited further inquiry, as in the example given here.

Area of development	*Key questions*
Classroom management – effective small group work with computers	To what extent do all members of a group share responsibilities in a set task? To what extent am I freed from more mundane routine roles in the classroom?

This posed more problems for teachers than any other part of the process. The instinctive tendency was to suggest solutions to perceived problems. Restricting the discussion to the identification of issues and subsequent questions for inquiry was a discipline which caused not only frustration but also annoyance at first. Where partners found real difficulties, they were encouraged to identify and express issues as 'dilemmas' – 'On the one hand . . . , but, on the other hand, . . . '.

However, when the questions were linked to specific forms of classroom observation (a statutory requirement within school teacher appraisal) the sense of the process became clearer. The notion of observation as a judgemental process by 'Appraisal Man' had been transformed to: 'What information do I need to enable me to answer this question with more confidence and thus determine further action and development?'

As one teacher said: 'We are used to collecting information to evaluate the success of an initiative but not to determine the shape and course of that initiative. I guess we are used to rushing, under pressure, into action. Reflection like this seems a luxury.'

CASE STUDY

The second part of this narrative describes how a primary school sought to incorporate the ideas and principles which emerged in appraisal training, as described above, into the development of IT teaching and learning in the curriculum.

My first discussion with the head teacher told a familiar story. There had been a number of IT initiatives in the school but, as the head said: 'It always seems that we are starting back at square one.' He went on: 'Initial enthusiasm and commitment has been quite high and we have had good support. We can't blame lack of equipment. But we have not really seen development or, if we have, it has been patchy. I can't, in all honesty, say that all the children are having a consistent experience in IT.'

The reasons, it appeared, were, in no particular order:

- the dependence on the skills and expertise of an individual enthusiast or leader – lost if that person leaves the school;
- lack of teacher self-confidence – hard gained but soon lost;
- the difficulty in getting the correct balance between the development of teacher skills and curriculum implementation.

This last point seemed crucial and was perhaps the key to the first two. Often the focus in school had been on developing teacher skills in computer use, with the aim of thus developing confidence. However, if these skills had been developed without reference to actual classroom practice – the variety of learning experiences available to children and how they could be incorporated into the curriculum – development of IT as a teaching and learning tool was likely to be limited. At the same time, if the use of IT in the curriculum was introduced without attention to the skills of teachers in their own IT use, they would lack the confidence to exploit its full potential. As the head teacher went on to say: 'If I look at my staff and their attitude towards the use of IT in their classrooms, I can see everything from enthusiasm, through guarded interest, to great caution and outright hostility.'

What, therefore, did he want? In terms of IT development he wanted:

- greater clarity of the school's aspirations and criteria of quality in relation to IT teaching and learning;
- a much closer link between the development of teacher skills and confidence, and the awareness of IT use in the curriculum and classroom;
- a recognition that, as in other areas of school activity, expertise in IT is a collective relying on the complementary skills and experience of teams of teachers and individuals;
- an understanding that development is a long-term process which has to work to realistic and manageable targets;
- highly supportive structures to allow individuals to develop their own skills with confidence.

In terms of school development he wanted:

- a process which would bring together existing procedures and activities to a convergent focus;
- an explicit link between whole school development and individual professional development;
- correlation between the guidance given to individual development and the school's own criteria for quality in IT teaching and learning.

The appraisal process which was being planned in the light of the training described above seemed to offer the 'tools' by which some of these targets could be achieved. The particular features which stood out were:

- the possibility of a clear and agreed structure which would allow teachers to explore their skills (and weaknesses) in a more explicit and supportive way;
- the strength of a partnership exploration, observation and analysis to ensure that action was preceded and mediated by reflection and identification of need;
- a means by which explicit techniques of identifying questions, gathering information, analysing information, forming hypotheses and determining action (effectively the process of 'action research') could be embedded into an INSET and professional training process;
- rigour brought not by an authoritarian structure of judgement but through 'critical friendship'.

A pragmatic note which formed a realistic 'political context' to these aspirations was, in the head's words: 'We've got to do appraisal whether we like it or not. Let's for heaven's sake make it of real use to us!'

Planning the process

The dilemma facing an appraisal system, which seeks convergence between whole school development and individual professional development, is the possible tension between the perceived rights of individuals to choose their own 'areas of focus' for appraisal and the desire of the school to introduce what amounts to a degree of prescription or, at the least, 'ring fencing'. This tension is reinforced by the powerful 'rules' of confidentiality which bind the products of the appraisal process. The key, as in the procedures used during training, seemed to be self-appraisal which was accorded a prime position in the recommended model for appraisal in Cambridgeshire (Figure 17.2).

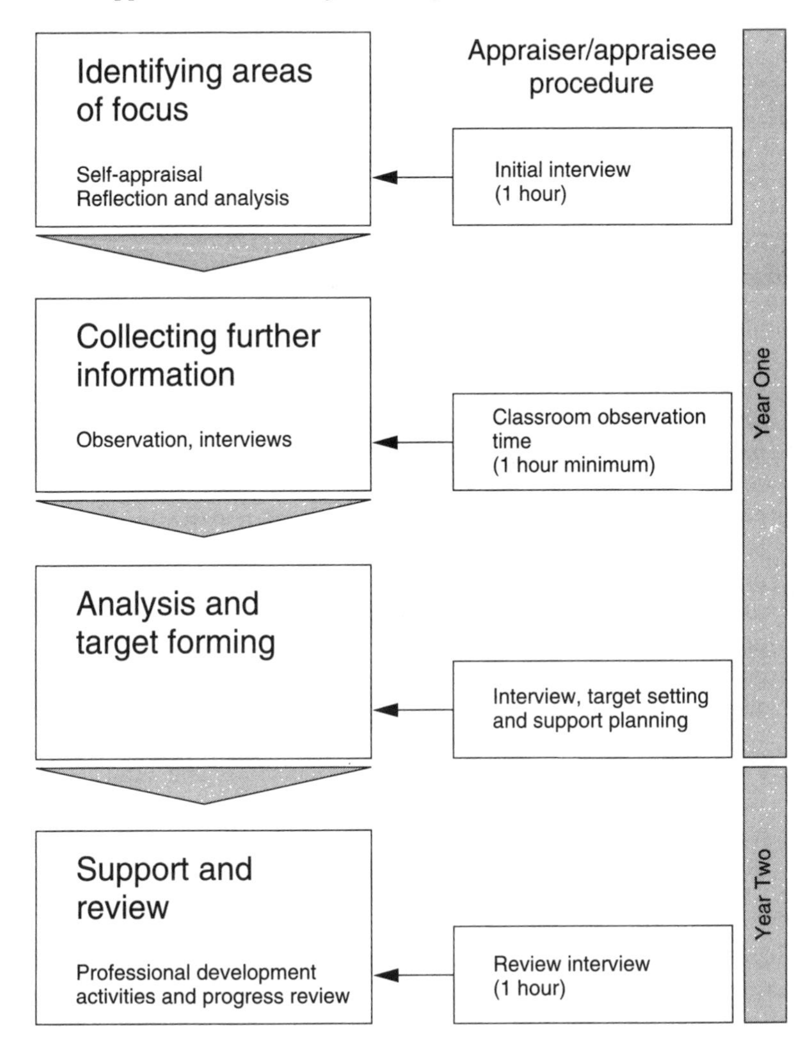

Figure 17.2 Appraisal phases

We planned to derive a self-appraisal mechanism, or 'tool,' that shared the following features:

- it would offer teachers genuine choice of specific areas of professional practice, albeit in relation to the use of IT;
- it would be derived directly from a detailed, explicit and agreed view of school development targets in IT;
- it would be transferable, in alternative guises and formats, to perform essential planning, monitoring and quality assurance functions for the school and would offer compatibility with external frameworks of evaluation such as OFSTED.

The first step was to produce 'aspirational' agreed statements of effective teaching and effective learning targets for the school. These were compiled using some NCET (1994) materials as a model but based upon individuals and then teams constructing lists based upon the starters: 'Effective learning in IT in this school would result in . . . ' and 'Effective teaching of IT in this school would demonstrate . . . '. The results are shown in the boxes below and opposite.

Effective learning in IT would result in:

- pupils asking more questions and offering hypotheses because IT makes it easier to answer or explore them;
- pupils showing a willingness to look for answers because IT makes information retrieval, data analysis and modelling easier;
- pupils showing a willingness to take risks because IT allows them to correct errors and/or to start again;
- pupils using and choosing a wider range of resources and media because IT facilitates organisation and retrieval;
- pupils showing an ability to learn by iteration rather than through one single attempt, because IT makes experimentation faster and easier;
- pupils showing better motivation towards their work because IT makes possible the capture/retrieval and analysis of real information and allows pupils to achieve high-quality presentation and to design systems which perform real tasks;
- pupils collaborating on tasks to produce outcomes and using IT to facilitate such collaboration;
- pupils becoming more autonomous because IT offers them tools they can control to perform jobs and tasks for them.

These immediately offered the senior management of the school a set of key criteria for quality assurance monitoring, not taken from some external prescription but constructed by staff themselves in language which they both owned and understood.

Effective teaching in IT would demonstrate that:

- individual lesson planning takes account of the school's agreed plan for the development of IT capability;
- lesson objectives identify specific opportunities for developing IT capability;
- teachers take pupils' prior experience with IT (gained in and out of school) into account when planning lessons;
- activities have built-in differentiation so that the tasks set match the needs and abilities of pupils;
- teachers use IT to motivate learning and to sustain pupils' interest;
- IT is used to enhance both teaching and learning in a range of subject contexts;
- teachers manage their classrooms to maximise the availability and use of IT resources;
- teachers use the IT expertise of colleagues to develop their own learning and that of their pupils;
- teachers consciously find ways to use pupils' own IT expertise to develop other pupils' learning;
- available support, such as technician or IT Special Educational Needs specialists, is used by the teacher to best effect;
- teachers use the available expertise of parents and other members of the community to enrich IT use in their classroom.

Features of effective learning in Information Technology To what extent are you confident that there is evidence of these features in your classroom?	*Very Confident*	*Confident*	*Uncertain*	*Very Uncertain*
pupils asking more questions and offering hypotheses because IT makes it easier to answer or explore them.				
pupils showing a willingness to look for answers because IT makes information-retrieval, data analysis and modelling easier				
pupils showing a willingness to take risks because IT allows them to correct errors and/or to start again				
pupils using and choosing a wider range of resources and media because IT facilitates organisation and retrieval				
pupils showing an ability to learn by iteration rather than through one single attempt, because IT makes experimentation faster and easier				
pupils showing better motivation towards their work because IT makes possible the capture/retrieval and analysis of real information and allows pupils to achieve high quality presentation and to design systems which perform real tasks				
pupils collaborating on tasks to produce outcomes and use IT to facilitate such collaboration				
pupils becoming more autonomous because IT offers them tools they can control to perform jobs and tasks for them				

Figure 17.3 Features of effective learning in Information Technology

Similarly, these criteria could be used as essential 'templates' at the level of both subject planning, as in the construction of schemes of work, and the planning of 'year teams' in constructing an integrated and complementary curriculum.

Critically, however, they were adapted as simple but clear self-appraisal tools for individual teachers to use to initiate the choosing of 'areas of focus' for their appraisal with their appraisers. Like the exercise in appraisal training described above, this simple structure allowed teachers to identify those aspects of IT teaching and learning which were priorities for their individual development, yet reassured them that these individual choices were directly connected with team and school planning. Moreover, the phrasing of the features of teaching and learning invited appraisees and appraisers to move on to discuss and agree appropriate methods for gathering further information about actual practice through classroom observation. This would-be observation focused not on superficial judgements of teacher competence but deployed to enrich and amplify teachers' own knowledge of their teaching and learning practice in IT.

The school used detailed profiles of pupil progression in IT capability in the National Curriculum IT attainment targets, *Communicating Information, Handling Information, Modelling* and *Monitoring and Control*, to generate check lists both for staff to evaluate their own capability and as a basis for recording systems for classroom observation (Table 17.1). Observation itself was supported by clear guidance and pro formas to ensure consistent and informed practice (Figure 17.4).

CONCLUSION

The outcomes of this carefully planned process are, at the time of writing, still to be revealed. However, it is noteworthy that the staff are committed to an appraisal process which offers a supportive and clear structure, maintains their individual rights of choice, and links their own development to that of their school as a community.

IT development in schools is difficult and is often led by enthusiasm rather than detailed planning. Enthusiasm is valuable but it can also be transient and, to others, intimidating rather than inspirational.

The responsibility on school management to initiate, implement, monitor and evaluate development is huge and we should not assume that the procedures and tools to achieve this are automatically in place.

There is a certain irony that 'Appraisal Man', with such unpromising and suspicious origins, may be the positive provider of the means by which busy schools, bombarded, as they would see it, with initiatives, can achieve clarity and bring together and focus the energies they need.

Tally Systems

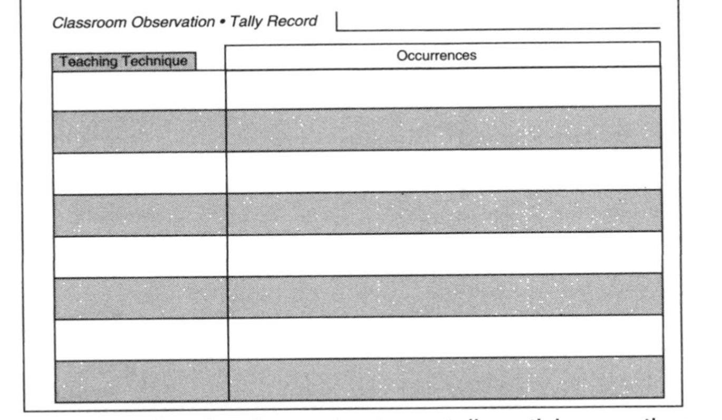

Classroom Observation • Tally Record

Teaching Technique	Occurrences

In this situation the observer enters a tally or tick every time agreed events take place. The purpose is to produce a pattern of action and behaviour which will show, for example, whether one particular behaviour dominates others.

The results are factual and exclude judgement, although they can inform later judgements.

It is important that the observer and teacher agree precise categories of behaviour or events beforehand and there is clear agreement as to what the categories mean.

The technique is useful to test subjective feelings of a teacher – e.g. 'I think I tend to pay more attention to the boys in my class compared with the girls'.

Classroom Observation • Questioning

Teaching Technique	Occurrences
Open questions to class/group	
Closed questions to class/group	
Open questions addressed to individuals	
Closed questions addressed to individuals	
Restating pupil response	
Elaborating pupil response	
Inviting response to pupil's answer	
Correcting child response	

Pros

- easy to use
- simple to apply
- excludes judgement
- systematic and supportive to observer

Cons

- limited in detail
- reveals little of quality of performance etc.
- no distinction between individual tallies

Figure 17.4 Tally systems

Table 17.1 Communicating information

Levels	*Program skills*	*Use of keyboard/ resources*	*Mouse control*	*Activities*	*Resources*
1 Work involves manipulating text, pictures or sounds to communicate meaning. Programs which allow the children to move pictures, build sentences using whole words or rearrange parts of a tune are appropriate. Support programs such as Talking Books will give CD-ROM experience.	Moving around the screen, selecting objects with the mouse	Use of: • RETURN key • Space bar • DELETE key	Click and point Keeping mouse on the mouse mat	1 Adding text to a picture 2 Matching sound to text or picture 3 Sorting pictures/text 4 Finding objects/text that don't belong	Colour screen computer Printer Mouse-driven software: CD and disc based
2 Work consists of actually creating information in the form of words, pictures or sounds (perhaps a simple story, a painting or an original tune made from basic components) and learning how to save and print their work with help from adult or older child.	LOAD • SAVE • PRINT With help	• Use of RETURN • Use of DELETE, CAPS LOCK Typing in some text unaided Recognition of upper and lower case Switch on computer	Improving controlled movement of the mouse Using mouse button(s) with increasing accuracy Scrolling windows	1 Name labels 2 Topic book titles 3 Writing addresses 4 Simple posters 5 Invitations 6 Captions	Colour screen computer Printer Software: • text processing • graphics • music
3 Work requires children to create longer pieces of writing, pictures or tunes, amend them, perhaps correcting	Start a fresh document – change fonts/sizes – change colours Load, print and save	Keying in information Edits by deleting and correcting capitals, full stops and spelling	Block text	1 Writing about ourselves 2 Posters in colour and layout 3 Front cover for topic	Colour screen computer Printer Software: • text processing

mistakes and improving word choice. They must be able to print and save work independently. The use of on-line services can be introduced through e-mail exchanges with a partner school.	program/document Block text moving Spellchecking Moving between windows on screen	Set up computer Switch on printer		4 Short descriptive writing 5 Reports 6 Book reviews 7 Tourist guides	• graphics • music • modem, e-mail and telephone connection
4 Children will use word processors, multimedia software, CD-ROM and on-line services independently to create electronic and paper presentations. Search & replace	Entering clip art into text Cut/paste marks; block text and copy Tabs; justification; sizing writing; using more than one page line resources	Increased awareness of the position of letters Setting up printer Choosing and saving text, sound and pictures to disc from CD-ROMs and from on-	Blocking text Use of icons to change and alter features	1 Poems – using layout to add to meaning 2 Magazines/newspapers 3 Factual reports 4 Card designs 5 Collaborative writing projects	DTP system with scanner/digitiser Multimedia software
5 Children will use software to enhance communication through the use of software features which allow the manipulation of text. They will combine different sorts of information. CD-ROM and on-line systems will be exploited as sources of information, text and pictures which will then be edited to match existing projects.	Creating clip art Entering clip art/charts/graphics into DTP packages Page layout and design Leading; sub/superscript Configuring a program Setting up templates Rulers; printing banners	Hot keys	Using mouse accurately and quickly in use of generic programs: • DTP • Word processor • Database • Graphics • Spreadsheet	1 Diagrams 2 Map work 3 Long stories with chapters 4 Writing for more than one audience 5 Play writing 6 Creating story using text, graphics and sound 7 Creating factual report	DTP system with scanner/digitiser Multimedia software Midi interface and keyboard Sound sampling equipment Video and still cameras

ACKNOWLEDGEMENTS

I wish to thank *The Times Educational Supplement* for permission to reproduce the cartoon 'Appraisal Man' by Bill Stott which appeared in the issue of December 1992. I also wish to thank Cambridgeshire Curriculum Agency for permission to reproduce parts of the *Schemes of Work Toolkit* and Cambridgeshire appraisal training materials.

REFERENCE

NCET (National Council for Education Technology) (1994) *Reviewing IT in the Primary School.* Coventry: NCET.

Chapter 18

Strategies for staff and institutional development for IT in education

An integrated approach

Niki Davis

The development of information technology in teachers' professional work and its development within organisations appears to occur in phases, rather than as one smooth transition. Evidence from around the world shows that it frequently starts with the adoption of an application or two by enthusiastic individuals. A middle phase involves leadership by a co-ordinator who frequently begins with an attempt to standardise hardware and software, then often changes the focus to the curriculum. At the end of the development an ideal situation can be the infusion of technology throughout the organisation, where it is used and developed by everyone, as and when appropriate. While this ideal state may remain unattainable, given the rapid development of the technology, this chapter describes strategies to move towards it. An additional, idealistic view is that teachers should be thoroughly prepared to use IT during their initial training. This chapter draws some lessons from those in universities and schools who have been working to achieve this. It reflects on a range of strategies they have explored and the underpinning models of professional development. It is divided into sections which deal, in turn, with strategies for individual development; additional issues arising for the development of practice across a group; and the necessary development of the organisation as a whole, including strategies which assist the development of this infrastructure.

DIMENSIONS OF PROFESSIONAL DEVELOPMENT

The process of professional development is approached from two interacting dimensions:

- the individual's personal view;
- the social context within which that person works.

John Butler (1992) emphasises the role of reflection in bringing these two dimensions together. The individual reflects on information gained personally, considering it within the social context of work where it may be employed.

The social context for teachers today, both inside and outside education, is clearly influenced by new technologies. Teachers already appreciate the role of IT to communicate information, for example through television and other media.

And they will appreciate its use to handle and control data which affect them, for example in money transactions. New technology also has the potential to change learning, teaching and its management. Teachers at all levels will need support to add the various IT tools and approaches to their professional practice. Teachers need new personal knowledge about IT and an appreciation of a range of applications to match their interests. They need to develop skills and strategies for their own professional practice. In addition, they need 'public knowledge' of the ways in which their institution(s) expect IT to be used and accessed. Given the low level of confidence and skill that many teachers start with and the rapid development of IT, the complexity of professional and institutional development in schools and teacher education institutions becomes apparent.

To unravel this complexity I will consider the individual first and then move on to groups and whole institutions.

PERSONALISED STRATEGIES FOR STAFF DEVELOPMENT

Teachers and trainers come across IT in many ways, but to progress to a stage where IT applications are adopted as naturally as a book or artefact to enhance learning can be a stressful process requiring commitment and support. One of my colleagues, Angela Horton (1992), once called this her 'pilgrim's progress'. The first step in professional development is to engage in it and, while this sounds obvious, it should be recognised that individuals are being asked to take a risk. Accepting that improvement is required may suggest that current practice is inadequate. Teachers must also take risks when they first apply new tools and technologies in their classrooms – they are taking on the unknown. A supportive environment with some counselling is therefore appropriate and important. To reduce the risk and to embed professional development in the knowledge and prior experience of individuals implies helping them to make links with associated and relevant practice. The links are between relevant IT applications, their curriculum interests or personal experience, and their approaches and values in teaching and learning. This approach considers professional development to be a form of learning. Hence professional development must be firmly embedded in past experience and the individual's prior knowledge, as was considered in Chapter 1.

The University of Exeter was one of the five institutions involved in Project INTENT with the aim of improving the use of IT in initial teacher education. The Exeter INTENT team included four people working together to develop courses, resources, staff and the institution generally. As part of this process we discussed and attempted to clarify strategies for the professional development of our colleagues. We agreed that the first and most common strategy was 'informal discussions and conversations'. This was seen as the key and yet was the hardest to quantify and evaluate because it was about listening to the concerns of individuals and counselling them.

We recognised that this strategy was used repeatedly and that staff development must mean that we, the agents of development, become more informed about the professional work of colleagues. It was clear that colleagues with limited knowledge and skills in IT were unable to describe what they wanted. The counselling involved the two dimensions: the individual's personal view and the social context within which that person worked. Individuals needed to build up their mental picture of what IT could do for them. Also, we needed to gain an understanding of individuals' environments and the way in which they taught: their social context. It is important to note that the professional development was not one-way. Each of the four INTENT team members also underwent professional development in both dimensions in terms of increased understanding of different disciplines and appropriate uses for IT within each discipline.

Let me illustrate this with an example which involved my colleagues with responsibility for the education of art teachers. Colleagues in this discipline needed to identify applications of IT which they found valuable. An early workshop using a painting package (Paintbrush) showed the diversity of their approach as artists, but it did not ignite their enthusiasm. One colleague produced a beautiful sketch and another a wonderful explosion of pattern and colour, but neither was satisfied with the tools, preferring the precision and feel of the pencil or the infinite variety of tone and colour possible with a traditional palette. A computer as a paintbrush was rejected because traditional media were more appropriate for what they wanted to teach. However, some time later we did find a tool that caught their imagination for an area within art where new demands required a new approach. The use of interactive video disks of museums and art galleries proved to be a far more effective means of studying 'the masters' than the traditional use of postcards and an occasional visit to an art gallery.

Having found a key IT tool, the second dimension of context had to be addressed. Other colleagues had to be convinced of the value of the video disks. New practices were required so that students could access the materials within the constraints of course time and location. An expensive resource could not be duplicated for each student and so course organisation, assessment and classroom management had to become more flexible. Instead of all students studying the same topic simultaneously, the teacher set small groups of students a topic to investigate and this concluded with the presentation of the topic to the whole group. The interactive video disk was a major resource for the task, so students booked time to use it. Their presentation to the whole group and the handout produced for their fellow students was assessed instead of the traditional essay. In this way my colleagues successfully adapted their classroom management and this process of change continues to evolve today.

PHASES OF PROFESSIONAL DEVELOPMENT

Professional development of the individual is a process which occurs in phases. Brown (1994) describes an evaluation of a teacher training programme in schools which sought to enhance management of IT and classroom applications of IT to enhance learning. He describes three phases:

> Typically novices are concerned in developing their own competence. Concern then switches to the tasks to be undertaken: for example they may focus upon the support necessary to get learners to use IT for particular tasks. The final stage can involve a more critical reflection on the use of IT: how it is used to enhance learning rather than just encourage its use *per se.*
>
> (Brown, 1994, p. 146)

In the USA, Berenson and Snyder (1991) have shown striking changes in final grades of a university course by adopting approaches to staff development first developed for schools. They describe a spiral of changes which started with tutors building knowledge of new tools and adopting a constructivist approach to teaching undergraduates. This approach encouraged students to construct their own knowledge in mathematics through using IT. The second stage of 'vision making' involved identifying tools and active student-centred strategies for using them. In the third stage staff 'took risks' to trial these new visions within their courses. The spiral continued as more knowledge-building occurred. Active learning strategies introduced were co-operative learning, class discussion, probing questioning, student-generated problem-solving and inquiry/guided practice. Use of IT included graphic calculators, computer graphics and laser disk. For example, calculus group projects became the basis for study groups and gave students the opportunity to communicate mathematically with each other (Berenson *et al.*, 1990).

Professional development may be stimulated by a range of factors. In schools there is often pressure from management to conform to new requirements, such as those imposed by a National Curriculum. However, most teachers also demand that changes benefit their students. Therefore the start, or a move to a new phase in the process, is the discovery of a key IT application which persuades them that IT is relevant to their purposes – that it does enhance teaching and learning.

Timing of events in these phases of professional development is also important. During Project INTENT I worked closely with Angela Horton, who led the teacher education of sixty primary student teachers. I describe in detail in another article this case of one university tutor's development (Davis, 1992). Angela's first course was planned and delivered jointly as a workshop for sixty student teachers with a circus of activities based on appropriate software and historical artefacts. Angela and I together led the session from our respective expertise in humanities and IT, with the collaboration of two other tutors. The second phase took place early in the following term. Angela noted the effect of the students' interest:

> This first experience of working with students has been a reasonable success in the light of its objectives. Moreover, when I saw the students' interest in what they were doing my enthusiasm for pursuing these issues and challenges increased.
>
> (Davis, 1992, p. 8)

Angela's decision to work with a second group fairly soon after the first one was important to her continued professional development. It was not a case of using more applications, but a new and more reflective approach to the old material. This time Angela, who had gained confidence, took the lead. My role was more like that of resource librarian, suggesting items of software and ways in which they might be applied. Angela had become more autonomous. She had also moved to a new phase in attempting to distil her approach to the use of IT in the primary classroom. She told me: 'I realised [after rewriting the student handout] that the task sheets didn't support the effects on children's learning. Therefore I rewrote them and recognised that I had developed. Like anything else, you have to learn from experience and you have to start somewhere.'

I diagnosed six phases in Angela's development:

1 competence with some software;
2 understanding the place of that software within the curriculum;
3 starting to distil this for student teachers;
4 enlarging range of practice;
5 clarifying enhanced learning through IT;
6 improving practice in courses, classroom and assessment.

Angela had time for consolidation of the first phase of professional development over the Christmas vacation and she was able to approach the second course with renewed vigour. Had there been a year between a repeat of the first and second attempts to integrate IT, she might well have forgotten too much. These points apply to professional development just as much as they do to student learning.

Similar phases in professional development occur in schools. The following example is taken from a secondary school. It involves a department of English and, as in the previous case, the head of department was already familiar with IT tools for his personal use. However, other members of the department did not have IT skills. The case is told through extracts from the IT co-ordinator's diary. We start with an early unsuccessful exploration of word processing in English. Clearly, it is not perceived as the critical encounter to motivate further developments in IT:

> Head of English attends another course, 'Word processing in English', and reports: 'I saw nothing that convinced me that word processors can be usefully applied to English.' Objections include: 'You can't cross things out and write comments at the side and you can't see the whole document in one go.'
>
> (October 1988)

Later the same teacher was encouraged when he started to teach students with special educational needs, using word processors to provide a stimulus and allow them to produce neat and correct work. However, the application which set a series of developments in motion was desktop publishing (DTP):

> An in-service course for the English department resulted in the comment: 'I can see possibilities with this.' Following this, the IT co-ordinator's classes began to produce some good work which was put on display in the IT room. The head of English commented: 'You can do some rather good things with this, can't you?!' He brought other members of the department to have a look.
>
> Following agreement to dedicate some equipment to the delivery of IT across the school in English and sustained support to develop teachers' personal skills in DTP, the English department placed IT firmly in their courses, using word processors and DTP. Special-needs students were taught to DTP.
>
> (January 1990)

This success story was not without subsequent pain, because many members of the department had yet to learn about classroom management of IT and, at that time, the students had a low level of IT literacy. The head of English complained to the IT co-ordinator:

> 'We've started on our DTP but it is just not working . . . the kids keep losing work and we need printouts at the end of each lesson so they can take them home and amend them . . . I give up! – there are too many problems. You can't ask people like X to do DTP with such problems.' The IT co-ordinator suggests that he should provide in-class support and for the first time it is accepted for X, who has relatively little IT experience. By the end of the first lesson all pupils had successfully saved their work and produced a printout.
>
> (January 1994)

This account of work in English shows that the first phase in the evolution of IT use at departmental level must be to establish the belief that IT can enhance the quality of learning. This is largely an individual process, described in the previous section, but enthusiastic colleagues will encourage other staff in the same department. The original lack of belief can be gradually transformed into a commitment to ensure that students receive a good experience. However, the process is not without its pain and those committed to IT have to persevere in arguing the case for its value, while attempting to avoid using externally imposed policies (such as criteria for course accreditation) to coerce colleagues. In the end, staff frequently admire the quality of students' work with IT and this will reinforce their new belief that all students should, can and will achieve competence with IT in their learning. Further evidence of this process has been gained in schools (Brown, 1994) and in other universities (Vaughan, 1991).

This case has moved our focus from the individual to a group of teachers and their support staff.

GROUPS AND INDIVIDUALS

In the USA, Neil Strudler (1991) describes four aspects of support that he ensures within his university, drawing on his doctoral research in elementary schools in Oregon:

- collaborative problem-solving;
- resource adding;
- training and follow-up support;
- organisation and preparation.

A more detailed list is provided in the box. It is derived from the list drawn up during Project INTENT by the Exeter staff development team. It is divided roughly into two: strategies to promote institutional development, and those suitable for an individual/group. It is important that the two occur in parallel in order to avoid problems commonly experienced by many IT co-ordinators and staff, such as lack of resources.

Demonstration followed by individual tuition has been one of the main modes used to introduce new applications. This support of an individual or small group permits greater in-depth needs analysis and a more individualised follow-up programme than could be provided for a large group. The description of Angela Horton's development illustrated this approach. In particular, the newer technologies (video disk, scanning, etc.) fit this style well. Such work often results in collaborative research and development, which increases opportunities for new resources. However, this type of listening and learning can be very time-consuming and in practice is not always possible. The third case of an English department in a school used a range of strategies, including in-service courses for staff.

The next example illustrates a number of approaches which have been merged together. It emphasises the opportunistic nature of staff development. Work in response to demands of the situation can be unfruitful, yet occasionally unplanned events prove fruitful in the end. Although derived from a real case in a university, this example is not untypical of development within a school department. It started from the need in modern languages to provide an introductory course for students. The course was designed collaboratively with the IT department. Informal discussions and conversations led to demonstrations of simulation software such as the virtual visit to *Granville* in France and the use of a Concept keyboard with *Meine Welt*. As staff tried to adopt these software applications within their specialist modern language resource area, spontaneous trouble-shooting and consulting were used to support them. At first, the modern language staff expected the IT tutor to take the lead with IT and to play little or no part themselves. Eventually, the major stimulus to their own professional development came when they perceived the enthusiasm of the student teachers. The IT tutor describes it thus:

> By chance, in order to deliver a message to the group, a tutor did join us during a session. She was accosted by two enthusiastic students who insisted

on explaining what they were up to. Once she saw the enthusiasm the students had got from what they were in the middle of, she stopped and took a closer look. When I went to talk to another colleague in that department, it had filtered through and a similar staff session was requested.

Work with this department continues. Recently IT resources have been purchased for the subject area and there has been a review of the central resource collection available to students. Overall, this has proved to be a truly eclectic approach to providing support, involving a wide range of strategies.

Strategies for staff development with information technology

Strategies for the institution

1 meetings which may be a group concerned with IT, or a subject or a course team, etc.;
2 work through senior management.

Strategies for the individual/group

Mainly introductory:

3 informal discussions and conversations;
4 courses provided for staff by staff developer;
5 demonstrations by staff developer to an individual or group.

Direct information/skill support

6 spontaneous support;
7 provision of information to suit the colleague's personal interests or needs;
8 consultation on general problems or provision of specific information;
9 provision of resources (hardware, software or other media);
10 workshop where colleagues have a chance to use IT;
11 trouble-shooting, mainly on technical problems;
12 curriculum development or collaboration which is often related to research.

Team teaching

13 teaching where both the colleague and staff developer are teaching;
14 join in classes taught by the staff developer or other IT competent/confident colleague.

Indirect staff development

15 work through students, whose work develops the colleague;
16 work through technicians who have received IT development;
17 work through the staff development unit.

The need for a link between short courses and more extensive requirements is clear. Although courses are usually well received they have limited outcome in terms of staff continuing to use the technology. The limitations are due to the shortness of the training that each individual receives, as well as the difficulty of arranging sufficient follow-up time with the right equipment to develop skills. (In the School of Education at Exeter, and in many schools, staff do not own computers which are capable of running the curriculum software.) However, staff attending short courses frequently do achieve a greater appreciation of what a computer can do. In-service training courses off the premises are also useful, but frequently focus on hardware and software which are inaccessible to the participants afterwards. In Devon this was addressed by the local education authority: it provided a computer and software for each participant to take away and develop within their own school. Occasionally this excellent approach backfired due to incompatibility of the equipment with the other equipment in the school, which in turn led to difficulties in technical support and curriculum coherence for the students.

It is also important to accept that a few colleagues may never take IT on board. Institutions should try to ensure that colleagues feel valued for the niche they have carved out, in which they are effective and play a valuable role. The lack of IT expertise in a small percentage of staff need not affect the quality of teaching and learning that students experience, if appropriate adjustments are made in the overall provision.

TECHNICIAN DEVELOPMENT AND INVOLVEMENT

Staff development is also important for support staff, especially for IT technicians to develop their knowledge and use of IT so that they can pass this on to other staff. This should include discussion of the ways in which technicians could assist teaching staff, particularly those who are relatively inexperienced. The IT technician needs to be supported and protected just as much as the tutors who are non-specialist users of IT. All staff need to recognise that teachers and technicians engage in a special sort of team teaching with shared responsibility for IT. Much of the teaching with IT depends on a workshop approach in which students use IT tools to develop their teaching plans and projects. Support staff appreciate adequate warning of the plans. As my colleague Penni Tearle commented:

> The quality of support provided by the technician in the primary teaching base was undoubtedly very important to this course. She provided a great deal of support, both when students were working with pupils and at times in between. She was kept fully informed by the IT tutors of likely requests from students, and also knew the curriculum requirements which were being addressed. She has worked with computers for some time and has been trained by the IT tutors to use the newer machines and interactive video bar-code systems.
>
> (Tearle and Davis, 1992, p. 13)

Other support staff also have an important role to play. Many teachers in university departments work very closely with assistants and regularly draw upon their expertise, particularly when it comes to the use of technology. These assistants gain an interesting overview of IT use and common problems, through working with both staff and students. Their feedback is very useful for IT co-ordination. Staff development provided by assistants includes careful organisation of the production of support materials, reviewing software, etc. In some schools a similar role is played by staff in a resource centre.

ORGANISATIONAL DEVELOPMENT

The development of organisations may take a variety of forms. Top-down planned directives and bottom-up natural development represent the two extremes of approach. However, a partnership model, in which senior managers work collaboratively with staff, recognising that there is inevitably some divergence of interest between the institution and the individual, is clearly more powerful. Working in this way in relation to IT often provides very effective staff development for senior managers. The many members of staff who sit on policy-making and resource committees are included in my category of senior managers.

A partnership approach to the development of IT within an organisation raises the awareness of the managers who are involved. They come to understand the ways in which IT co-ordinators, or those with a responsibility for staff development, can assist them to achieve management objectives. The work done by IT co-ordinators often goes unrecognised until attention is drawn to it through developing this kind of partnership approach. Once it is in place, managers often respond by raising the priority for resources to support the development of IT, including hardware, software, time and support staff. They have access to formal decision-making bodies. This is important because strategies for organisational development must work at policy and committee level, both within departments and across the institution as a whole. Resources are allocated in line with policy as it evolves. Colleagues' expectations of what they can do to improve teaching and learning with IT will be – or have been – raised by strategies already discussed, and they need resources with which to implement the new approaches. An appropriate strategy is to focus effort and resources on one area or department at a time, thus establishing local expertise which will sustain the innovations when, in due course, the focus moves on to another department.

Information technology affects all departments within an institution, but the role IT plays depends upon the needs of the discipline and the approach to staff development. Few resources will be available unless allocation is negotiated, because the colleagues who make decisions will not be aware of the special needs of departments. One pressing need within all educational organisations is therefore to communicate effectively across departments (or age-related teaching groups, in the case of primary schools). For university departments of education, it is also important to raise awareness of the needs of teacher training within the larger institution. The IT co-ordinator is therefore a key member of the institution's IT or resources committee and may raise issues there, when appropriate. In the early phases the members of this committee could be invited to the department to view the work in context.

It is also important to ensure that the senior management team is aware of guidelines for practice and resourcing laid down by outside bodies. For schools in England, Wales and Northern Ireland, IT is an integral part of the National Curriculum, just as it is of the 5–14 curriculum in Scotland; throughout the UK it is a statutory right for students with special needs, to whom it can give greatly improved access to the curriculum. Effective, educational uses of IT are also a requirement for initial teacher education programmes throughout the UK. Newly qualified teachers should have achieved a level of competence in IT. As the Trotter Report (DES, 1989) recommends:

> The IT capability of all students completing their initial teacher training should be sufficient for them to make effective use of IT in the classroom and at the same time provide a sound basis for their subsequent development in this field.
>
> (Trotter, 1989)

Institutions may have their own internal reports and policies relating IT to teaching quality and administration. Careful wording of these documents often makes it possible to pass on the coercive pressure from outside the institution and retain a partnership model within the institution.

The IT (or resources) committee appears to evolve through phases, which are naturally related to the phases of development noted for individuals. The first phase at Exeter appears to be typical. A working party of enthusiasts joined together with the aim of improving resources: hardware, accommodation and staff. One result was my appointment as the first lecturer in IT in education. I then became a key member of the group and led the development of the first IT policy, a brief document clarifying aims for IT but without specifying any strategy. As a result of this, the committee changed from a group of volunteers to a more formally constituted body representing interest groups within the organisation. Finally, as the IT activities and responsibilities increased and there was need for more specialised computing expertise, the committee needed to reduce its work with hardware and software by forming a subcommittee to deal with those aspects. The main committee now focuses on achieving institutional objectives through the use of IT. Future policy is likely to emphasise the need for monitoring, evaluation and strategic planning for IT development. The committee receives regular reports on staff development and supports both staff development and course development. It continues to report directly to the top committee in the organisation.

Committees other than IT are also important. A curriculum committee can negotiate a minimum number of hours for IT to enable the development of courses suited to students' needs and encourage the adoption of IT to suit the demands of teaching, learning and administration. Monitoring and evaluation of IT is also appropriate through course committees. In schools, co-ordination of the students' IT experience is often through the strands of IT competence such as 'using it to communicate information'. This responsibility is often spread across the subject departments after discussion at both the school IT committee level and at subject level. In this way use of IT can be designed to serve both subject and IT needs, as recommended by several directives including the National Curriculum for England and Wales.

In many institutions IT co-ordination has not followed the pattern of development outlined above. There are many reasons for this, but the indication is that often the co-ordinator has been preoccupied by technical issues and side-lined as a result of low status in the formal management hierarchy. In a survey of IT co-ordinators in schools, Colin Kirkman's analysis of their greatest problems puts the emphasis on shortage of time and lack of professional development opportunities, as shown in Table 18.1.

In Kirkman's list the interrelationship of strategies is clear. Equipment allocation has implications for improving staff attitudes; availability of time has implications for staff training; overload of the co-ordinator has implications for practical support in using resources and curriculum co-ordination – and all of these have implications for each other.

Gavin Owen's (1992) survey of secondary school co-ordinators concludes that the development of policy is far too important to be left to the technologists. IT as an infrastructure for learning must be directed by subject specialists right across the organisation. An important strategy will therefore be to empower the IT co-ordinator to undertake strategic planning. This can be done by teaming the technical IT expert with a member of the senior management team. Alternatively the IT co-ordinator could be promoted to the level of a head of subject department. This would permit negotiations with heads of departments

Table 18.1 The greatest problems of IT co-ordinators

Need more equipment/finance	15
Practicalities in using resources	14
Time	31
Attitude of staff	5
Staff awareness/training	17
IT co-ordinator overload	4
Promotion of IT	7
Co-ordination/delivery issues	8
National Curriculum	12
Other	3

Source: Kirkman (in preparation)

to take place on level ground, rather than requiring the IT manager to depend on personal charisma or technical expertise.

THE WAY AHEAD

This chapter has provided a wide-ranging view of strategies which are continuing to evolve over time, partly in response to the IT co-ordinators' own staff development. Many of the institutions whose work is represented here have moved a long way in a short time. This is clear just from the quality of the questions asked by staff. In the early days my colleagues at Exeter asked questions such as 'How do I use a word processor?' Questions are now more precise and more closely associated with education, rather than technology. For example: 'How can we develop an appreciation of colour and form using IT?' However, some of the old areas of concern remain: the need is still there to support all teachers in becoming confident and competent users of IT; the monitoring of student experience remains problematic; and there have been rapid developments in the field of technology itself.

In addition, there are new demands from government policies. The arrangements for increased school-based teacher education are a particular case in point. NCET (1994) provides a guide to the responsibilities of each partner and an indication of appropriate strategies. This lays out a continuum of responsibilities for seven elements of IT capability, which are the same as those listed for teachers in the introduction to Part One of this book – higher education takes the major role in developing basic technical capability whereas schools take the major role in developing an ability to manage IT use in the classroom.

Clearly, teachers in schools will be keen to set a good example to their students, and students should be prepared to help teachers take on new resources and ideas. These partnerships could become an important source for the ongoing professional development of teachers, as Malcolm Bell and Colin Biott suggest in Chapter 10 of this book. Teaching is an excellent learning strategy because we understand more deeply as we explain and demonstrate. The same applies to professional development. In my opinion, supporting the development of colleagues is the very best way to enhance your understanding of the role and importance of their subject within education as a whole.

New strategies will be required in the future, but the aim will remain the same: to improve the quality of teaching and learning. The overarching process will also be the same: change agents and those undergoing professional and institutional development are learners constructing new practice in both personal and social contexts.

ACKNOWLEDGEMENTS

My own professional development, upon which this chapter is based, would not have been possible without the support and collaboration of my colleagues in

Exeter, especially Penni Tearle, Chris Taylor and Bruce Wright, and all those in Project INTENT. School-focused description has been enhanced considerably by my doctoral students, especially Colin Kirkman and Gavin Owen. My thanks to all.

An earlier version of this chapter was published as Niki Davis, Colin Kirkman, Penni Tearle, Chris Taylor and Bruce Wright, 'Development of teachers and their institutions for IT in education: an integrated approach', *Journal of Information Technology and Teacher Education*, 4 (1), 1996.

REFERENCES

Berenson, S.B. and Snyder, S.S. (1991) 'Case study: changing undergraduate teacher preparation in science and mathematics education.' Paper presented at the 16th annual conference of the Association of Teacher Education in Europe, Amsterdam, September.

Berenson, S.B., Stiff, L.V. and Sims, L.B. (1990) 'Preparation of mathematics and science teachers for the twenty first century at North Carolina State University: a first year report submitted to the National Science Foundation, Grant Number TPE–8850634.'

Brown, A. (1994) 'Processes to support the use of information technology to enhance learning', *Computers in Education*, 22 (1/2): 145–53.

Butler, J. (1992) 'Teacher professional development: an Australian case study', *Journal of Education for Teaching*, 18 (3): 221–7.

Davis, N.E. (1992) 'Reflecting on professional development for IT: in-depth support', in *Developing IT in Teacher Education*, DITTE no. 1. Coventry: National Council of Educational Technology, pp. 17–26.

DES (Department of Education and Science) (1989) *Information Technology in Teacher Training: Report of the IT in ITT Expert Group* (Chair: Janet Trotter). London: HMSO.

Horton, A. (1992) 'Exploring IT for teaching and learning in the humanities', in *Developing IT in Teacher Education*, DITTE no. 1. Coventry: National Council of Educational Technology, pp. 5–15.

Kirkman, C. (in preparation) PhD thesis, University of Exeter.

NCET (National Council of Educational Technology) (1994) *Training Tomorrow's Teachers in Information Technology: A Partnership between School and Higher Education.* Coventry: NCET.

Owen, G. (1992) 'Whole school management of information technology', *School Organisation*, 12 (1): 29–40.

Strudler, N. (1991) 'Education faculty as change agents: strategies for integrating computers into teacher education programs', in D. Carey, R. Carey, D. Willis and J. Willis, *Technology and Teacher Education Annual.* Charlottesville, Va: AACE, pp. 275–8.

Tearle, P. and Davis, N.E. (1992) 'Bringing children, students and IT together in the primary base at Exeter University', in *Developing IT in Teacher Education*, DITTE no. 4. Coventry: National Council of Educational Technology, pp. 5–15.

Vaughan, G. (1991) 'Can professional development be achieved through course development?', *Developing IT in Teacher Education*, DITTE no. 4, Coventry: National Council of Educational Technology, pp. 73–82.

Index

A-levels 72
Acorn Computers 74, 138, 236
action research 5, 97, 114–15, 119–22, 128, 142–3, 223
Adams, Tony 174
adventure games 104, 105–6
Aitken, Roy 200
Alderson, G. 55
Almond, L. 120
Alred, G. 152
America *see* USA
Anne, Queen of Denmark 86
Apple Macs 78
appraisal: action or reflection 244–5; case study 245–52; development or improvement 244; inspection 239–40; role of partner 243; structure clarity 242–3; training 240–2
'Appraisal Man' 238–9, 245, 252
Archimedes computer 74, 75
art and design 12, 73–84; computer-aided design 109; IT and the National Curriculum 81–3; National Curriculum pressures 83–4; role for computer in art class 75–7; teacher competence 157–8
Art and Information Technology – Key Stage 3 83
Art: Non-statutory Guidance 82
Arthur Mellows Village College (AMVC) 73–81, 83
ARTISAN 75–81
AT&T Learning Network 170, 172
Athey, C. 90
Attwood, G. 175
authenticity 24

Baggott, Linda 177
Barton, Roy 12, 66, 105
BBC computers 144; BBC 'B' 138–9, 211; BBC Master 74, 211
Bell, Malcolm 98, 266
Bereiter, C. 24, 32, 38
Berenson, S.B. 257
Bigum, C. 143
Biott, Colin 98, 266
Birmingham University 211
Blenkin, G.M. 93
Bolter, J. 108
Bone, D. 183
Brasell, H. 66
Breese, C. 29
Bridges, D. 148
Britain *see* UK
British Telecommunications (BT) 170, 172
Brown, A. 257, 259
Brown, Erica 116
Brown, J.S. 24, 143
Brown, Roger 217
browsing 90
Bruner, J.S. 46
Bullock, E. 223
Bullock Report 189
Bush, Tony 197, 225
Butler, John 254
Butt, P.J. 59
Byrne Hill, G. 98, 152

CAD (computer-aided design) 109, 161–2
Calkins, L. 29
Cambridge University 174–5
Cambridgeshire LEA 5, 73, 74, 116
Cameron Jones, M. 132
Campus 2000 176
Campus Connect 170
CampusWorld 172, 176

Canada 174, 176
Case, R. 90
case competitions 173–4
CD-ROM: data sources 18–19, 106–7, 112, 162; education potential 107; encyclopedias 105, 107, 111; simulations 105; use in drama 158
Chandler, D. 51
change: approach to 5–6; institutional 187–207; leadership 224–5; management 187; management in educational institutions 210–26; management issues 221–3; partnership in management 190–3; useful ideas for management 204–7
Chester College 4
Choosing and Using IT Equipment 236
Civilization 106
classroom: culture 21–2, 24–6; knowledge 102; structure (pre-computer) 101–3
Cochran-Smith, M. 29, 110
Cockburn, A. 22
Collins, J. 106
communications, electronic 167–79; applications 168–70; budgeting implications 179; continuing professional development 175–8; cross-curricular applications 175; effective use 178–9; potential audience 18; potential for professional development 173–5; potential for teaching and learning 170–3; within companies 109; *see also* e-mail
compartmentalisation 188–9
computer: access to 128–9, 130; as catalyst for educational change 107–8; as cognitive tool 123–5; as curriculum resource 103–7; as neutral tool 123; as tutor 123; classroom 229; clusters 230–1; conferencing 104 (Table 8.1), 105, 111; health and safety issues 232; laboratory 229; portable *see* portable; single 230; skills for educational purposes 140–1
Concept keyboards 22, 40, 46
conferencing, computer 104, 105, 111
confidence, creating 143–6
CONNECT 177
control 20–1
Cornish, M. 127–8
Council for National Academic Awards (CNAA) 196, 211, 213–14, 216
COUNTER 42, 45–6
Coveney, Rod 184–5, 204
Coventry University 211, 216
cultural alienation 188

Daiute, C. 29
data: logging 63–4, 71–2, 104 (Table 8.1), 105, 155; simultaneous collection and presentation 66–7
databases 12; acceptability to teachers 131; children's approach to questioning 58–9; children's use of 51–61; educational characteristics 103, 104 (Table 8.1); hierarchical 50; issues for teachers 59–60; national 112; relational 18; remote 104 (Table 8.1); structures used in schools 50–1; tabular 50, 51
DataKing 52
Davies, Richard 15, 25, 60, 118, 143
Davis, Niki 4; (1988) 176; (1992) 257–8; (1994) 105, 172–3; (this volume) 185, 230; Somekh and (this volume) 98; Tearle and (1992) 262
Davison, Bob 116
De Vries, R. 90
'decision tree' software 18
Department for Education (DfE) 83, 127, 151, 163, 218
Department for Education and Employment (DfEE) 167
Department of Education and Science (DES): teacher education criteria 125; publications: (1975) 189; (1988) 29; (1989 – *Approval of Courses*) 190, 222; (1989 – *Revised Criteria*) 151; (1989 – Trotter Report) 4, 225, 264; (1990) 163; (1991) 81–2; (1992) 82,
Department of Employment 187, 218
Desforges, C. 22
design, computer-aided (CAD) 109, 161–2, *see also* art and design
design and technology 161–2
desktop publishing 18, 104, 155, 159, 162, 259
Dickinson, D. 29
DiMauro, V. 176–7
Division of Quality Audit (DQA) 212–13
Donaldson, M. 43, 87
Doyle, W. 21–2, 23
drama 158–9
Dreyfus, S.E. 206

drill and practice programs 104, 106

Easdown, G. 131
East Anglia, University of (Centre for Applied Research in Education) 4
Ebbutt, D. 143
ECCTIS 168
Education Reform Act (1988) 81
electronic communications *see* communications, electronic
Elliott, John 115, 143, 191–2, 205–7
e-mail 104, 105, 111, 172–3, 174–5
encyclopedias 104, 105–6, 111
English teaching: desktop publishing 259; IT competence 159–60; word processing 258–9
Enterprise Awareness in Teacher Education 218
Essex LEA 5, 73, 116
European Union 228
Exeter: Multimedia Communication Centre 177, 231–2, 234, 236, 260, 264, 266; School of Education 262; University 4, 175, 177, 255

Fawlty Towers 147, 230
Fisher, R. 28
Flexible Learning Project 160
Ford Teaching Project 115
frequency bar charts 50, 55–8
Front Page Extra 230
Fullan, Michael G. 115, 122, 190–3, 205–7

Galpin, B. 54
Garth Hill 189
GCSE 162
gender 188
Ghaye, A.L. 223
Godber, Juliet 74
Goldsmiths' College, University of London 4, 144, 150–4, 157, 163–5; IT in Teacher Education Committee 153–4
Goodchild, Stanley 189
Gordon, G. 216
graphics packages 103, 104, 157
graphs: children's work with 55–8; databases 51; information handling 18; interpretation of 12; skills 67–8; velocity 18, 20
Graves, Donald H. 17, 29
Greenwich Park 86
Griffin, Elaine 117
group: processes 60; tuition 260–2
Guha, M. 87

hacking 234–5
Halpin, David 196
Handy, Charles 200
hardware, buying 235–6
Hargreaves, Andy 201
health and safety 232
Heaney, P. 51
Hein, A. 87
Henriquez, A. 176
Heppell, S. 85
Her Majesty's Inspectorate (HMI) 81, 81, 151, 153, 164, 188, 192, 214
Higher Education Funding Council 224, 226
Higher Education Quality Control Council (HEQC) 211, 212–14, 216–17, 225, *see also* Division of Quality Audit
histograms 50, 55, 56
historical inquiry 18
Hodgkinson, K. 164
Holt, J. 90
Honey, M. 175–6
Horton, Angela 255, 257–8, 260
House, Ernest R. 117, 122
Hoyle, Eric 196–7, 206
Hurst, Vicky 12–13, 93, 105
Hutt, J.J. 89
hypertext: educational characteristics, 104; example 85; instructional 106; novels 108; use with primary-age children 12–13, 86–93

ICL (International Computers Ltd) 184
ideas processors 103, 104
Images of Organization 206
Impact of information technology on Children's Achievements in Primary and Secondary Schools (ImpacT) 69
individuals: power of 206; tuition 260, 261
information handling 18–19
Information Superhighway 98, 108, 167
Information Technology in Initial Teacher Education 225
Initial Teacher Education and New Technology Project (INTENT) 183–5; aims 190, 191–2; Exeter, 255–7, 260; formation 4; funding 4, 192, 204,

218; Goldsmiths' College 151, 153; in action 197–204; ITTEs 193–6; managers 195–6, 198–204; management of change 204–7; organisation 4; publications 5; selection of team 197; staff development project 218–21; Worcester 210–26
Inner London Educational Computing Centre (ILECC) 144
input devices 22–3
INSET 74, 246
inspection 239–40
inspector, resident 239
institutional change 187–207
intellectual tools *see* tools
INTENT *see* Initial Teacher Education and New Technology Project
interaction, pupil/teacher 68–70
interactivity, software 25
Internet 167, 169–70, 177, 221
Isenberg, D.J. 221–2, 226

Jackson, P.W. 21
JANET 221
Jessel, John 12–13, 35, 105
Jones, A. 106
Jones, Inigo 86

Kelly, A.V. 93
Kent, T.W. 174
Kerslake, D. 56
Kidsnet 169
Kingman Report 29
Kirkman, Colin 265
Kist, J. 51
knowledge: classroom/adult 102; redefinition of public 108–9
Kohlberg, L. 90
Kozma, R.B. 17
Krajcik, J.S. 67

LabNet 176–7
Landow, G.P. 108
languages, modern 160–1
leadership 224–5
Learning from Audit 217
Lewis, R. 141
light pens 22
Linkoping, University of, 174–5
Linn, M. 68
literacy 16
Liverpool Polytechnic 4
local area network 146, 147
LOGO: modelling environment 19; number concept study 42, 44–5, 103; role in mathematics learning 136, 202; mathematics teacher competence 155–6; Spaceship task 44–5; teacher–student partnership 135–6; turtles 106, 135
Lomax, P. 183

McAleese, R. 85, 90
McGowan, John 12, 74, 77, 109–10
'Making ready for change: acquiring enabling skills' 148
Malen, Betty 197
Mammals of the World: a Key Datafile 52, 58–9
Markham, E.M. 53
Mason, R. 168
mathematics: early years education 40–8; teacher competence 155–6
Maxted, D. 29
Maybin, J. 110–11
Mead, G.H. 140, 144
Meaning of Educational Change, The 191
measurement 20
Mehan, H. 29
Mercer, N. 68, 106
'messiness' 205–6
Micros and Primary Education (MAPE) 59
Microsoft Word 140, 236
Microsoft Works 235
MIT's 90s Research Group 184
modelling 19–20; software packages 103, 104; teacher competence 155
modern languages 160–1
Mokros, J.R. 66
Moore, A. 160
Moran, C. 37
multimedia 85, 106–7, 177–8
Mulvey, Rod 139
Murphy, R. 151
Muscella, D. 176-7
music 18; software 103, 104; teacher competence 156–7

Nachmias, R. 68
Nakhleh, M.B. 67
NASA 168
National Council for Educational Technology (NCET): Flexible Learning Project 160; INTENT funding 4, 192, 204, 218; PALM 5,

73; publications (1991) 160; (1993) 155–62, 164; (1994 – *Networks for Learning*) 168; (1994 – *Portable Computers*) 231; (1994 – *Reviewing IT*) 248; (1994 – *Training Tomorrow's Teachers*) 266; (1995 – *Choosing and Using IT Equipment*) 236; (1995 – *Managing IT*) 179, 183–4; (1995 – *Training Today's Teachers*) 12; (1995a) 158; (1995b) 162; (1995c) 160; (1995d) 156; (1995e) 161; (1995f) 157; (1995g) 155
National Curriculum (NC): art and design 81–4, 157; computer teaching requirements 50; constraints 100; graphing skills 67; influence of requirements 257, 264–5; IT assessment point 3; IT attainment targets 188, 249; IT capability 163; IT enhancement 130; Science IT requirement 64; software needs 235; timetabling pressures 73
National Curriculum Council (NCC) 82
National Maritime Museum 93
National Vocational Qualifications 3
Netherhall software developers 138–9
network: local area (LAN) 146, 147, 230; wide area (WAN) 230
networking, electronic 107–8, 111–12
New Meaning of Educational Change, The 205
Norfolk LEA 5, 73, 116, 187
Northumbria, University of 127
number, concept of 40–1, 47–8
nursery-age children 12

OFSTED (Office for Standards in Education) 184, 239–40, 248
Olsen, J. 110
open-ended software packages 103–5
Open University 175, 176, 210
outliners 103
Owen, Gavin 233, 265

Paddle, A. 51
Paintbrush 256
painting software 157
PALM *see* Pupil Autonomy in Learning with Microcomputers Project
Papert, Seymour 19
Parker, Z. 183
Parliamentary Office of Science and Technology (POST) 15
Partington, P. 216
partnership 206
Passey, D. 114
Pea, R.D. 25
Peacock, M. 29
Personal Knowledge 23
Phillips, R.J. 55, 56
Piaget, J. 88
pie charts 18, 50, 55, 57
Pirsig, R. 141–2
Polanyi, M. 23
portable computers 12, 21, 35, 231
Portable Computers in Schools project 64, 71
Pratt, Jon 74, 116, 118, 185
presentation packages 103, 104
primary-age children 12, 245
programming languages 103, 104, *see also* LOGO
Project INTENT *see* Initial Teacher Education and New Technology Project
'projects' 204–5
Proposals for art, 5–14 81
Pupil Autonomy in Learning with Microcomputers Project (PALM) 116–18; action research 5, 97, 114–15, 119–22, 142, 143, 223; aims 5, 73–4; approach, 97; Arthur Mellows Village College 73–4, 78, 81; funding, 5, 73; innovation 183; publications 5, 118, 121; subject disciplines of teachers carrying out action research in PALM 118 (Table 9.1); teachers' approaches 122–5; teachers' level of competence with computers 118 (Table 9.2)

Quality Audit 212–18
quality learning 14–15, 23–4
Quee, J. 58, 59
Queen's House 86, 91–3

Reflective Practitioner, The 115
ResCue 176
research, action see action research
resources: allocation of 189; flexible use of IT 234; organisation in educational institutions 228–36
responsibility 189–90
Reuters 169
Reynolds, M. 11
Ridgway, J. 114

Riel, Margaret 171
ROAMER 42, 47
Robinson, Bernadette 105
Robinson, Brent 105
robots 19, 20, 40
Ross, A. 51, 58
Roszak, T. 51
Rothery, Andrew 220–1
Ruopp, R. 176
Ruthven, K. 151

Salomon, G. 25
Salters, M. 11
scaffolding 110–11
Scardamalia, M. 24, 32
Schilling, M. 54
Schön, Donald 115
School Curriculum and Assessment Authority (SCAA) 56, 82–3, 155–62, 164
science, practical: conventional 65; with computers 65–6
Scottish Council for Educational Technology (SCET) 177, 231
screens: focus effect of 67; touch 22
Scrimshaw, P. 35, 97, 103, 105, 108
secondary pupils 12
self-teaching 141–3
Sellinger, M. 175
Sharples, M. 29
Sheingold, K. 25
Shuard, H. 48
Shuker, Leon 144
SimCity 106
simulations 20, 104, 105–6, 131, 155
SIP (Support for Innovation Project) 187
situated cognition 143
skills, computer: enabling 143–8; for educational purposes 140–1; performance and self 138–9; transferable 141–3
Smith, Helen 12, 51, 108
Smith, R. 152
Snyder, S.S. 257
social studies 162–3
software: buying 235; choice 100; 'decision tree' 18; interactivity 25; National Curriculum needs 235; open-ended 103–5; tackling a new package 145; teachers' use of 109–10; types 103–7 (Table 8.1); Windows 146
Somekh, Bridget 4–5, 74, 148; (1983) 120; (1988) 187; (1989) 176; (1990a) 118; (1990b) 118; (1991a) 118, 142; (1991b) 118; (1993 – 'Flies on their classroom walls') 118; (1993 – *Project INTENT*) 190; (1994a) 118; (1994b) 118; (this volume) 97; and Davies (1991) 15, 25, 60, 118, 143; and Davis (this volume) 98, 138; and Whitty and Coveney (this volume) 184; *et al.* (1992) 151, 197
Spavold, J. 58
speech-sensitive devices 22
Spoken Language and New Technology (SLANT) project 68–9
spreadsheets 19–20; educational characteristics 103, 104 (Table 8.1); teacher competence 155, 162
staff: development project 218–21; development strategies 261; support 262–3; support for 231–2
Steadman, S. 107
Stenhouse, Lawrence 22
stereotyping 188
stories 32–4
Stradling, B. 64, 71
Straker, A. 103
Stratta, E. 223
Strudler, Neil 160
student teachers: co-learning partnerships 133–6; dimensions of placements 129–32; nature of professional learning 131; Northumbria 127–8; placement characteristics 132–3; problem of IT in placements 128–9; teacher support strategy 131–2
Suffolk LEA 187
support staff 262–3
Supporting Teacher Development Through Action Research 121
Sylva, S. 89

talking books 104, 105, 107
task, authenticity of 24
Taylor, Chris 185, 234
Taylor, Graham 215
Taylor, Rod 83
teachers: approaches to using computers in teaching 122–5; professional development 173–8, 206–7, 254–9; role 109–12; willingness to use IT with students 130

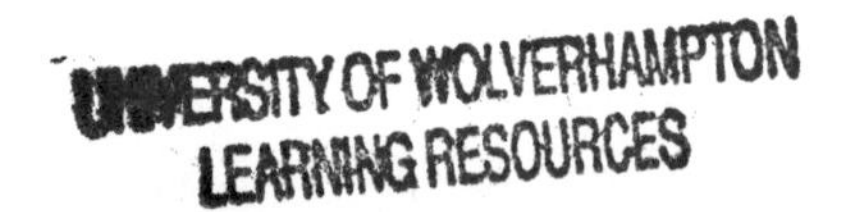